Volume 2 of the Empire Blueprint Series: Case Studies for
Business Success

70 Case Studies in Leadership, Innovation, and Resilience

ALSO BY AUTHORSDOOR GROUP

Volume 2 of the Empire Blueprint Series: Case Studies for
Business Success

---

70 Case Studies in Leadership, Innovation, and Resilience

Building a Thriving Enterprise

L. A. MOESZINGER

AuthorsDoor Group
an imprint of The Ridge Publishing Group

Library of Congress Control Number: 2024922968

70 Case Studies in Leadership, Innovation, and Resilience: Building a Thriving Enterprise / by L. A. Moeszinger

ISBN 978-1-956905-41-0 (e-book)
ISBN 978-1-956905-40-3 (softcover)

1. Business & Economics / Entrepreneurship. 2. Business & Economics / Small Business. 3. Business & Economics / Management. 4. Self-Help / Motivational & Inspiration. 5. Business & Economics / Leadership. I. Title. II. Series

Printed in the United States of America

Dedicated to the visionary leaders, bold innovators, and resilient changemakers who inspire us to push boundaries, embrace challenges, and create lasting impact.

AuthorsDoor Group
Coeur d'Alene, Idaho

INTRODUCTION.TO THE
AUTHORSDOOR LEADERSHIP PROGRAM

The AuthorsDoor Leadership Program, separate from the Builders Empire Series, is a new initiative designed to empower authors and publishers with the skills to effectively sell books. It features three tailored series: (1) AuthorsDoor Series: *Publisher & Her World*, (2) AuthorsDoor Advanced Series: *Publisher & Her World*, and (3) AuthorsDoor Masterclass Series: *Publisher & Her World*; each series is meticulously structured to guide participants from foundational concepts to advanced strategies in selling books, book by book, in a chronological format. The courses, offered for free on our YouTube channels—Publisher & Her World at Ridge Publishing Group, AuthorsDoor Group: Publisher & Her World, and Authors Red Door #Shorts—complement the books and workbooks, each providing unique and valuable teachings.

Explore additional resources to enhance your journey:

- Follow our blog at AuthorsRedDoor.com.
- Subscribe to our Newsletters at AuthorsDoor.com.
- Join our AuthorsDoor Strategy Forum Facebook Group.
- Connect with our Facebook Page at AuthorsDoor Group.
- Become a fan on our social media channels @AuthorsDoor1.

For feedback or questions, contact us at info@authorsdoor.com. We are here to support your journey from writing to successfully selling your books.

Warm regards,

L. A. Moeszinger #PubHerWorld

Contents

Introduction

70 Case Studies in Leadership, Innovation, and Resilience

In today's dynamic business landscape, leadership, innovation, and resilience are the driving forces that separate thriving enterprises from those that falter. This second volume of the Empire Blueprint Series provides 70 case studies that dive into the essential qualities, strategies, and decisions required to build sustainable, impactful businesses. Whether you're leading a startup, scaling a growing company, or refining your leadership approach within an established organization, this volume offers practical lessons and inspiration from real-world success stories.

Leadership: The Core of Impactful Enterprises

The book opens with case studies that demonstrate leadership strategies that drive change and inspire action. These stories show how exceptional leaders influence their teams, foster alignment, and achieve meaningful outcomes by leading with integrity, empathy, and vision. You'll explore how influential figures manage not just people but also culture and performance, setting the tone for long-term impact.

Resilience and Adaptability: Thriving Amid Uncertainty

A thriving enterprise must be able to adapt to rapid change and unexpected challenges. The section on resilience focuses on companies and individuals who bounced back from setbacks, using adversity as an opportunity to innovate. From navigating market disruptions to pivoting in uncertain times, these case studies demonstrate that resilience is not just about surviving but growing stronger through adversity.

Negotiation, Collaboration, and Influence

Success in business often comes down to the ability to collaborate effectively, influence key stakeholders, and negotiate strategically. This section provides insights into real-world negotiations—whether with partners, employees, or investors—and shows how the art of collaboration can lead to breakthroughs and win-win outcomes.

Corporate Culture, Communication, and Ethics

A thriving enterprise is built on a strong foundation of corporate culture and ethics. These case studies examine how successful companies create cultures that foster trust, creativity, and accountability, while also addressing the role of ethics in decision-making. Clear communication and effective networking are essential components, and this section provides practical strategies for building lasting connections and high-performing teams.

Innovation and Technology: Keys to Growth

Innovation is at the heart of every thriving business. The section on innovation offers stories of how companies stayed ahead of the curve by embracing creativity and new ideas. You'll explore the role of technology in driving business growth, learning how leaders integrate cutting-edge tools and systems to remain competitive in a fast-changing marketplace.

Digital Marketing, SEO, and Online Success

No modern business can succeed without digital marketing and SEO strategies. This section dives into how organizations leverage digital tools to build brand awareness, engage customers, and grow their online presence. From mastering search engine optimization to launching effective social media campaigns, the case studies here provide step-by-step guidance on digital success.

Legal and Financial Foundations for Sustainable Growth

Behind every successful business is a solid legal and financial foundation. This section highlights the importance of sound financial management, compliance, and legal frameworks that allow businesses to scale and thrive safely. The case studies provide insights into fundraising, risk management, and financial planning, offering valuable lessons for businesses at every stage.

Creating a Lasting Legacy

The final section focuses on building businesses that endure beyond their founders, exploring what it takes to create a legacy. These case studies offer insights into how visionary leaders embed purpose and impact into their companies, ensuring that their work leaves a meaningful mark on their industries and communities.

A Practical Toolkit for Leaders and Innovators

This volume is more than a collection of case studies; it's a comprehensive toolkit for leaders, innovators, and professionals seeking to build resilient, impactful enterprises. Whether you're working on your leadership skills, seeking inspiration for innovation, or navigating complex business challenges, the stories in this volume provide practical guidance and proven strategies for success.

No matter where you are on your journey—leading a team, building a company, or striving for long-term growth—these 70 case studies will help you develop the skills and mindset needed to thrive. With insights into leadership, innovation, resilience, and legacy creation, this book will equip you to make bold decisions, inspire others, and build a thriving enterprise for the future.

Each story reflects the unique journey behind every success, revealing strategies, lessons learned, and moments of resilience. Some businesses were built from humble beginnings, others disrupted industries, but all demonstrate that success is rarely a straight line—it is forged through creativity, persistence, and a relentless pursuit of vision.

As you immerse yourself in these pages, may these stories inspire new ideas and ignite the drive to pursue your own entrepreneurial goals. Let them remind you that no matter the obstacles, success is possible—and often just one bold step away.

A Focus on Adaptive Leadership
for Modern Challenges

The business world today is marked by rapid change, disruption, and uncertainty, requiring leaders to adopt an adaptive leadership approach to remain effective. Adaptive leadership goes beyond traditional command-and-control models by emphasizing flexibility, innovation, and continuous learning. In this section, we explore case studies that demonstrate how leaders thrive in volatile environments by embracing change, empowering their teams, and responding quickly to shifting market dynamics.

Adaptive leaders understand that they must pivot strategies in real time, make data-driven decisions, and foster a culture where creativity and experimentation are encouraged. These case studies reveal how forward-thinking leaders build resilient organizations by engaging in open communication, encouraging feedback, and collaborating across departments. In doing so, they create agile enterprises capable of navigating economic shifts, technological disruptions, and unexpected crises.

In addition, the case studies showcase how adaptive leadership prioritizes team empowerment. Leaders focus not just on individual performance but on building collective capacity, fostering trust, and nurturing leadership within teams. By encouraging employees to take initiative and adapt, these leaders build organizations that can respond to uncertainty with confidence and clarity.

Key to adaptive leadership is the ability to stay emotionally balanced in times of change, using setbacks as opportunities for learning and growth. Several examples in this section illustrate how leaders build personal resilience while supporting their teams through challenges, such as sudden market shifts or organizational restructuring. This approach ensures that the entire enterprise is prepared to innovate and evolve, rather than reactively managing crises.

Through these stories, readers will discover the value of leading with humility and curiosity, recognizing that leadership is not static—it's a skill that evolves in response to changing realities. Adaptive leadership prepares individuals and organizations to move forward with purpose, even in uncharted territory. This section offers both strategic insights and practical tools for becoming an adaptive leader in today's fast-changing world.

The Role of Emotional Intelligence in Leadership and Collaboration

Emotional intelligence (EQ) plays a vital role in effective leadership and collaboration, influencing how leaders connect with their teams, navigate challenges, and foster a productive work environment. EQ involves self-awareness, empathy, emotional regulation, and interpersonal skills, all of which are crucial for building trust, motivating others, and maintaining healthy communication within an organization.

Leaders with high EQ understand their emotions and manage them effectively, ensuring that their decisions are not clouded by stress or frustration. This self-awareness helps them remain calm under pressure and respond thoughtfully to challenges. Through emotional regulation, these leaders create a positive atmosphere where team members feel supported and engaged, even during difficult times.

Empathy—the ability to understand and share the feelings of others—is another key component of EQ. Empathetic leaders connect with their employees on a personal level, recognizing their struggles and offering appropriate support. This fosters trust and loyalty, making it easier to inspire collaboration and cooperation across teams. In addition, leaders who practice empathy are better equipped to resolve conflicts and build consensus, ensuring that team dynamics remain strong.

Effective collaboration also requires strong interpersonal communication. Leaders with high EQ are skilled at listening actively, providing constructive feedback, and communicating with clarity and compassion. They encourage open dialogue and inclusivity, creating environments where employees feel heard and valued. This, in turn, promotes innovation, as individuals are more likely to share their ideas and take creative risks when they feel respected and understood.

Several case studies in this section illustrate how emotionally intelligent leaders use influence and collaboration to drive results. Whether negotiating with partners, resolving internal conflicts, or fostering cross-functional teamwork, these leaders leverage EQ to build meaningful relationships that contribute to long-term business success.

In a rapidly evolving business landscape, emotional intelligence is not just a soft skill—it's a strategic asset. The case studies in this section demonstrate how EQ allows leaders to balance the demands of leadership with empathy, fostering a collaborative culture that promotes growth and resilience. By developing emotional intelligence, leaders are better equipped to inspire trust, enhance communication, and create environments where teams can thrive.

Innovation as a Continuous Process

Innovation isn't a one-time breakthrough—it's a continuous process that fuels long-term success. In today's fast-changing world, companies must constantly evolve to stay relevant. This section highlights case studies of businesses that have embraced innovation as an ongoing journey, using creativity and adaptability to respond to challenges, enter new markets, and shape future trends.

Continuous innovation requires leaders to cultivate a mindset of experimentation within their teams, encouraging employees to take calculated risks and explore new ideas. Many of the organizations featured in these case studies demonstrate how fostering a culture of innovation—where creative problem-solving is encouraged—results in breakthrough products, services, and strategies. These companies show that successful innovation happens incrementally, with small but impactful changes over time, rather than relying on isolated eureka moments.

The role of customer feedback is critical in the innovation process. Many of the businesses featured here actively engage with their customers, using their input to refine products, improve services, and develop solutions that align with emerging needs. This approach allows them to stay ahead of market trends and maintain a competitive edge, ensuring that their innovations are both relevant and impactful.

Technology also plays a pivotal role in continuous innovation. Leaders must leverage digital tools, data analytics, and emerging technologies to streamline operations, optimize customer experiences, and create new opportunities for growth. The case studies demonstrate how integrating technology into everyday operations creates new pathways for scalability and efficiency.

A common theme across the case studies is the importance of resilience and agility in innovation. Many of the companies featured faced setbacks and market disruptions but used these challenges as opportunities to innovate further. By staying agile and open to change, these organizations demonstrate that continuous innovation is not just about survival—it's about thriving in any environment.

This section provides practical lessons for business leaders on how to embed innovation into their organizations' DNA. Through structured experimentation, customer engagement, technological integration, and adaptability, these stories show how innovation can become a routine practice that drives long-term growth. Whether introducing small improvements or launching groundbreaking new initiatives, embracing innovation as a continuous process is essential for building a thriving enterprise.

Digital Transformation and Its Impact on Leadership

In the digital age, effective leadership demands more than traditional skills—it requires leaders to embrace digital transformation to keep pace with evolving technologies and shifting market expectations. Digital transformation impacts every level of an organization, from customer engagement and operations to internal collaboration and decision-making. This section explores how leaders harness technology to reshape their businesses, foster innovation, and stay competitive in a rapidly changing world.

Digital transformation requires leaders to rethink strategies, processes, and organizational structures. The case studies in this section highlight how businesses integrate AI, automation, cloud technology, and data analytics to streamline operations, improve customer experiences, and scale efficiently. Leaders who succeed in this space view technology as a core enabler of growth rather than a peripheral tool.

The shift toward remote work and virtual collaboration has also redefined leadership. Effective digital leaders prioritize building strong communication channels, fostering trust, and maintaining team cohesion across dispersed teams. Many of the case studies explore how businesses have adopted cloud-based tools, project management platforms, and virtual collaboration strategies to support employee engagement and productivity in remote work environments.

However, digital transformation is not just about technology—it's about cultural change. Leaders must cultivate a mindset of adaptability and continuous learning within their teams, empowering employees to adopt new tools and processes. Several stories in this section showcase how businesses successfully implemented change management strategies, helping employees transition smoothly into digital-first operations.

The role of data-driven decision-making is another key theme. Digital leaders rely on insights from big data and analytics to anticipate market shifts, identify new opportunities, and optimize performance. The case studies reveal how companies have used data to personalize customer interactions, drive innovation, and mitigate risks, demonstrating that leveraging information effectively is essential for staying ahead.

Finally, digital transformation demands a forward-looking mindset. Leaders must balance immediate operational goals with long-term strategic vision, continuously innovating to stay relevant in fast-moving markets. The case studies highlight how businesses align technology with their broader missions, showing that successful digital transformation requires a combination of leadership, strategy, and agility.

This section provides readers with valuable insights into how leaders across industries navigate the complexities of digital transformation. It emphasizes the importance of embracing change, fostering collaboration, and leading with data, preparing businesses to thrive in a world increasingly shaped by technology.

The Intersection of Ethics, Sustainability, and Business Success

In the modern business landscape, success is no longer measured solely by profits. Ethics and sustainability have become central pillars for companies aiming to thrive in today's marketplace. This section explores how purpose-driven enterprises integrate ethical practices and environmental responsibility into their core strategies, fostering trust, loyalty, and long-term value.

Ethical leadership involves more than compliance with regulations—it requires transparent communication, fair practices, and integrity at every level. The case studies in this section highlight leaders who have prioritized honesty and accountability, creating organizations where trust is a competitive advantage. These companies understand that building a reputation for ethical conduct enhances their brand image and attracts both customers and talent.

Sustainability, once seen as an optional initiative, is now a business imperative. Companies that focus on reducing their environmental impact, adopting sustainable practices, and contributing to social good position themselves as industry leaders. Many of the businesses featured here show how green innovations and sustainable models can enhance efficiency while aligning with consumer values. These organizations prove that profits and purpose can coexist—driving economic growth while preserving the planet.

Moreover, ethical and sustainable business practices are key to building customer loyalty and engagement. Today's consumers prefer to support companies that share their values and act responsibly. These case studies demonstrate how companies leverage their ethical commitments to engage customers on a deeper level, forging connections that extend beyond transactional relationships.

The intersection of ethics, sustainability, and business success also requires a long-term mindset. Leaders must balance short-term gains with future impact, ensuring that their decisions contribute positively to society and the environment. This section explores how companies embed ethics and sustainability into their mission and culture, creating a foundation for resilient growth that benefits stakeholders, employees, customers, and communities alike.

These case studies offer valuable insights into how organizations can thrive by doing well while doing good. Whether it's adopting sustainable practices, leading with transparency, or embedding social responsibility into everyday operations, the stories in this section illustrate that ethical and sustainable businesses are better positioned for long-term success in a world that increasingly values responsibility and impact.

Tools for Readers to Apply Insights In Real Time

This section emphasizes the importance of turning knowledge into action by providing practical tools for readers to apply the insights from these case studies immediately. Learning becomes meaningful only when it translates into real-world changes, and this volume is designed to empower readers to implement what they learn step by step.

Self-Assessment and Goal-Setting Exercises

Throughout the chapters, readers are encouraged to reflect on their current challenges and strengths. Incorporating guided self-assessment exercises will help you identify areas for improvement, develop action plans, and set short- and long-term goals aligned with your vision and strategy.

- **Example**: Use goal-tracking templates to monitor progress in leadership development or innovation projects.

- **Prompt**: *What is one area in your leadership that needs refinement based on the case studies?*

Checklists, Templates, and Frameworks for Immediate Use

Each case study offers key takeaways that can be turned into actionable checklists or templates. Whether you're building a social media strategy, refining your brand, or negotiating deals, these tools allow you to stay organized and focused.

- **Leadership checklist**: Daily habits to build influence and foster team trust.

- **Digital marketing templates**: Plan social media campaigns using tools aligned with the book's strategies.

Discussion and Peer Collaboration Opportunities

For even greater impact, consider engaging with others to discuss the case studies. Use this book as part of a mastermind group or business book club, where participants share experiences and exchange ideas on how to apply the insights in real-time scenarios. Collaborative discussions can uncover new perspectives and solutions that might not arise in individual learning.

- **Example**: Host monthly reflection sessions where participants compare progress and brainstorm improvements.

Progress-Tracking Tools for Accountability

Maintaining momentum is crucial for long-term success. Use habit trackers, digital tools, or spreadsheets to stay accountable and ensure the insights from the book are being implemented regularly. A monthly progress review can keep you on track, making it easier to refine strategies over time.

- **Example**: Create a progress-tracking spreadsheet to monitor key performance metrics related to your goals.

Supplemental Online Resources and Continued Learning

To deepen your understanding, readers can access additional resources and exercises, such as workbooks, online courses, or guided workshops. Engaging with related content across other volumes of the Empire Blueprint Series will provide continuity, allowing you to explore advanced strategies at your own pace.

By using these tools to apply the insights in real-time, readers will not only gain a deeper understanding of the material but also experience tangible results in their leadership, innovation, and resilience efforts. This section serves as a practical bridge between knowledge and action, equipping readers to build thriving enterprises through continuous improvement and accountability.

Building Personal Resilience Alongside Business Success

Success in business is not just about strategy and execution—it also requires the ability to build personal resilience. Leaders and entrepreneurs often face setbacks, challenges, and high-pressure environments that can test their endurance. Developing resilience ensures that they not only recover from obstacles but emerge stronger, both personally and professionally.

The case studies in this section reveal how successful individuals balance mental well-being with business goals. They demonstrate the importance of managing stress, avoiding burnout, and maintaining a positive mindset during difficult times. Resilient leaders understand that setbacks are part of the journey and view challenges as opportunities for learning and growth.

Self-care practices play a significant role in sustaining resilience. Many of the leaders featured prioritize physical health, mental wellness, and time for reflection, recognizing that personal well-being is essential for sustainable business performance. This balance helps them make clear, level-headed decisions even under pressure.

Additionally, building a support system is a key element of resilience. The stories highlight how leaders seek mentorship, partnerships, and team collaboration, leaning on others for guidance and strength. They cultivate open communication and trust within their teams, fostering environments where employees also develop resilience through shared challenges and support.

Another important theme is the ability to stay adaptable. Resilient individuals pivot when necessary, adjust strategies quickly, and remain open to change, ensuring they thrive in uncertain environments. Mindset shifts—such as focusing on progress over perfection and embracing failure as part of growth—are essential tools for leaders on this journey.

This section offers practical lessons for readers on nurturing personal resilience while building business success. It encourages entrepreneurs and professionals to view challenges as stepping stones, not roadblocks, and provides strategies for maintaining focus and energy over the long term. With resilience as a foundation, leaders are better equipped to stay the course, lead with strength, and create lasting impact.

How to Use This Volume

This book, *70 Case Studies in Leadership, Innovation, and Resilience: Building a Thriving Enterprise*, is designed to offer both inspiration and actionable insights. You can engage with the material in ways that suit your goals, whether you are reading sequentially or focusing on specific topics. Below are suggestions for how to get the most from this volume:

1. Read Sequentially for a Comprehensive Overview

If you are looking to develop a holistic understanding of leadership, resilience, and business growth, reading the book chapter by chapter will provide a progressive framework. Start with leadership principles and follow through to innovation strategies and legacy creation.

2. Focus on Relevant Sections for Immediate Solutions

This book covers a variety of topics—from corporate culture to digital marketing. If you're facing specific challenges, such as improving team collaboration or refining your business's digital presence, target the sections most relevant to your needs.

3. Take Notes and Apply Lessons in Real Time

Each case study contains practical takeaways you can apply directly to your business. Use a notebook or digital journal to jot down insights, ideas, and action steps as you read. Refer to the tools and templates provided throughout the book to help integrate these lessons into your daily operations.

4. Use as a Discussion Guide or Group Learning Tool

This volume is ideal for team discussions, business book clubs, or mastermind groups. Use the case studies as conversation starters to spark ideas and inspire collaboration. Consider holding weekly meetings or workshops to review chapters together and apply the strategies as a team.

5. Reflect on Challenges and Monitor Progress

The book emphasizes personal and business resilience. Set aside time to reflect on challenges you've faced and how the strategies in the book apply to your situation. Track your progress over time, using the lessons in this volume to pivot and adapt as needed.

6. Cross-Reference with Other Volumes and Series

This book is part of a larger Empire Blueprint Series. Consider referencing Volume 1 and Volume 3 for deeper insights into branding, growth, and legacy-building. Additionally, related material in the AuthorsDoor and Masterclass Series offers complementary tools for expanding your business knowledge.

By using this volume strategically—whether for personal learning, group discussions, or direct application—you will be equipped to lead with confidence, innovate continuously, and build a resilient, thriving enterprise.

Conclusion: A Roadmap to Leadership, Innovation, and Resilience

This volume, "70 Case Studies in Leadership, Innovation, and Resilience: Building a Thriving Enterprise," serves as both a guide and inspiration for those seeking to lead, innovate, and build businesses that withstand challenges. The insights within these case studies provide practical tools and strategic frameworks for navigating the complexities of modern business while maintaining personal and organizational resilience.

Whether you are striving to develop as a leader, foster a culture of innovation, or build a legacy of impact, this book offers the wisdom and lessons from real-world experiences. It challenges you to reflect on your journey, embrace adaptability, and align your strategies with a vision that not only achieves success but creates sustainable growth.

As you engage with these stories, remember that leadership is not a destination—it's a continuous process of learning, growing, and evolving. Use this volume as a companion and resource, returning to its pages whenever you encounter new challenges or seek inspiration for your next move. The path to thriving in business is filled with opportunities to pivot, innovate, and lead with purpose, and this book equips you to navigate that path confidently.

With the insights gained here, your business journey can become one of resilience, adaptability, and lasting success—turning challenges into opportunities and ideas into legacies. Let this volume be the beginning of your journey toward creating a thriving enterprise.

CHAPTER ONE

Leadership That Drives Impact

L eadership transcends mere titles or positions of authority; it embodies the ability to inspire others, instigate meaningful change, and cultivate an environment where individuals and organizations can flourish. Effective leaders go beyond task management; they align vision with action, making a lasting impact on their teams, customers, and communities. In this chapter, we delve into the qualities, strategies, and practices that define impactful leadership, equipping you with the tools to lead with purpose and achieve transformative results.

John C. Maxwell, a celebrated authority on leadership, asserts, "Leadership is not about titles, positions, or flowcharts. It is about one life influencing another." Impactful leadership begins with personal influence—leaders who empower their teams to grow, innovate, and exceed expectations. Whether in startups or established corporations, those who engage meaningfully with their people inspire loyalty and commitment, paving the way for sustained success.

Visionary leadership also entails translating strategy into action. Stephen R. Covey emphasizes that "Leadership is not just about doing things right; it's about doing the right things." This chapter explores how leaders craft compelling visions and foster a shared sense of purpose, motivating teams to chase ambitious goals with enthusiasm and unity.

Strategic thinking is another hallmark of effective leadership. Henry Mintzberg famously stated, "Strategy is not just about foreseeing the future but about creating it." Exceptional leaders anticipate challenges, capitalize on opportunities, and remain adaptable in shifting markets. They establish resilient organizations that thrive amidst uncertainty, equipping their teams with the tools and mindset to navigate changing landscapes.

Emotional intelligence is vital for building strong relationships and fostering trust. Patrick Lencioni notes, "The best leaders are the ones who care about their team's well-being." Leaders who prioritize the development and well-being of their teams create supportive cultures where employees feel valued and motivated to excel. This chapter provides insights into how emotional intelligence enhances leadership, driving engagement and innovation.

Operational excellence requires leaders to cultivate efficiency without compromising quality. Ursula Burns, former CEO of Xerox, highlights, "You can't have a good business without a good operational strategy." Leaders who implement intelligent processes and prioritize continuous improvement ensure that their organizations remain competitive and sustainable.

Leadership also calls for courage and adaptability. Dale Carnegie reminds us, "Most of the important things in the world have been accomplished by people who have kept on trying when there seemed to be no hope at all." This chapter emphasizes how leaders embrace change, make bold decisions, and learn from setbacks to propel long-term success.

Collaboration is crucial in impactful leadership. Mary Barra, CEO of General Motors, asserts, "You cannot be successful in business without great partnerships." Effective leaders cultivate teamwork and partnerships, leveraging diverse perspectives to tackle complex challenges and uncover new opportunities.

This chapter offers actionable strategies for building collaborative teams and achieving collective success.

Ultimately, great leadership is about creating a lasting legacy. Leaders who embody ethical practices foster trust and respect, understanding that their influence extends beyond the present moment, shaping the future for those who follow.

In this chapter, you'll gain practical insights from leaders such as John C. Maxwell, Henry Mintzberg, Patrick Lencioni, and Mary Barra on cultivating leadership that drives impact. Whether leading a small team or an entire organization, the principles explored in this chapter will help you develop the skills, mindset, and strategies needed to inspire others, execute effectively, and leave a lasting mark on your business and industry.

John C. Maxwell's Success Story: From Pastor to Global Leadership Expert

"Leadership is not about titles, positions, or flowcharts. It is about one life influencing another." — JOHN C. MAXWELL, LEADERSHIP EXPERT AND AUTHOR

John C. Maxwell stands as one of the world's foremost leadership experts, transforming the way people think about personal and organizational growth. From his early days as a pastor to becoming an internationally renowned author, speaker, and mentor, Maxwell's journey has been defined by a commitment to developing leaders at every level. His philosophy that "leadership is influence" has resonated with millions across industries, inspiring countless professionals to embrace personal growth and cultivate leadership skills. With a portfolio of bestselling books and a network of leadership training programs that span the globe, Maxwell's work has touched lives far beyond the business world, shaping leaders in churches, nonprofits, and corporations alike. His story exemplifies the power of vision, perseverance, and the belief that everyone has the potential to grow into a leader who can inspire others.

Humble Beginnings and the Power of Purpose
John C. Maxwell began his career as a pastor, where he discovered his passion for leadership. Raised in Ohio, Maxwell grew up in a family deeply rooted in faith, which shaped his philosophy of servant leadership. Early in his ministry, he realized that leadership principles could transform not only churches but also businesses and individuals seeking personal growth. Driven by the idea that leadership is a skill that can be learned and improved, Maxwell set out to inspire others beyond the pulpit.

Writing His First Books and Finding His Voice
Maxwell's journey into the world of writing began with a desire to share leadership wisdom with a broader audience. His first books, such as *Developing the Leader Within You* and *Becoming a Person of Influence*, were met with enthusiasm, establishing him as a thought leader in the leadership development space. These books provided readers with practical frameworks for personal and organizational growth, resonating with audiences looking for actionable guidance.

Building a Leadership Empire
In the 1990s, Maxwell founded organizations like INJOY and the John Maxwell Team to expand his reach. These initiatives were designed to equip leaders with training, mentorship, and tools to foster leadership in their own communities and workplaces. Through seminars, coaching programs, and global leadership events, Maxwell began cultivating a vast network of leaders. His focus on teaching individuals to grow both personally and professionally allowed his philosophy to transcend industries.

Global Influence and Recognized Success
Maxwell's leadership frameworks became the foundation for countless businesses, nonprofits, and government organizations seeking positive change. With more than 100 books to his name—many of them bestsellers—he has reached millions of readers around the world. His works, including *The 21 Irrefutable Laws of Leadership*, became cornerstones for leadership development, earning accolades and recognition across sectors.

Legacy of Impact and Leadership Beyond Borders
John C. Maxwell's success lies not only in his bestsellers but in the thousands of leaders he has mentored and empowered along the way. As a speaker, coach, and

mentor, Maxwell continues to travel the world, sharing his message that leadership starts from within. His influence spans industries, and his teachings remain relevant as organizations adapt to an ever-changing world. His vision is simple: to develop leaders who, in turn, develop others—creating a ripple effect of positive change across generations.

Maxwell's enduring message is that leadership is not about titles or positions but about empowering others, leaving a legacy of growth, and serving with integrity.

Henry Mintzberg's Success Story: Redefining Management Thinking

"Strategy is not just about foreseeing the future, but about creating it. A true strategic leader doesn't just follow roads—they build them." — HENRY MINTZBERG, RENOWNED MANAGEMENT EXPERT

"Termination of a contract should be approached with the same careful consideration as its inception, ensuring that ending an agreement is as respectful and strategic as its formation." — HENRY MINTZBERG, MANAGEMENT EXPERT AND PROFESSOR

Henry Mintzberg is a trailblazer in the field of management, whose innovative ideas have reshaped the way businesses and organizations operate. Known for his groundbreaking perspectives on leadership, strategy, and managerial roles, Mintzberg has consistently challenged traditional approaches to business education and management theory. His belief that strategy emerges through action, rather than rigid planning, has provided leaders with a new framework for navigating uncertainty. With a career spanning decades, including influential works like *The Nature of Managerial Work* and *Strategy Safari*, Mintzberg has become a guiding force in modern management. His legacy continues to inspire leaders to embrace collaboration, adaptability, and reflective learning in an ever-changing world.

Early Life and Educational Foundations

Henry Mintzberg, a renowned scholar and thought leader in management, was born in Montreal, Canada, in 1939. His early education reflected a curiosity about the world, but it was at McGill University where Mintzberg found his passion for understanding organizations. He earned a mechanical engineering degree, which sparked his interest in problem-solving and complex systems. However, his fascination with human behavior and leadership led him to pursue further studies in management.

Shaping a New Perspective in Management

Mintzberg continued his academic journey at the MIT Sloan School of Management, where he earned his Ph.D. His groundbreaking dissertation challenged the conventional view of managers as planners and decision-makers. Instead, Mintzberg proposed that management is an art, comprising diverse roles and practical actions performed in real-time. This idea laid the foundation for his widely acclaimed book *The Nature of Managerial Work* (1973), where he introduced his famous model of managerial roles, including interpersonal, informational, and decisional roles.

Impact on Management Theory

Throughout his career, Mintzberg has been a vocal critic of traditional business education, advocating for more practical and reflective approaches. His innovative ideas on emergent strategy—where strategy evolves through actions rather than deliberate planning—have influenced how organizations navigate uncertainty. Mintzberg's publications, such as *Mintzberg on Management* and *Strategy Safari*, became essential reading in both academic and professional circles. His ideas have resonated particularly with leaders seeking alternative approaches to rigid corporate structures, emphasizing adaptability and learning through doing.

Founding the International Masters for Health Leadership (IMHL)

Driven by his passion for blending education and real-world experience, Mintzberg co-founded the International Masters for Health Leadership (IMHL) at McGill University. This program brought together leaders from across the health sector, reinforcing his belief in the importance of diverse, collaborative learning environments. Mintzberg's dedication to education has also extended to the

International Masters in Practicing Management (IMPM), which offers a unique take on executive education, integrating reflection with practical leadership challenges.

Legacy and Continued Influence
Henry Mintzberg's contributions have redefined how we understand management and leadership. His advocacy for decentralized, collaborative organizations has inspired leaders worldwide to rethink how businesses operate. Even as the management landscape evolves, Mintzberg remains a pivotal figure, continuing to influence through his teaching, writing, and consulting.

Mintzberg's story is one of relentless curiosity and a desire to challenge the status quo, leaving a legacy that extends far beyond his books and theories. His work embodies a lifelong dedication to helping organizations navigate complexity, making him one of the most influential thinkers in the field of management.

Patrick Lencioni's Success Story: Transforming Leadership with Teamwork and Trust

"Building a team is like weaving a tapestry. Each thread must be strong alone, but it's how they intertwine that creates something truly magnificent."
— PATRICK LENCIONI, BUSINESS MANAGEMENT EXPERT

Patrick Lencioni is a visionary in the field of organizational health, known for revolutionizing how businesses think about teamwork, leadership, and trust. With a unique blend of storytelling and practical insights, Lencioni has empowered leaders to build high-functioning teams through his bestselling books, including *The Five Dysfunctions of a Team*. As the founder of The Table Group, Lencioni has dedicated his career to simplifying complex leadership challenges, helping companies foster trust, accountability, and clarity. His influential work continues to guide organizations of all sizes, proving that success stems not just from strategy but from a healthy, cohesive culture where people work well together.

Early Inspiration and Humble Beginnings

Patrick Lencioni's journey to becoming a renowned author, consultant, and thought leader in business began with a deep fascination with human behavior and organizational dynamics. Raised in the San Francisco Bay Area, Lencioni discovered his passion for teamwork and leadership at a young age. His early professional experiences included working in management consulting at Bain & Company and Oracle, where he witnessed firsthand the struggles organizations face with internal alignment and leadership dysfunction.

Founding The Table Group

In 1997, driven by a desire to make a tangible impact, Lencioni founded The Table Group, a management consulting firm specializing in organizational health. His goal was to help businesses overcome dysfunction, foster trust, and create cultures of clarity and accountability. From the beginning, Lencioni's approach emphasized simplicity—cutting through jargon to address the root of organizational challenges with practical solutions.

The Breakthrough with *The Five Dysfunctions of a Team*

Lencioni's breakthrough came with the release of *The Five Dysfunctions of a Team* in 2002, a book that quickly became a bestseller and established him as a leading voice in business strategy. The book presented a powerful framework for diagnosing and overcoming the key challenges teams face, such as lack of trust, fear of conflict, and poor accountability. His storytelling approach, using relatable business fables, set his work apart from traditional management books and resonated with leaders worldwide.

Expanding Influence and Thought Leadership

Following the success of *The Five Dysfunctions of a Team*, Lencioni continued to build his reputation with books like *The Advantage*, *The Ideal Team Player*, and *Death by Meeting*. These works expanded on his core themes of trust, teamwork, and effective leadership, providing actionable frameworks for organizations to implement. His ideas became staples in leadership training programs and executive coaching initiatives around the globe.

Legacy of Organizational Health

Today, Lencioni is widely recognized as one of the foremost experts in organizational health and teamwork. Through The Table Group, he has worked with a diverse range of clients, from Fortune 500 companies to small nonprofits, helping them build cohesive leadership teams and healthy work environments. His influence extends to keynote speaking engagements and workshops, where he continues to inspire leaders to prioritize trust, clarity, and alignment within their organizations.

Impact and Continuing Journey
Patrick Lencioni's career is a testament to the power of passion, simplicity, and empathy in business. His work has transformed how leaders think about teamwork and organizational health, providing them with tools to unlock their team's full potential. With a philosophy that leadership is less about processes and more about relationships, Lencioni's influence endures, helping businesses cultivate healthy cultures that drive long-term success.

Stephen R. Covey's Success Story: The Principles-Driven Path to Global Influence

"The key is not to prioritize what's on your schedule, but to schedule your priorities." — STEPHEN R. COVEY, AUTHOR AND EDUCATOR

"Strength lies in differences, not in similarities." — STEPHEN R. COVEY, AUTHOR AND EDUCATOR

Stephen R. Covey, the author of the legendary book *The 7 Habits of Highly Effective People*, left a profound mark on leadership, self-development, and personal success. His journey to becoming one of the most influential thought leaders in the world is a story of faith, education, and the relentless pursuit of principles-based living. Covey's success came not just from his books but from his ability to distill timeless truths into practical guidance, inspiring millions to lead more intentional and meaningful lives.

Early Life and Education: Laying the Foundation
Stephen R. Covey was born on October 24, 1932, in Salt Lake City, Utah. Covey's upbringing in a faith-based environment instilled in him a strong sense of values and responsibility from a young age. As a teenager, he faced personal challenges,

including being sidelined from sports due to a severe health issue. This obstacle forced Covey to focus on academics and personal growth, helping him develop a love for learning and self-discipline that shaped his future.

Covey pursued business and education degrees, earning a bachelor's degree in Business Administration from the University of Utah and an MBA from Harvard Business School. His interest in how leadership and ethics intersect led him to earn a Doctorate of Religious Education (DRE) from Brigham Young University, where he studied how timeless spiritual principles apply to leadership, self-management, and success.

Academic and Corporate Leadership: The Beginnings of a Thought Leader
Covey initially began his career in academia as a professor at Brigham Young University, where he taught organizational behavior and business management. His teaching emphasized the importance of principles-based leadership—the idea that success comes from aligning personal behavior with enduring truths such as integrity, honesty, and service.

While teaching, Covey also worked as a consultant for various organizations, where he witnessed firsthand the leadership and management challenges faced by businesses. Covey observed that many professionals focused too much on efficiency at the expense of effectiveness—achieving short-term goals without long-term vision or alignment with personal values.

These insights laid the foundation for what would become his life's work: teaching people to achieve not just external success, but also internal fulfillment through timeless principles.

The 7 Habits of Highly Effective People: A Global Phenomenon
In 1989, Covey published "The 7 Habits of Highly Effective People," which quickly became a global bestseller. The book introduced a paradigm shift in personal and professional development by focusing not on quick fixes but on cultivating core habits rooted in character and values. The 7 habits Covey outlined are:

1. **Be Proactive:** Take responsibility for your actions and choices.

2. **Begin with the End in Mind:** Define your vision and long-term goals.

3. **Put First Things First:** Prioritize what matters most.

4. **Think Win-Win:** Seek mutually beneficial outcomes.

5. **Seek First to Understand, Then to Be Understood:** Practice empathetic listening.

6. **Synergize:** Collaborate to create better solutions through teamwork.

7. **Sharpen the Saw:** Continuously renew yourself physically, mentally, emotionally, and spiritually.

The 7 Habits framework struck a chord with readers worldwide, offering a clear, actionable roadmap for improving relationships, career performance, and personal well-being. Unlike traditional self-help books, Covey's focus on character ethics, long-term vision, and principle-based living resonated with people across cultures, industries, and roles.

The book sold over 40 million copies and was translated into dozens of languages, becoming one of the most influential works in the personal development field. Covey's ability to blend timeless wisdom with practical insights made the book a cornerstone in leadership programs, corporate training, and personal growth journeys worldwide.

Building the Covey Leadership Empire

Following the success of *The 7 Habits of Highly Effective People*, Covey co-founded FranklinCovey, a global consulting and training company, in 1997. The company merged Covey's leadership teachings with Franklin Quest, a company specializing in time management tools. Together, they created a comprehensive personal and organizational development platform that focused on both productivity and personal fulfillment.

FranklinCovey became a trusted partner for businesses, governments, and educational institutions, offering training in areas such as leadership, goal-setting, and team collaboration. Covey's influence extended beyond corporate boardrooms, impacting educators, students, and families. Programs based on the 7 Habits framework were integrated into school curricula, helping young people develop the skills needed to lead meaningful lives.

Principle-Centered Leadership and Additional Works

Covey's thought leadership expanded with additional books, including "Principle-Centered Leadership" and "The 8th Habit: From Effectiveness to Greatness." In *The 8th Habit*, Covey argued that in the modern world, success requires more than just effectiveness—it requires finding one's voice and inspiring others to do the same. This book encouraged individuals to go beyond personal success and become leaders who create positive change in the world.

Covey's message of servant leadership and purpose-driven living became especially relevant in an era marked by rapid change, technological disruption, and shifting societal expectations. His work emphasized that authentic leadership comes from personal integrity—leading oneself before leading others.

Challenges and Personal Philosophy

While Covey achieved remarkable success, his journey was not without challenges. As an entrepreneur, author, and public speaker, he faced the complexities of balancing work, family, and personal commitments. Covey was candid about his struggles with time management and personal renewal, which inspired the creation of "Sharpen the Saw," the seventh habit focused on continuous self-care and growth.

Covey's personal philosophy was deeply rooted in faith and family. A devout member of The Church of Jesus Christ of Latter-day Saints, Covey often spoke about how his spiritual beliefs shaped his leadership philosophy. He believed that living according to universal principles—such as integrity, love, and service— was the key to a meaningful life.

Awards, Impact, and Legacy

Throughout his career, Covey received numerous awards, including Time Magazine's designation as one of the 25 Most Influential Americans. His work influenced leaders, entrepreneurs, and educators across the globe, becoming a staple in leadership training programs and business schools.

Covey's impact extended beyond the professional world into personal relationships and family dynamics. Many families adopted the 7 Habits framework to improve communication, strengthen bonds, and build shared values. Covey often said that his greatest success was his role as a husband, father, and grandfather, reflecting his belief that family is the most important leadership role anyone can have.

Stephen Covey's Passing and Continuing Legacy
Stephen Covey passed away on July 16, 2012, at the age of 79 due to complications from a bicycle accident. Though he is no longer with us, his teachings live on through FranklinCovey's programs, his books, and the countless lives he touched. The 7 Habits framework continues to inspire individuals to lead lives of purpose and integrity, shaping future generations of leaders.

His legacy is not just about achieving success but about living with intention, aligning actions with principles, and making a positive impact on the world. Covey's principles-centered approach remains as relevant today as ever, offering timeless guidance for navigating life's challenges with wisdom, humility, and purpose.

Key Lessons from Stephen R. Covey's Success

1. **Align with Timeless Principles:** Covey's message emphasizes that true success comes from aligning behavior with universal truths like integrity, empathy, and service.

2. **Focus on Character, Not Just Results:** Personal effectiveness comes from building strong character, not just achieving outcomes.

3. **Continuous Growth is Essential:** Covey's "Sharpen the Saw" principle highlights the importance of lifelong learning and renewal.

4. **Begin with the End in Mind:** Having a clear vision and aligning daily actions with long-term goals ensures a purposeful life.

5. **Balance Personal and Professional Roles:** Covey believed that true leadership starts at home, with family relationships being the most important responsibility.

Conclusion: A Life of Meaningful Impact
Stephen R. Covey's story is one of faith, vision, and service. His principles-based teachings have transcended industries, cultures, and generations, helping millions lead more intentional and meaningful lives. From corporate boardrooms to

classrooms, Covey's message remains a guiding light for those seeking personal and professional fulfillment.

His legacy serves as a reminder that success is not just about achieving goals but about living with integrity, empowering others, and contributing to the greater good. Through the 7 Habits, Covey gave the world a blueprint for living a life of purpose and significance, ensuring that his influence will endure for generations to come.

Dale Carnegie's Success Story: The Pioneer of Personal Development and Influence

"Mastering the art of the conversation starter is crucial in digital communication; it's about crafting messages that not only capture attention but also encourage active engagement and build community." — DALE CARNEGIE, AUTHOR AND DEVELOPER OF FAMOUS COURSES IN SELF-IMPROVEMENT, SALESMANSHIP, CORPORATE TRAINING, PUBLIC SPEAKING, AND INTERPERSONAL SKILLS

"True influence isn't about controlling the conversation; it's about shaping it in a way that leaves others eager to follow your lead." — DALE CARNEGIE, AUTHOR OF HOW TO WIN FRIENDS AND INFLUENCE PEOPLE

Dale Carnegie is widely regarded as a pioneer in the field of personal development, celebrated for his ability to unlock human potential through communication and interpersonal skills. Born into humble beginnings, Carnegie's path was far from easy, yet his challenges shaped his understanding of what it takes to succeed. His bestselling book, *How to Win Friends and Influence People*, revolutionized the way people think about influence, empathy, and leadership. With the creation of Dale Carnegie Training, his teachings became a global movement, inspiring millions to develop confidence, build meaningful relationships, and lead with integrity. Carnegie's work remains a cornerstone in the personal growth landscape, proving that success lies not just in what we achieve but in how we connect with and inspire others along the way.

Early Life and Humble Beginnings

Dale Carnegie was born in 1888 on a small farm in Maryville, Missouri. Raised in a modest household, Carnegie faced financial challenges early on, but he found solace in learning and personal growth. He honed his public speaking skills in high school debates, eventually enrolling at the State Teacher's College in Warrensburg. Despite his interest in communication, Carnegie's early career didn't begin in a glamorous setting—he worked as a traveling salesman, struggling to find stability.

The Turning Point: Public Speaking and Personal Growth

In 1912, Carnegie's life took a pivotal turn when he began teaching public speaking classes for adults at the YMCA in New York City. Observing how fear of speaking held people back, he developed techniques to help individuals overcome stage fright and express themselves confidently. Carnegie quickly realized that success was not just about what people knew—it was about how effectively they could communicate and connect with others.

Drawing on his experiences and research, Carnegie formulated practical principles to enhance interpersonal skills. His early lessons focused on the power of persuasion, the importance of listening, and building authentic relationships—insights that would become the cornerstone of his legacy.

Writing a Masterpiece: *How to Win Friends and Influence People*

In 1936, Carnegie published his most iconic work, *How to Win Friends and Influence People*. This groundbreaking book, filled with timeless advice on communication, empathy, and influence, became an instant bestseller. It offered readers a fresh perspective on personal and professional success, teaching that listening, showing appreciation, and finding common ground were essential to thriving in both life and business. Carnegie's approachable style and practical wisdom resonated across industries, making the book an enduring success.

Building a Global Legacy

Carnegie's methods soon evolved into a formal program. He founded Dale Carnegie Training, an institution dedicated to personal development, leadership, and effective communication. His courses empowered individuals and businesses to develop confidence and foster meaningful relationships, cementing his reputation as a pioneer in self-improvement.

Over time, Dale Carnegie Training expanded globally, influencing millions across more than 90 countries. Carnegie's legacy remains influential, as his techniques are still taught to leaders, entrepreneurs, and professionals aiming to refine their interpersonal skills and build impactful careers.

Lasting Impact and Influence

Dale Carnegie's philosophy continues to inspire people worldwide. His work emphasizes that success lies not only in talent or knowledge but in how individuals relate to and inspire others. Carnegie's enduring message—that kindness, empathy, and strong communication are keys to influence—has solidified his place in history as a transformative figure in personal development. Even today, his books and teachings remain essential reading for anyone seeking to lead with integrity and connect with people on a deeper level.

Ursula Burns' Success Story: From Intern to Industry Leader

"In the realm of trademark disputes, success is measured by your ability to secure your intellectual property while maintaining business relationships. It's essential to resolve conflicts in ways that foster cooperation and respect." — URSULA BURNS, FORMER CEO OF XEROX

Ursula Burns's rise from humble beginnings in the Lower East Side of Manhattan to becoming the first Black woman to lead a Fortune 500 company is a story of resilience, hard work, and visionary leadership. Born to a single mother and driven by a passion for engineering, Burns broke barriers throughout her career at Xerox, transforming the company during a critical period of change. Her tenure as CEO not only reshaped Xerox's future but also set new standards for diversity and inclusion in corporate leadership. Burns's journey is a testament to the power of determination, adaptability, and innovation, inspiring future generations to challenge limits and embrace new possibilities.

Early Life and Education

Born on September 20, 1958, Ursula Burns grew up in the public housing projects of the Lower East Side of Manhattan. Raised by a single mother who worked tirelessly as a cleaning woman and ran a home daycare, Burns was instilled with values of hard work, education, and resilience. Determined to break the cycle of poverty, she excelled in school and discovered a passion for mathematics. She earned a Bachelor's degree in Mechanical Engineering from the Polytechnic Institute of New York and later completed a Master's in Mechanical Engineering from Columbia University.

Joining Xerox: The Start of a Historic Career

In 1980, Burns joined Xerox as a summer intern, unaware that this position would mark the beginning of a groundbreaking journey. She worked her way up through the ranks, holding various engineering and product development roles. Burns's early career was defined by a willingness to take on challenging projects and a no-nonsense approach to solving problems, quickly earning her a reputation as a dynamic and effective leader.

Breaking Barriers: Becoming the First Black Woman CEO

Burns's talent and leadership did not go unnoticed. By 2000, she was named Senior Vice President of Corporate Strategic Services, leading key efforts to transform Xerox's business model. At a time when Xerox was struggling with declining revenue and fierce competition, Burns played an instrumental role in reshaping the company's future.

In 2009, Burns was named CEO, making history as the first Black woman to lead a Fortune 500 company. Her promotion not only marked a personal triumph but also broke significant barriers for women and minorities in the corporate world. Under her leadership, Burns shifted Xerox's focus from traditional printing services to business services, acquiring companies such as Affiliated Computer Services to drive innovation and long-term growth.

Innovative Leadership and Business Transformation

Burns understood the importance of adapting to changing market dynamics. During her tenure, she championed technological innovation and digital transformation. She also focused on creating a more inclusive and diverse workplace, a value she had upheld throughout her career. Burns took bold steps to streamline operations, eliminate inefficiencies, and expand Xerox's portfolio beyond printing technology into business outsourcing and services.

Her ability to lead through uncertainty and steer the company in a new direction earned widespread respect. Burns's focus on sustainability and corporate responsibility also made Xerox a leader in environmental initiatives, further strengthening the company's reputation.

Stepping Down and Expanding Influence

In 2016, Burns stepped down as CEO but continued to serve as Chairman of the Board until Xerox separated into two companies: Xerox and Conduent. She then became an advocate for diversity, leadership, and education, using her platform to inspire future generations. Burns serves on the boards of several prominent companies, including Uber and ExxonMobil, and remains an influential voice in business, tech, and social causes.

Legacy and Impact

Ursula Burns's journey from an intern to the CEO of Xerox embodies the power of persistence, courage, and adaptability. Her success challenged stereotypes and set new precedents for women and minorities in leadership. Through her tenure at Xerox, Burns not only transformed a company but also redefined what it means to be a leader in the modern world—emphasizing the importance of vision, inclusion, and strategic innovation. Today, she continues to inspire others with her story, proving that with determination and courage, no barrier is insurmountable.

―――――――

Mary Barra's Success Story: A Trailblazer in the Automotive Industry

"Maintaining a trademark requires the same attention and care as nurturing a leading brand. Regularly renew, monitor, and enforce your trademarks to ensure they remain a potent symbol of your company's quality and reputation." — MARY BARRA, CEO OF GENERAL MOTORS

Mary Barra's journey from inspecting fenders on a factory floor to becoming the first female CEO of General Motors is a story of grit, determination, and vision. With a lifelong connection to the automotive world and a passion for engineering, Barra steadily climbed the corporate ladder at GM, taking on key leadership roles in manufacturing, engineering, and human resources. Known for her ability to balance technical expertise with empathetic leadership, Barra transformed GM during turbulent times, leading the company through a safety crisis and spearheading its transition to electric vehicles. Her inspiring leadership style and bold strategies have reshaped GM's future, making her a pioneering figure in both the automotive and business worlds.

Early Life and Education: Building a Foundation

Born in 1961 in Royal Oak, Michigan, Mary Barra grew up in a family that was deeply connected to the automotive industry. Her father worked for Pontiac, a division of General Motors (GM), which fostered her early fascination with cars. Barra developed a strong work ethic and love for engineering early on, which led her to pursue a degree in electrical engineering from Kettering University (formerly General Motors Institute). She later earned an MBA from Stanford University, sponsored by GM, which laid the groundwork for her future leadership roles.

Rising Through the Ranks: Learning GM from the Inside

Barra began her career at GM as a co-op student at the age of 18, inspecting fenders and working on the factory floor. This experience gave her an invaluable perspective on GM's operations and a deep understanding of its workforce. Over the years, she took on various roles in manufacturing, engineering, and human resources, steadily climbing the corporate ladder. Her commitment to operational efficiency and innovation did not go unnoticed.

One of Barra's most critical assignments came when she was named Vice President of Global Manufacturing Engineering. In this role, she oversaw production processes across GM's global network, streamlining operations and improving vehicle quality. Her ability to balance technical expertise with leadership skills made her a standout executive.

Breaking Barriers: Becoming GM's First Female CEO

In 2014, Mary Barra shattered the glass ceiling by becoming the first female CEO of a major global automaker. At the time, GM was facing numerous challenges, including a federal investigation into faulty ignition switches that had led to several deaths. Barra's handling of the crisis—with transparency, accountability, and empathy—earned her respect within the industry and beyond. She prioritized customer safety and reformed the company's safety culture, ensuring GM could regain public trust.

Transforming GM: Electric Vehicles and Innovation

Under Barra's leadership, GM pivoted toward the future of transportation. She spearheaded the company's shift from traditional combustion engines to electric vehicles (EVs), aiming to make GM a leader in sustainable mobility. Barra announced bold plans for the automaker to transition to an all-electric future, with a goal of phasing out gasoline-powered vehicles by 2035.

Barra also expanded GM's focus on autonomous driving technologies through partnerships and acquisitions, such as the investment in Cruise Automation. Her strategic vision has positioned GM to compete with tech companies and new market entrants in the race toward innovation.

Legacy and Leadership Style

Mary Barra is known for her collaborative and inclusive leadership style, emphasizing accountability, teamwork, and continuous learning. She is committed to diversity and inclusion, advocating for more women and underrepresented groups in leadership roles within GM and the industry. Her ability to lead through change, manage crises, and inspire innovation has set a new standard for corporate leadership.

Conclusion: Leading GM into the Future

Mary Barra's journey from the factory floor to the top office of General Motors is a testament to perseverance, adaptability, and strategic vision. As a trailblazer in a male-dominated industry, she has not only redefined what it means to lead but also steered GM toward a more sustainable and innovative future. Barra's story continues to inspire, proving that with hard work and determination, barriers can be broken and new paths can be forged.

CHAPTER TWO

Resilience and Adaptability

In today's ever-changing business landscape, resilience and adaptability are vital qualities that define successful entrepreneurs and leaders. The ability to bounce back from setbacks and pivot strategies in response to evolving markets distinguishes thriving businesses from those that falter. This chapter explores how resilience and adaptability can serve as foundational pillars of business success, equipping you with the tools to navigate uncertainty, embrace challenges, and turn obstacles into opportunities.

Max McKeown, a prominent business strategist, asserts, "Adaptability is about the powerful difference between adapting to cope and adapting to win." Businesses that embrace change, viewing it as an opportunity rather than a threat, foster a mindset that cultivates innovation and growth. Those who recognize that adaptability is not merely a survival mechanism but a pathway to thriving in competitive environments will position themselves for success.

The success stories of companies like Airbnb and Warby Parker illustrate how resilience and innovation can reshape entire industries. These businesses have navigated challenges by continuously evolving their models and embracing feedback from their customers. Their journeys demonstrate that understanding and responding to market dynamics are critical for sustained growth.

Emily Weiss, founder of Glossier, exemplifies how a customer-centric approach can enhance adaptability. By listening to her audience and creating products that resonate with their needs, she transformed her beauty brand into a community-driven powerhouse. This chapter provides practical insights into how you can adopt an adaptable mindset and build agility into your business model, ensuring that your strategies align with customer expectations.

Brendan Kane, a digital strategist and author, emphasizes the importance of leveraging technology to adapt in a fast-paced world. His insights reveal that embracing technological advancements allows businesses to streamline operations and effectively reach their audiences. As companies like Warby Parker demonstrate, innovation is often the key to maintaining relevance in a rapidly changing marketplace.

The chapter also highlights the historical resilience of figures like Amelia Earhart, who faced societal challenges with unwavering determination. Her legacy inspires entrepreneurs to cultivate a mindset that embraces risk and innovation, proving that adaptability is essential for overcoming obstacles and achieving groundbreaking success.

Martha Stewart's journey from homemaking to becoming a media mogul exemplifies how adaptability can lead to enduring influence. By continuously reinventing her brand and expanding into new markets, she has maintained relevance across generations, showcasing the power of resilience in navigating the complexities of business.

Through the insights of leaders such as Max McKeown, Emily Weiss, and Brendan Kane, this chapter offers practical guidance for cultivating resilience and adaptability. You'll learn how to develop a mindset that embraces change, build a flexible business structure, and leverage setbacks as opportunities for growth. Resilience and adaptability aren't just survival mechanisms—they are essential qualities that empower you to lead your business through uncertainty and emerge stronger on the other side.

———————

Max McKeown's Success Story: The Architect of Innovation and Strategic Insight

"Adaptability is about the powerful difference between adapting to cope and adapting to win." — MAX MCKEOWN, AUTHOR AND BUSINESS STRATEGIST

Max McKeown is a visionary strategist and thought leader whose work bridges the gap between innovation, strategy, and leadership. Known for his ability to simplify complex business concepts, McKeown has authored influential books that inspire organizations to embrace change and unlock their full potential. With a background in psychology and innovation management, he offers a unique perspective on how businesses can thrive in an ever-evolving landscape. Through his books, consulting work, and speaking engagements, McKeown has empowered countless leaders and companies to foster creative thinking and implement practical strategies for sustainable growth. His insights continue to shape the way businesses approach innovation, driving transformative success in a world of constant disruption.

Early Life and Academic Beginnings
Max McKeown's journey to becoming a world-renowned business strategist and innovation expert started with an insatiable curiosity for understanding what makes people, teams, and organizations succeed. Born in the UK, McKeown developed an early fascination with human behavior and strategy, which led him to pursue studies in psychology, strategy, and innovation management. His academic background equipped him with unique insights into both the human and technical aspects of business.

Discovering the Power of Innovation
While working in various consulting roles with global businesses, McKeown identified a recurring challenge: most companies were struggling to adapt to change and unlock their creative potential. He realized that even the most brilliant ideas could fail without strategic alignment and execution. This observation became the cornerstone of his professional focus—helping businesses unleash their potential through innovation and well-defined strategy. McKeown's early

work with companies across industries shaped his understanding of the barriers to innovation and strategic success.

Writing to Influence

McKeown's breakthrough came with his acclaimed books, starting with *The Strategy Book* and *The Innovation Book*. His accessible yet profound writing resonated with business leaders and entrepreneurs, offering practical strategies for innovation, leadership, and adaptation. These works became bestsellers, empowering readers to implement actionable change within their organizations. His signature approach was to blend rigorous research with engaging storytelling, making complex business theories relatable and easy to apply.

A Global Thought Leader

As McKeown's reputation grew, he became a sought-after speaker, consultant, and advisor to some of the world's largest organizations. He was invited to speak at international conferences, sharing his ideas on how companies could thrive in an era of constant disruption. His talks emphasized that innovation isn't limited to technology—it's a mindset that permeates culture, strategy, and leadership. McKeown also embraced digital platforms, using social media to reach a wider audience and engage with followers on innovation trends and business transformation.

The Legacy of Innovation

Max McKeown's contributions to the fields of business strategy and innovation are widely recognized, not only through his books but also through his consulting work with high-profile clients. His ability to demystify strategy and inspire creative thinking has helped countless businesses and leaders unlock their potential. Today, McKeown continues to influence future generations of entrepreneurs, managers, and executives through his writing, speaking engagements, and consulting projects.

Impact and Influence

McKeown's lasting impact lies in his philosophy that innovation is a choice and a responsibility. He believes that organizations must embrace change proactively and that every individual has the power to contribute to innovation. His work serves as a reminder that with the right strategy, mindset, and leadership, businesses can not only survive but also thrive in a fast-changing world.

Airbnb Success Story: From Air Mattresses to Global Hospitality Giant

"Build something 100 people love, not something 1 million people kind of like." — BRIAN CHESKY, THE VISIONARY ARCHITECT OF COMMUNITY-DRIVEN INNOVATION

"Constraints are a gift. They force creativity and problem-solving in ways you'd never explore otherwise." — JOE GEBBIA, THE CREATIVE MIND BEHIND PROBLEM-SOLVING CONSTRAINTS

"Success isn't about being first—it's about being the best at solving real problems." — NATHAN BLECHARCZYK, THE STRATEGIC ENGINEER OF PRACTICAL SOLUTIONS

Airbnb's story is one of creativity, resilience, and an unconventional approach to solving a problem. What began as an idea to make a few extra dollars by renting out air mattresses turned into a multi-billion-dollar company that transformed the travel and hospitality industry.

The Beginning: A Simple Idea Born from Necessity
Airbnb was founded in 2008 by Brian Chesky, Joe Gebbia, and Nathan Blecharczyk in San Francisco. The idea for Airbnb came out of necessity. Chesky and Gebbia, two friends who had recently graduated from the Rhode Island School of Design, were struggling to pay rent in their expensive San Francisco apartment.

In October 2007, a major design conference was coming to town, and all the hotels were fully booked. Seeing an opportunity, Chesky and Gebbia decided to rent out space in their apartment to conference attendees. To make it work, they set up three air mattresses in their living room and offered breakfast in the morning. This "Air Bed and Breakfast" concept became the seed for what would later become Airbnb.

They quickly realized that their idea could solve a real problem for travelers looking for affordable and unique lodging options while helping homeowners and renters make extra money.

The Struggles of a Startup

Like most startups, Airbnb did not take off immediately. In fact, the early days were full of struggles. The founders launched the initial website, airbedandbreakfast.com, in 2008, but it failed to gain traction. The economic recession was in full swing, and convincing people to rent out their homes to strangers was a tough sell.

At one point, the co-founders were broke and resorted to selling cereal boxes— limited edition Obama O's and Cap'n McCain's during the 2008 U.S. presidential election—to raise money for the business. This clever marketing stunt raised $30,000, which helped them keep the company afloat.

However, the turning point came when the founders were accepted into Y Combinator, a startup accelerator program in Silicon Valley. With the guidance of Paul Graham, they learned to refine their idea and improve the platform. Y Combinator gave them $20,000 in seed money, but more importantly, the confidence and mentorship to scale their business.

Expansion and Growth

One of the key strategies that helped Airbnb grow was its focus on user experience. The founders realized that professional photos of rental properties made a big difference in how listings were perceived. So, they flew to New York to personally photograph their hosts' homes. This small action led to more bookings and set a precedent for quality control on the platform.

As Airbnb expanded, it began offering unique stays like treehouses, castles, and even private islands. This focus on offering not just a place to sleep but a unique experience resonated with travelers who were looking for more than just a hotel room.

Airbnb also built a trust system through reviews, host profiles, and guest profiles, making people more comfortable with the idea of staying in someone else's home or renting out their space to strangers. This community-driven approach helped create a sense of trust and safety, which was critical for the company's success.

By 2011, Airbnb had reached 1 million bookings and expanded to international markets, growing rapidly in Europe, Asia, and Latin America.

Overcoming Challenges and Disrupting the Industry
Airbnb disrupted the traditional hotel industry by providing more affordable and diverse accommodation options. However, its rise was not without challenges. Many cities and governments raised concerns over regulation, safety, and taxation as Airbnb properties multiplied in urban areas, often competing with local hotels and rental properties.

Despite these hurdles, Airbnb continued to grow. It worked with local governments to create frameworks for hosts to pay taxes and comply with regulations. The company also added features to ensure guest safety, including a $1 million host guarantee and 24/7 customer support.

IPO and Current Success
By 2020, Airbnb was one of the most anticipated IPOs (Initial Public Offerings) in the tech world. Despite the COVID-19 pandemic significantly impacting travel, Airbnb showed resilience by pivoting to longer-term stays and offering virtual experiences. When it went public in December 2020, Airbnb's IPO valued the company at over $100 billion, marking one of the most successful tech IPOs of all time.

Key Factors in Airbnb's Success:

- **Unique Value Proposition**: Airbnb offers a diverse range of accommodations, from spare bedrooms to luxurious mansions and even unusual properties like treehouses and yurts.

- **Community and Trust**: The company built a platform based on trust through verified reviews, user profiles, and host guarantees, fostering a sense of safety for both hosts and guests.

- **Global Expansion**: Airbnb quickly expanded internationally, tailoring its platform to different markets and capitalizing on the growing trend of experiential travel.

- **Adaptability**: The company has successfully navigated regulatory challenges and industry disruptions by working with governments and constantly evolving its business model.

- **Focus on Experience**: Airbnb positioned itself not just as a booking platform but as a way for travelers to **live like locals** and have unique, memorable experiences.

From its humble beginnings with air mattresses on a living room floor to becoming a global hospitality leader, Airbnb's story is a testament to innovation, persistence, and the power of community. Today, it connects millions of travelers with hosts around the world, creating a marketplace that offers something for everyone—from budget travelers to luxury seekers.

Emily Weiss' Success Story: From Beauty Blog to Beauty Empire

"Success doesn't come from waiting for the perfect moment. It comes from starting messy, learning as you go, and believing in the power of your vision." — EMILY WEISS, BEAUTY DISRUPTOR AND FOUNDER OF GLOSSIER

Glossier is a beauty brand that has revolutionized the industry by focusing on a customer-first, digital-native approach. Its rise to success is deeply intertwined with the vision of its founder, Emily Weiss, who saw an opportunity to change the way beauty products were marketed and sold.

The Beginning: From Blog to Brand

Emily Weiss started her career in fashion as an intern for Teen Vogue and later as a fashion assistant at Vogue. In 2010, while still working in fashion, she launched Into the Gloss, a beauty blog that featured in-depth interviews with women about their beauty routines. The blog quickly gained popularity due to its authentic, behind-the-scenes look at how real women, celebrities, and beauty insiders used products. Weiss built a community around the blog, creating a space where beauty enthusiasts could share tips, advice, and experiences.

This online community, combined with Weiss' insider knowledge of the beauty industry, planted the seed for a bigger idea: creating a beauty brand that would be directly influenced by the consumers who used the products. She saw a gap in the market for products that were designed based on real feedback from users, and thus, Glossier was born.

The Launch of Glossier

In 2014, Weiss launched Glossier with a small selection of four products: a cleanser, a moisturizer, a balm, and a skin tint. These were marketed as essentials for a simple, natural beauty routine, which resonated with women tired of overly complicated beauty regimens. Glossier's products were minimalist, sleekly packaged, and affordable—a contrast to many luxury beauty brands at the time.

One of the key factors that set Glossier apart from traditional beauty brands was its digital-first strategy. Glossier was launched as an e-commerce brand with a focus on direct-to-consumer sales, leveraging its strong online community for marketing and product development. Instead of traditional advertising, Weiss and her team relied on social media and word-of-mouth marketing to build buzz.

Glossier's Instagram page became a key tool in its growth, showcasing real customers using the products and encouraging them to share their own experiences. This authentic, user-generated content helped Glossier build a cult following, with customers who felt like they were part of something bigger than just a beauty brand.

Customer-Centric Approach

At the heart of Glossier's success is its customer-centric approach. From the start, Weiss has emphasized the importance of listening to customers. Glossier frequently polls its community for feedback, asking them what products they want to see next. This direct feedback loop allows the brand to develop products that meet real customer needs, creating a sense of co-creation between the brand and its consumers.

This philosophy led to the launch of some of Glossier's most popular products, such as the Boy Brow, a brow grooming product that quickly became a bestseller, and Cloud Paint, a gel-cream blush that gained cult status.

Expansion and Growth

As Glossier's popularity grew, so did its product line. The brand expanded from skincare to include makeup, fragrances, and body care, all while staying true to its minimalist, no-fuss aesthetic. Glossier also began to experiment with pop-up shops and eventually opened permanent stores in cities like New York and Los Angeles, creating immersive, Instagram-worthy retail experiences that drew in fans.

By 2018, Glossier had raised $100 million in funding and was valued at over $1 billion, making it one of the fastest-growing beauty companies in the world. Weiss' vision of building a beauty brand that put customers first and focused on inclusive, natural beauty resonated with a generation looking for authenticity in their purchases.

Social Media and the Power of Community

Glossier's use of social media has been instrumental to its success. The brand has built a massive online following by focusing on real people and real stories, rather than relying on traditional celebrity endorsements. Instagram, in particular, has been a key platform for Glossier, where its hashtag #glossier has thousands of posts from customers sharing their experiences with the brand.

By empowering its customers to be brand advocates, Glossier has created a marketing machine that runs on word-of-mouth and user-generated content. This grassroots approach not only builds trust but also fosters a deep sense of community among Glossier users.

The Future of Glossier

Glossier's success shows no signs of slowing down. In addition to expanding its product offerings, the company has announced plans to continue opening more brick-and-mortar stores and expanding its international presence. Weiss has also hinted at future innovations, with the brand focusing on more skincare products and continuing to develop new, inclusive beauty offerings.

From its beginnings as a beauty blog to its status as a billion-dollar beauty empire, Glossier's story is a testament to the power of community, innovation, and customer-first thinking. Weiss' vision of disrupting the beauty industry by focusing on authenticity and direct-to-consumer strategies has changed the game, proving that with the right approach, even the most established industries can be revolutionized.

Key Takeaways:

- **Community-driven:** Glossier's success is rooted in its deep connection with its customers and the beauty community.

- **Digital-first strategy:** Glossier revolutionized beauty by relying on e-commerce and social media instead of traditional retail models.

- **Customer-focused product development:** Listening to consumers and incorporating their feedback into product launches has been a winning strategy for Glossier.

Glossier is more than just a beauty brand—it's a movement that has redefined how beauty companies interact with their customers.

Brendan Kane's Success Story: From Digital Strategist to Social Media Growth Guru

"Engagement isn't luck—it's strategy. Master the art of grabbing attention, and you'll unlock limitless potential." — BRENDAN KANE, DIGITAL STRATEGIST AND AUTHOR OF ONE MILLION FOLLOWERS

Brendan Kane is a name synonymous with explosive social media growth and innovative digital strategies. He has built a reputation as a master of helping brands, celebrities, and businesses grow their social media presence at record speeds, thanks to his unique understanding of how to create viral content and engage audiences effectively.

Early Career: Building a Foundation in Digital Strategy
Brendan Kane's journey to success began in the entertainment industry. After graduating from college, he moved to Los Angeles to work in film. He quickly realized the power of digital media to help entertainment brands expand their reach. Kane worked on digital platforms for major studios like Paramount

Pictures, Warner Bros., and Lionsgate, helping them develop digital strategies to promote their films.

Kane's early experience in the film industry exposed him to the massive impact of digital marketing and social media growth. It was during this time that he developed a passion for understanding how content could be optimized to reach millions of people. He knew that if he could figure out how to create content that went viral, he could build significant online audiences for brands and individuals.

Social Media Success and Celebrity Collaborations

After working with major film studios, Brendan decided to branch out and apply his skills beyond the entertainment industry. He started consulting for celebrities, influencers, and Fortune 500 companies, helping them navigate the rapidly changing world of social media.

His big breakthrough came when he used his growth hacking techniques to build 1 million followers on Facebook in just 30 days. This remarkable feat was not just a milestone in his own career, but also a testament to his ability to generate viral content and understand how to leverage social media algorithms. This success propelled Kane into the spotlight as a social media expert and allowed him to secure high-profile clients.

Some of the major figures and brands Kane has worked with include Taylor Swift, Rihanna, and MTV. He helped these global icons optimize their social media presence to better engage with their massive fan bases and grow their reach exponentially. His experience with A-list celebrities further cemented his status as a go-to expert for digital strategy.

Author and Speaker: Sharing His Knowledge

With years of success under his belt, Brendan Kane decided to share his insights with a broader audience. In 2018, he published his book "One Million Followers: How I Built a Massive Social Following in 30 Days," which became a bestseller. The book is a practical guide that reveals the strategies Kane used to rapidly grow social media followings and create viral content. It became especially popular among entrepreneurs, influencers, and marketers looking to scale their online presence.

Kane's approach is built around iterative testing—trying out different strategies quickly, analyzing the results, and adjusting based on what works best. He encourages people to think of social media growth as a science, where results are driven by data and constant optimization.

Following the success of his first book, Kane released *Hook Point: How to Stand Out in a 3-Second World* in 2020. In this book, he addresses the challenge of grabbing attention in a crowded digital landscape. With so much competition for attention online, Kane explains how brands and individuals can create impactful content that captures interest in just a few seconds—crucial for standing out on social media platforms.

Key Strategies Behind Brendan Kane's Success

- **Data-Driven Growth:** Kane's success comes from his commitment to analyzing data and constantly testing new ideas. His approach is grounded in metrics, which allows him to optimize content for maximum engagement.

- **Understanding Algorithms:** Kane is a master of social media algorithms, allowing him to create content that aligns with platform trends and maximizes organic reach.

- **Content that Resonates:** He emphasizes creating value-driven content that resonates with specific audiences. Whether it's for brands, celebrities, or influencers, Kane's strategy is about building authentic connections through content.

- **Failing Fast, Learning Faster:** Kane encourages a mindset of "failing fast and learning faster," where constant experimentation and adaptation are key to growth. His methods focus on quick iterations to discover what works.

Entrepreneurial Ventures and Future Vision

Brendan Kane has also founded Strike Social, a company that provides AI-powered solutions for social media advertising, and Hook Point, his consulting and education company, through which he continues to help brands and individuals navigate the complexities of social media growth. His vision for the future involves continuing to empower businesses and creators by teaching them how to stay relevant in an ever-evolving digital world.

Conclusion: A Master of Digital Growth

Brendan Kane's journey from digital strategist to social media guru is one of adaptation, experimentation, and relentless learning. Through his unique approach to social media growth and content creation, he has built a successful career that spans industries and continents. Kane continues to be a pioneering force in the digital marketing world, proving that with the right strategy, anyone can build an engaged and massive online audience.

===

Warby Parker's Success Story: Visionary Disruptor Revolutionizes Eyewear

"Doing good is good for business. Our mission isn't just about selling glasses; it's about creating impact and making the world see better." — WARBY PARKER, PIONEERS OF DIRECT-TO-CONSUMER EYEWEAR AND SOCIALLY CONSCIOUS BUSINESS

Warby Parker's journey from a simple idea to a billion-dollar disruptor is a story of innovation, purpose, and perseverance. Founded in 2010 by Neil Blumenthal, Dave Gilboa, Andrew Hunt, and Jeffrey Raider while they were students at the Wharton School of Business, Warby Parker set out to solve a problem they all experienced firsthand: the exorbitant cost of eyeglasses. Fueled by a desire to democratize access to stylish, affordable eyewear, the founders crafted a direct-to-consumer model that would cut out middlemen, passing savings onto customers. But Warby Parker's mission went beyond profit—they built a brand that merged business with social impact, offering a "buy one, give one" program to help those in need. From leveraging e-commerce and social media to scaling into physical retail and becoming a public company, Warby Parker's ascent illustrates how strategic innovation and a customer-first approach can turn a frustration into a thriving, socially-conscious empire.

The Idea: A Solution Born from Frustration

Warby Parker was founded in 2010 by four friends—Neil Blumenthal, Dave Gilboa, Andrew Hunt, and Jeffrey Raider—who met while studying at the Wharton School of Business. The idea for the company came from a shared frustration: eyeglasses were far too expensive, often costing hundreds of dollars for a single pair. They realized the eyewear industry was dominated by a few large players, keeping prices artificially high, and saw an opportunity to disrupt the market with a direct-to-consumer model.

Their vision was simple: make stylish, high-quality eyewear affordable and accessible to everyone. By cutting out the middleman and designing glasses in-house, Warby Parker could sell their products at a fraction of the traditional retail price, starting at $95.

The Business Model: Disruption and Innovation

What set Warby Parker apart from the beginning was its innovative business model. The founders were inspired by companies like Zappos and TOMS, focusing on a customer-centric approach with an emphasis on social good. They adopted a "buy one, give one" model, where for every pair of glasses sold, a pair would be donated to someone in need. This social mission resonated with consumers who were increasingly seeking brands with a purpose.

The founders also recognized that buying glasses online could be a challenge since most people prefer to try on frames before making a decision. To address this, they launched a home try-on program, where customers could select five pairs of glasses to try on at home for free. This simple yet game-changing idea revolutionized the online shopping experience and helped build trust with skeptical customers.

Early Success: Word-of-Mouth and Virality

Warby Parker launched in February 2010, and the company quickly gained traction. They initially aimed to sell 15,000 pairs of glasses in the first year, but within just a few weeks of launching, they had sold out of their inventory and were forced to create a waitlist of 20,000 customers.

Much of Warby Parker's early success came from its savvy use of social media and word-of-mouth marketing. The founders reached out to influential bloggers, stylists, and fashion publications, which helped them gain exposure in the early days. The company also benefited from viral growth through customer recommendations, as people were excited about the combination of style, affordability, and social good.

Growth and Expansion: From E-commerce to Brick-and-Mortar

Despite being a digital-first company, Warby Parker recognized the value of physical retail. As the business grew, they opened their first brick-and-mortar store in New York City in 2013. This allowed customers to try on glasses in person and created a more immersive brand experience. The company's physical stores were designed to feel like libraries, with shelves lined with glasses instead of books—a creative and inviting environment that encouraged customers to linger.

By combining online convenience with an enjoyable in-store experience, Warby Parker was able to create a seamless omnichannel approach. As of 2024, Warby Parker operates more than 150 stores across the United States and Canada, while still maintaining a strong online presence.

The Secret Sauce: Customer Experience and Innovation

Warby Parker's focus on customer experience has been one of the key factors in its success. The company is known for its excellent customer service, hassle-free returns, and fast shipping. They've also continued to innovate by introducing features like virtual try-on technology and expanding into other areas like prescription sunglasses and contact lenses.

Additionally, Warby Parker has stayed true to its social mission. As of today, they have donated millions of pairs of glasses to people in need through partnerships with organizations like VisionSpring. This commitment to social impact has helped the company build a loyal customer base and solidify its reputation as a purpose-driven brand.

Becoming a Billion-Dollar Brand

By combining style, affordability, and a focus on social good, Warby Parker quickly became a billion-dollar company. In 2021, the company went public via a direct listing on the New York Stock Exchange, solidifying its status as a leader in the eyewear industry.

Warby Parker's story is a testament to the power of disruption, innovation, and customer focus. The company has proven that even in industries dominated by legacy players, there's always room for a challenger with a fresh perspective and a commitment to making things better for consumers.

Warby Parker continues to evolve and expand, with the same mission that started it all: to offer affordable, stylish eyewear while making a positive impact on the world.

Amelia Earhart's Success Story: Soaring into History

"Launching a book without a pre-launch checklist is like piloting a plane without a pre-flight check—risky and unadvised. Tick every box, and you're not just ready to fly—you're ready to soar."
— AMELIA EARHART, PIONEERING AVIATOR

Amelia Earhart, a trailblazing aviator and fearless adventurer, redefined what was possible for women in the early 20th century. Born with an insatiable curiosity and a rebellious spirit, Earhart pursued her passion for flying at a time when the skies were largely closed to women. Her daring achievements, including becoming the first woman to fly solo across the Atlantic Ocean, captivated the world and established her as an enduring symbol of courage and determination. Beyond aviation, Earhart used her fame to advocate for gender equality, inspiring generations to challenge societal limitations. Though her mysterious disappearance during her attempt to fly around the world remains unsolved, her legacy soars on, reminding us that dreams are meant to be pursued—even against the odds.

Early Life and Passion for Aviation

Born on July 24, 1897, in Atchison, Kansas, Amelia Earhart's fascination with flight began at a young age. Raised in an unconventional household, she was encouraged to explore her curiosity and resist societal expectations for women. After attending a flying exhibition in 1920, where she took her first airplane ride,

Earhart was captivated by aviation. Determined to learn how to fly, she saved money working odd jobs and took her first flying lessons in 1921, with female aviator Neta Snook as her instructor.

Breaking Barriers and Achieving Firsts

Earhart earned her pilot's license in 1923, becoming one of the first women in the world to do so. Undeterred by financial challenges and societal limitations, she set her sights on record-breaking flights to inspire others. Her breakthrough came in 1928 when she became the first woman to fly across the Atlantic as a passenger, garnering international fame. Though this flight earned her admiration, Earhart remained determined to make a solo transatlantic journey to truly prove her abilities.

In 1932, she made history by becoming the first woman to fly solo nonstop across the Atlantic Ocean. Braving icy conditions, fatigue, and mechanical challenges, Earhart landed in Ireland after a 15-hour flight, cementing her place as an aviation icon. This achievement inspired a generation of women to pursue careers in aviation and other male-dominated fields.

Expanding Horizons and Inspiring a Nation

Throughout the 1930s, Earhart continued to break records, including becoming the first person—man or woman—to fly solo from Hawaii to California. She leveraged her fame to advocate for women's rights and promote aviation. Earhart was also an active member of The Ninety-Nines, an international organization for female pilots, dedicated to promoting opportunities for women in aviation.

In addition to her flights, Earhart wrote books and gave lectures, using her platform to encourage others to dream big. She emphasized perseverance, courage, and independence, becoming a symbol of progress and empowerment for women.

The Final Flight and Enduring Legacy

In 1937, Earhart embarked on her most ambitious adventure yet: a flight around the world. Along with her navigator Fred Noonan, she successfully completed much of the journey, covering two-thirds of the globe. However, on July 2, 1937, her plane vanished over the Pacific Ocean en route to Howland Island. Despite an extensive search, no definitive traces of Earhart or her aircraft were ever found, sparking enduring intrigue and countless theories about her disappearance.

Impact and Lasting Influence

Amelia Earhart's life and legacy are defined by courage, innovation, and an unwavering spirit. Her achievements shattered gender norms and proved that women could excel in fields once dominated by men. Though her life was tragically cut short, Earhart's adventurous spirit continues to inspire dreamers, trailblazers, and risk-takers worldwide. Her story reminds us that greatness is achieved not just by success, but by daring to explore the unknown.

Martha Stewart's Success Story: From Cater to Icon of Domesticity

"Without an open mind, you can never be a great success." — MARTHA STEWART, QUEEN OF LIFESTYLE AND DOMESTIC INNOVATION

Martha Stewart is a self-made businesswoman, television personality, and author, widely recognized as the ultimate domestic expert. From humble beginnings to becoming a household name, Stewart built a lifestyle empire that encompasses cooking, home décor, gardening, and entertaining. Her story is one of ambition, reinvention, and resilience.

Early Life and Influences

Born as Martha Kostyra on August 3, 1941, in Jersey City, New Jersey, Stewart grew up in a Polish-American family. She was introduced to the art of cooking, canning, and gardening at a young age by her mother, who taught her traditional Polish recipes and home-keeping skills. Stewart's father was an avid gardener, and he passed on his love of cultivating plants, a passion that would become central to Martha's later career.

Stewart attended Barnard College in New York City, where she earned a degree in European History and Architectural History. She initially began her career in a completely different field—modeling, which helped support her through college, and then as a stockbroker on Wall Street. However, the stock market wasn't her passion, and after the birth of her daughter Alexis, Stewart transitioned into her next chapter: home catering.

The Start of Her Empire: Catering and "Entertaining"
In the early 1970s, Stewart moved with her family to Westport, Connecticut, where she started a catering business from her home kitchen. Her creativity, attention to detail, and ability to turn everyday meals into luxurious events earned her a reputation for quality. Her catering business grew quickly, and she eventually partnered with a friend to launch Martha Stewart, Inc.

It wasn't long before her catering skills caught the attention of Alan Mirken, head of Crown Publishing Group, who asked her to publish a book. In 1982, Stewart released her first book, "Entertaining," which became an instant success. This marked the beginning of Stewart's journey to becoming the queen of domesticity. The book's blend of recipes, decorating ideas, and event-planning tips set the tone for Stewart's signature style.

Expanding Her Brand
Throughout the 1980s and 1990s, Stewart's empire grew rapidly. She authored dozens of books on cooking, entertaining, gardening, and decorating, including "Martha Stewart's Quick Cook," "Martha Stewart's Weddings," and "The Martha Stewart Cookbook." Her approachable yet elevated take on homemaking resonated with millions of readers.

In 1990, she launched Martha Stewart Living, a magazine that became the cornerstone of her brand. Filled with ideas for seasonal recipes, home projects, and decorating tips, it was an instant hit. The magazine's success led to the creation of her television show, "Martha Stewart Living," which aired in 1993 and turned Stewart into a beloved TV personality.

Stewart's meticulous attention to detail and her ability to anticipate lifestyle trends cemented her position as a lifestyle guru. Her name became synonymous with elegance, creativity, and high standards in home life.

Going Public and Building a Media Empire
In 1997, Stewart took her brand to new heights by founding Martha Stewart Living Omnimedia, an umbrella company that consolidated her various ventures, including publishing, TV shows, and merchandising. This move allowed Stewart

to control all aspects of her brand. In 1999, she took the company public, becoming the first female self-made billionaire in the United States. The IPO was incredibly successful, further fueling her fame and influence.

Her company expanded into merchandising, with Martha Stewart-branded products available in major retailers like Kmart and later Macy's. From cookware to linens, her product lines brought her home expertise into everyday homes, making her a true icon in the retail space.

Legal Troubles and Comeback

In 2001, Stewart's career faced a major setback when she was implicated in an insider trading scandal. Accused of selling her shares in ImClone Systems based on non-public information, Stewart was convicted of conspiracy and obstruction of justice in 2004. She served five months in federal prison and was forced to step down as CEO of her company.

Despite the public fallout, Stewart's resilience shone through. After serving her sentence, she made a comeback, returning to her television show and re-establishing her position as a business leader. Her brand remained strong, and her media presence grew once again with new television shows like "Martha" and collaborations with other companies.

The Modern Martha Stewart Brand

Today, Martha Stewart continues to expand her brand through partnerships, media appearances, and new product lines. She has embraced the digital age, creating a robust online presence through social media and her website. Stewart has also developed an unlikely yet successful partnership with rapper Snoop Dogg, co-hosting "Martha & Snoop's Potluck Dinner Party," which has garnered both media attention and widespread fan appeal.

Martha Stewart's legacy as a self-made entrepreneur and lifestyle expert continues to inspire generations of homemakers, entrepreneurs, and fans. Her story is one of hard work, innovation, and reinvention, proving that setbacks can be overcome with determination and vision.

Conclusion: The Domestic Mogul

Martha Stewart's journey from a catering business owner to a billion-dollar lifestyle empire is a remarkable example of building a brand that stands the test of time. Through her books, TV shows, magazines, and product lines, Stewart revolutionized the way we think about home life, entertaining, and DIY culture. Today, her name remains synonymous with creativity, style, and the art of living well.

CHAPTER THREE

Negotiation, Influence, and Collaboration

Success in business often hinges on the ability to negotiate effectively, wield influence with integrity, and foster meaningful collaborations. Whether striking deals with partners, managing team dynamics, or expanding into new markets, the skills of negotiation and influence are essential. This chapter explores how mastering these skills enables leaders to navigate complex business relationships, unlock growth opportunities, and cultivate long-term collaborations that drive sustainable success.

Michele Jennae, an expert in the art of negotiation, emphasizes that "influence is about making connections that create value." Effective negotiators know how to find common ground, ensuring that both parties leave the table with a sense of achievement. This chapter provides practical techniques for preparing for negotiations, understanding opposing perspectives, and securing mutually beneficial outcomes.

Influence is the ability to inspire others to follow your lead—not by force, but by building trust and communicating effectively. Blake Mycoskie, the founder of TOMS, notes, "When you lead with purpose, you inspire others to join you." Leaders who influence others through shared values and a clear mission create a sense of purpose that attracts followers and aligns efforts toward common goals.

Collaboration is equally vital, as no business can thrive in isolation. Otis Chandler, co-founder of Goodreads, reminds us, "Collaboration expands our horizons and multiplies our opportunities." This chapter delves into the importance of building partnerships that enhance your strengths, create synergies, and open doors to new ventures.

Mastering negotiation and influence requires preparation, adaptability, and active listening. Stephen R. Covey, author of The 7 Habits of Highly Effective People, famously asserted, "Seek first to understand, then to be understood." This principle forms the foundation of successful negotiations, encouraging business leaders to engage with empathy and address the needs of all parties involved.

Collaboration transcends transactional interactions; it fosters trust and mutual respect. Prince Ea, a motivational speaker and filmmaker, emphasizes, "True collaboration happens when people come together with a shared vision." This chapter offers insights into how you can build authentic, collaborative relationships that foster innovation and mutual success.

Navigating power dynamics is another key element of negotiation. Tobias Lütke, co-founder of Shopify, emphasizes the importance of flexibility: "Be firm on your values, but flexible on your methods." Leaders must balance firmness with adaptability, knowing when to push for their objectives and when to modify their approach to secure long-term partnerships. This chapter provides actionable advice for managing difficult conversations, overcoming objections, and finding win-win solutions.

Collaboration is particularly critical in today's interconnected business world. Henry Ford famously stated, "Coming together is a beginning; keeping together is progress; working together is success." As businesses increasingly rely on cross-functional and cross-industry partnerships, collaboration becomes a powerful tool for achieving strategic objectives.

The influence of negotiation and collaboration extends beyond external relationships to internal dynamics as well. Lee Crow, an organizational development expert, remarks, "Building a team is about creating a culture where collaboration thrives." Leaders must foster a collaborative culture within their organizations, empowering teams to work together toward shared goals.

This chapter draws from the experiences of industry leaders such as Michele Jennae, Blake Mycoskie, and Tobias Lütke, offering practical strategies for mastering negotiation and influence. You'll learn how to develop rapport quickly, leverage influence without manipulation, and cultivate partnerships that generate sustainable success. Whether you're closing a business deal, managing team relationships, or building strategic alliances, the insights provided in this chapter will equip you to lead with confidence and collaboration.

By the end of this chapter, you'll understand that negotiation, influence, and collaboration aren't just isolated skills—they are essential pillars for building a successful business. You'll discover how these elements work together to create a powerful framework for navigating challenges, driving growth, and forging lasting connections. In an increasingly interconnected world, mastering these skills will enable you to unlock new possibilities and elevate your business to new heights.

Michele Jennae's Success Story: A Champion of Authentic Networking and Meaningful Connections

"Networking is not about just connecting people. It's about connecting people with people, people with ideas, and people with opportunities." — MICHELE JENNAE, NETWORKING EXPERT AND AUTHOR

Michele Jennae is a thought leader and advocate for reimagining networking as a practice grounded in authenticity, generosity, and long-term relationships. With a passion for helping others thrive through meaningful connections, Michele's career has been defined by her unique philosophy: networking is not transactional, but transformational. Through her book *The Connectworker: Networking in the New Economy*, public speaking engagements, and coaching sessions, she has guided countless individuals and professionals to embrace relational intelligence as the foundation for personal and professional success. Michele's work continues to inspire people to build influence, foster collaboration, and lead with empathy in a world where genuine connection has become more valuable than ever.

The Beginning: Recognizing the Power of Relationships

Michele Jennae's journey began with a profound insight—true success isn't just about individual achievement but about building meaningful connections with others. As a communications specialist and leadership development coach, Michele discovered early in her career that the key to thriving in both personal and professional life lay in cultivating authentic relationships. Inspired by this realization, she embarked on a mission to teach others how to harness the power of networking and personal connection.

Launching "The Connectworker"

In 2013, Michele Jennae published *The Connectworker: Networking in the New Economy*, a book that quickly resonated with readers. In it, she redefined networking from a transactional process to one grounded in trust, generosity, and long-term relationships. Michele's approach was revolutionary, shifting the focus from "what can I get?" to "how can I help?" This philosophy aligned perfectly with the needs of professionals navigating an increasingly interconnected, yet impersonal, digital landscape.

Expanding Her Influence

Michele leveraged the success of her book to build a brand as a thought leader in networking, leadership development, and relationship-building. She became a sought-after speaker, delivering workshops and seminars for businesses, entrepreneurs, and organizations. Her presentations provided actionable strategies for making genuine connections in a world dominated by social media and online communication, encouraging people to lead with empathy and value.

Thought Leadership and Coaching

In addition to writing and public speaking, Michele Jennae expanded her influence through one-on-one coaching, where she mentored professionals on how to develop leadership skills rooted in relational intelligence. Her coaching focused on helping clients not only grow their networks but also use those connections to build influence and create collaborative opportunities. Michele's guidance empowered individuals to align their networking efforts with their personal and professional goals, resulting in sustainable success.

Building a Legacy Through Connection

Michele's ability to inspire connection and foster collaboration has been at the heart of her career. Her work continues to emphasize the importance of leading with integrity, sharing value without expectation, and nurturing meaningful relationships over time. Through her writing, coaching, and speaking engagements, Michele Jennae has become a leading voice in networking and relationship-building. Her career is a testament to the belief that success is not a solo journey—it is the result of meaningful connections, shared value, and a commitment to lifting others along the way.

Today, Michele Jennae's influence extends far beyond her initial work, as she continues to inspire professionals around the world to master the art of authentic networking, cultivating relationships that are as rewarding personally as they are professionally.

===

Blake Mycoskie's Success Story: Creator of the One-for-One Movement

"Start something that matters." — BLAKE MYCOSKIE, VISIONARY ENTREPRENEUR BEHIND TOMS AND THE ONE-FOR-ONE MOVEMENT

Tony Robbins is one of the world's most famous motivational speakers, authors, and life coaches. Known for his boundless energy, larger-than-life presence, and transformative seminars, Robbins' journey to the top was far from easy. His story is one of overcoming hardships, self-discovery, and a relentless desire to help others achieve their fullest potential.

The story of TOMS Shoes begins with Blake Mycoskie, an entrepreneur who was inspired to create a business that would make a difference in the world. In 2006, while traveling in Argentina, Mycoskie witnessed the struggles of children without shoes. Many children in underdeveloped areas were unable to afford shoes, which exposed them to injury and disease. This experience sparked an idea that would later become TOMS Shoes.

The Inspiration: A Simple, Powerful Idea

Rather than starting a traditional charity, Mycoskie decided to create a for-profit business with a social mission. His idea was simple: for every pair of shoes sold, TOMS would donate a new pair of shoes to a child in need. This became known as the One for One model. The company's first product was a version of the Argentinian alpargata, a simple, comfortable canvas shoe that fit with the brand's laid-back, ethical ethos.

The Birth of TOMS

With a desire to create sustainable change and offer a stylish, comfortable shoe, Mycoskie launched TOMS out of his apartment in Los Angeles. The business initially faced challenges—Mycoskie had to personally visit stores and pitch the shoes, with many retailers reluctant to take on an unknown brand with a unique social mission.

However, the brand's story and mission resonated with consumers. After Mycoskie's appearance on "The Amazing Race" and early coverage in media outlets like *Vogue*, TOMS quickly gained popularity. Consumers were drawn to the brand's simplicity and its promise that each purchase would make a difference.

The One for One Model: Social Impact and Success

TOMS' One for One model became a revolutionary idea in the world of social entrepreneurship. By aligning profits with a greater purpose, the brand grew rapidly, with customers feeling that they were contributing to a good cause with every purchase. The shoes themselves became trendy, comfortable, and easy to wear, which further fueled their success.

As the company grew, so did its philanthropic efforts. By 2013, TOMS had donated over 10 million pairs of shoes to children in need across the globe. The One for One model expanded beyond shoes—TOMS later introduced eyewear, clean water initiatives, and even coffee, with each product connected to a specific charitable cause. For instance, TOMS eyewear purchases helped fund vision treatments, including glasses and surgeries.

Challenges and Evolution

While TOMS saw rapid early success, the company also faced challenges as it expanded. Some critics questioned whether simply donating shoes was a sustainable long-term solution to poverty, raising concerns about the potential economic impact on local shoemakers in areas receiving donations.

In response, TOMS evolved its model to focus on local production, creating jobs in the communities they were helping and expanding their charitable efforts into new areas like clean water and health. Additionally, in recent years, the company has worked to become more transparent about its supply chain and social impact.

Legacy and Continued Impact

TOMS has become a leading name in social entrepreneurship, proving that businesses can be profitable while also addressing global social issues. The company has helped inspire a new generation of mission-driven businesses, blending philanthropy with commerce in innovative ways.

Though Mycoskie stepped down as CEO in 2015, TOMS continues to grow and impact millions of lives worldwide. As of today, TOMS has given away more than 100 million pairs of shoes and expanded its charitable efforts into over 70 countries, including initiatives in education, health, and environmental sustainability.

TOMS' story is one of innovation, compassion, and entrepreneurship, demonstrating that a simple idea can not only grow into a global brand but also make a lasting difference in the world.

Otis Chandler's Success Story: From Passion Project to Book Lover's Haven

"Build something people love, and the rest will follow." — OTIS CHANDLER, PIONEER OF DIGITAL READING COMMUNITIES

Goodreads started as a simple idea born out of one person's love for reading. In 2006, Otis Chandler, a software engineer, and entrepreneur, launched Goodreads with the goal of creating an online community where people could discover new books, share reviews, and connect with fellow book lovers. Today, Goodreads is the world's largest platform for readers and book recommendations, boasting over 90 million members.

The Inspiration: From Frustration to Innovation

The idea for Goodreads came to Chandler after a conversation with his then-girlfriend (now wife). They were discussing the difficulty of finding new books to read, especially ones that came with personal recommendations. Chandler realized that while there were some book review sites out there, there wasn't a true social network dedicated to books—where people could share, rate, and discuss what they were reading.

Chandler, who had a background in technology and a strong entrepreneurial spirit (his grandfather had founded The Los Angeles Times), decided to merge his love for reading with his tech skills. He envisioned a platform that would allow users to discover books through friends' recommendations, in the same way people often find books by word-of-mouth in real life. In December 2006, Chandler launched Goodreads from his living room with the hope that it would bring readers closer together.

Early Growth: A Community of Readers

Goodreads quickly gained traction, as people were drawn to its unique blend of social networking and book discovery. Users could create bookshelves, write reviews, and see what their friends were reading. This ability to see recommendations from friends and the broader community of readers helped create a strong sense of connection and engagement on the platform.

One of the reasons for Goodreads' success was its user-driven nature. The content—book reviews, recommendations, and lists—was generated entirely by users. This not only made the site highly interactive but also created a vast repository of book-related content that attracted more users.

In addition, Goodreads became a hub for book clubs and discussion groups, further fostering community engagement. Readers who loved discussing books offline found a new online space where they could interact with like-minded individuals.

The Power of Data: Personalized Book Recommendations
Another key factor in Goodreads' rise was its use of data to provide personalized recommendations. Users could rate books they had read, and Goodreads would then recommend similar titles based on their preferences. This feature, combined with the community's shared reviews and ratings, made it much easier for users to find books they were likely to enjoy.

Goodreads became more than just a place to catalog books—it became a place where users could discover their next favorite read, driven by both data and human curation.

Acquisition by Amazon
In 2013, Goodreads was acquired by Amazon, the giant online retailer and owner of Kindle, the leading e-reader. This acquisition gave Goodreads access to Amazon's vast resources and infrastructure, allowing it to grow even further. The integration with Kindle made Goodreads accessible directly from Kindle devices, enabling users to share what they were reading and rate books in real-time.

The acquisition also allowed Goodreads to leverage Amazon's vast database of book information, making the site even more robust in terms of book availability and discovery features. Despite fears that the acquisition might change the independent feel of the platform, Goodreads has remained user-focused and community-driven.

Key Features and Success Factors
Goodreads' success can be attributed to several key factors:

1. **Community Engagement**: Goodreads built a community where readers felt they could connect and share with others. Discussion forums, book clubs, and challenges keep users engaged.

2. **User-Generated Content**: The platform relies heavily on user-created reviews, lists, and recommendations, which makes the content dynamic and constantly updated.

3. **Data-Driven Recommendations**: By allowing users to rate books and providing personalized book suggestions based on those ratings, Goodreads ensures that users are continuously discovering new reads.

4. **Integration with Kindle**: Being able to rate and share books directly from Kindle devices has helped expand Goodreads' user base and keep readers engaged.

5. **Author Interaction**: Goodreads allows authors to create profiles, interact with readers, and promote their books, creating a two-way communication channel between readers and writers. This is especially popular for book launches and author Q&A sessions.

A Global Reading Platform

Since its inception, Goodreads has grown into the world's largest site for readers and book recommendations. With its vast catalog of books, personalized recommendations, and engaged community, the platform has helped millions of people discover new books, connect with authors, and share their love for reading. Goodreads has also introduced features like the Goodreads Choice Awards, where users can vote for their favorite books each year.

From its humble beginnings as a passion project to its position today as the go-to site for book lovers, Goodreads has transformed the way people read, discover, and discuss books.

Conclusion: A Haven for Book Lovers

Goodreads' journey from a small idea in Otis Chandler's living room to a global reading platform shows the power of community, innovation, and a genuine love for books. With its ability to bring readers together, recommend great reads, and provide a space for authors and readers to interact, Goodreads has solidified its place as an indispensable resource for anyone who loves books.

———————

Prince Ea's Success Story: Messenger of Mindfulness and Social Change

"The only way to change the world is to change yourself first."

— PRINCE EA, PHILOSOPHER OF PURPOSE

AND TRANSFORMATION

Prince Ea, whose real name is Richard Williams, is a spoken word artist, filmmaker, and motivational speaker known for his thought-provoking videos that touch on social, environmental, and personal issues. He rose to fame by blending his passion for rap, philosophy, and social justice into powerful messages that resonate with millions of people worldwide. Here's how he got his start and became successful:

Early Life and Rap Beginnings

Born and raised in St. Louis, Missouri, Prince Ea grew up with a passion for rap music and poetry. He studied anthropology at the University of Missouri-St. Louis, and during his college years, he developed a keen interest in not only music but also self-education in various philosophical and psychological subjects.

Prince Ea started his career as a rapper, releasing a series of mixtapes and songs that garnered attention in the underground hip-hop community. In 2009, he won a VIBE Magazine contest, which helped him gain some initial recognition as a skilled lyricist. However, while his rap career was progressing, Prince Ea became increasingly disillusioned with the music industry. He felt that commercial rap had moved away from meaningful content and focused more on superficial topics, which conflicted with his deeper desire to create art with a purpose.

The Shift: From Rapper to Philosopher

In 2011, Prince Ea made a dramatic shift in his career. Disillusioned by the mainstream music industry, he decided to focus more on creating content that was uplifting, inspirational, and focused on social change. He began writing and performing spoken word poetry, tackling issues such as environmental degradation, self-love, technology's impact on society, and mental health.

This shift helped Prince Ea distinguish himself from traditional rappers and allowed him to reach a broader, more diverse audience. His content started spreading across social media platforms, especially YouTube and Facebook, where his videos gained millions of views.

Viral Success

Prince Ea's big break came with a series of **viral videos** that resonated with people on a global scale. Some of his most famous works include:

- **"Why I Hate School But Love Education"**: This video challenges the traditional education system, sparking a global conversation about the value of self-education and lifelong learning. It amassed millions of views and helped solidify his voice as a motivational speaker.

- **"Dear Future Generations: Sorry"**: This powerful video highlights the impact of environmental destruction and urges people to take action to protect the planet. It resonated deeply with audiences concerned about climate change and sustainability.

- **"Can We Auto-Correct Humanity?"**: In this video, Prince Ea discusses the negative effects of technology and social media on human relationships, addressing how modern society is becoming more disconnected despite being constantly "connected" online.

These videos combined thought-provoking messages with compelling visuals, creating a unique format that captivated viewers worldwide.

The Power of Storytelling and Positivity

One of the key elements of Prince Ea's success is his ability to tell stories in a way that is both personal and universal. His videos often tackle complex issues like racism, mental health, and personal development, but they do so in a way that is accessible and relatable. He uses a mix of spoken word, music, and visual storytelling to convey his messages, making his content not only impactful but also engaging.

In addition to his social and environmental activism, Prince Ea promotes personal growth and mental well-being. He frequently shares messages of self-awareness, gratitude, and mindfulness, encouraging people to live more authentically and to focus on what truly matters in life.

Impact and Ongoing Success

Prince Ea's success has gone beyond social media. He has been invited to speak at TEDx talks, conferences, and universities around the world. He has also collaborated with brands and organizations that align with his values, using his platform to promote causes he believes in.

Through his online presence, Prince Ea has built a community of millions of followers across various platforms, including YouTube, Instagram, and Facebook. His videos have been viewed over a billion times, making him one of the most influential online creators in the self-help and social awareness space.

Legacy and Influence

What sets Prince Ea apart is his ability to use art as a vehicle for change. His messages of love, peace, and personal empowerment have inspired countless individuals to reflect on their lives and strive to make a positive impact on the world. His unique blend of creativity, philosophy, and activism continues to inspire people to think critically about the world and their place in it.

From his beginnings as a frustrated rapper to becoming a voice for global change, Prince Ea has shown that art can be a force for good when used with purpose and passion. He has redefined success on his own terms by focusing on what matters most to him: making the world a better place through his words and actions.

Tobias Lütke's Success Story: From Snowboards to E-Commerce Empire

"The best businesses come from people's bad personal experiences. If you just keep your eyes open, you're going to find something that frustrates you— and then you think, 'Well, I could fix that.'" — TOBIAS LÜTKE, ARCHITECT OF E-COMMERCE INNOVATION

Shopify, one of the most successful e-commerce platforms today, had a humble beginning rooted in an entirely different business idea—snowboards. The story of Shopify's meteoric rise is a perfect blend of entrepreneurial grit, technological innovation, and a visionary founder determined to solve a real problem.

The Beginnings: A Frustrated Entrepreneur

In 2004, Tobias Lütke, a German-born computer programmer, along with Scott Lake, co-founded Snowdevil, an online store that sold snowboarding equipment. Lütke, passionate about snowboarding, wanted to launch an e-commerce site to sell gear but found that the existing platforms were clunky, expensive, and lacked customization options.

Instead of using one of the limited e-commerce solutions available, Lütke decided to build his own platform from scratch. Using his programming skills, he developed the website for Snowdevil using Ruby on Rails, a web development framework that allowed for more flexibility and control.

Though Snowdevil didn't become a massive success, something important came out of the experience: Lütke realized that the real opportunity wasn't in selling snowboards—it was in selling the platform that powered their online store.

The Birth of Shopify

In 2006, Lütke and Lake decided to pivot from selling snowboards to selling the e-commerce software that Lütke had built. They rebranded the company as Shopify and began offering it as an all-in-one solution for entrepreneurs to easily create their own online stores. Shopify's mission was clear from the start: make commerce better for everyone by simplifying the process of building and running an online business.

Shopify provided small and medium-sized businesses with the tools they needed to set up an online store without the hassle of learning to code or managing complex systems. It quickly stood out for its user-friendly interface, customizable templates, and the ability to handle all the back-end technicalities like payments, shipping, and taxes.

Growth and Innovation

From the outset, Shopify's focus on ease of use and scalability set it apart from competitors. Lütke and his team continued to improve the platform, adding features like Shopify Payments, which simplified the payment process for merchants, and the Shopify App Store, which allowed developers to create plugins to expand the functionality of Shopify stores.

In 2009, Shopify launched Shopify API and the App Store, which opened the door for developers to create apps and add-ons for the platform. This was a game-changer as it allowed businesses to customize their stores with additional features like marketing tools, accounting software, and inventory management systems. The developer ecosystem became a huge part of Shopify's success, enabling third-party developers to extend the platform's functionality, which helped Shopify evolve into a robust e-commerce ecosystem.

Shopify's freemium business model, which allowed users to start for free and pay as they grew, made it accessible to aspiring entrepreneurs with limited resources. This model attracted a wide range of users, from small businesses to high-growth startups, all looking for an affordable, flexible way to sell online.

Going Public and Becoming a Tech Giant
In 2015, Shopify went public on the New York Stock Exchange (NYSE) and Toronto Stock Exchange (TSX) under the ticker symbol "SHOP." The IPO raised $131 million, valuing the company at over $1 billion at the time. The IPO marked a major milestone in Shopify's journey, but the company was just getting started.

Post-IPO, Shopify continued to grow exponentially. The platform attracted thousands of merchants who wanted to tap into the booming world of e-commerce, particularly as the shift to online shopping accelerated. Shopify expanded globally, offering localized versions of its platform and adding new features to meet the needs of larger businesses. By 2021, Shopify had surpassed 1 million merchants in over 175 countries and was widely recognized as one of the leading e-commerce platforms worldwide.

Shopify Plus and Scaling for Enterprises
As Shopify's platform matured, it began catering not only to small businesses but also to larger, more established brands. In 2014, Shopify introduced Shopify Plus, an enterprise version of its platform that offered more advanced features, support, and scalability for high-growth brands. This allowed companies like Kylie Cosmetics, Gymshark, and Allbirdsto build their brands on Shopify and handle large volumes of traffic and sales.

Resilience During the COVID-19 Pandemic

The COVID-19 pandemic accelerated the shift toward e-commerce, and Shopify emerged as a critical tool for businesses forced to go digital. As physical stores closed, many retailers turned to Shopify to keep their businesses afloat by selling online. Shopify quickly adapted, launching new features like Shopify Balance, a business banking service for merchants, and Shopify Capital, which provided cash advances to businesses struggling during the pandemic.

During the pandemic, Shopify's stock price soared as more businesses went online, and the company solidified its position as a leader in e-commerce. By 2021, Shopify had a market capitalization of over $150 billion, making it one of the most valuable companies in Canada and one of the leading players in the global tech scene.

Key Factors in Shopify's Success:

- **Focus on Simplicity**: Shopify's user-friendly interface and easy setup made it accessible for entrepreneurs with little technical expertise.

- **Developer Ecosystem**: The launch of the Shopify App Store allowed developers to build plugins and expand the functionality of the platform, fostering innovation and customization.

- **Freemium Business Model**: Shopify's pricing model allowed entrepreneurs to start small and scale their business as they grew.

- **Global Reach**: Shopify expanded its platform to cater to international markets, making it easier for businesses worldwide to sell online.

- **Support for Small and Large Businesses**: From small businesses to enterprise clients, Shopify's flexible platform could accommodate merchants at any stage of growth.

Conclusion: A Leader in E-Commerce

Today, Shopify powers more than 1.75 million businesses in over 175 countries, helping entrepreneurs and established brands alike build and grow their online presence. With its commitment to innovation and user-centric approach, Shopify has revolutionized the e-commerce landscape and continues to shape the future of online business.

From selling snowboards to becoming one of the most important e-commerce platforms in the world, Shopify's story is a testament to the power of solving real problems and continuously evolving to meet the needs of a rapidly changing market.

Henry Ford's Success Story: The Visionary Who Put the World on Wheels

"Coming together is a beginning, staying together is progress, and working together is success." — HENRY FORD, FOUNDER OF FORD MOTOR COMPANY

Henry Ford, a visionary entrepreneur and industrialist, forever changed the way the world moves and manufactures. Born on a Michigan farm in 1863, Ford's fascination with machinery ignited a journey that would revolutionize the automotive industry. Known as the pioneer of the modern assembly line, Ford's ability to turn innovative ideas into practical solutions made automobiles accessible to ordinary people, reshaping society in the process. Through persistence, bold thinking, and a commitment to efficiency, Ford built one of the most influential companies in history, leaving behind a legacy that extends far beyond cars—one rooted in the principles of innovation, affordability, and the power of possibility.

Early Life and Foundation of Curiosity
Henry Ford was born on July 30, 1863, on a farm in Greenfield Township, Michigan. From a young age, Ford displayed a fascination with machinery and engineering. His curiosity was sparked by the farm equipment he encountered daily, and by age 15, he had built his first steam engine. Ford's desire to escape the monotony of farm life motivated him to move to Detroit, where he worked as an apprentice machinist, immersing himself in the mechanical world that would define his legacy.

Early Career and Path to Invention

In the 1890s, Ford worked as an engineer at the Edison Illuminating Company, eventually rising to the position of chief engineer. This role provided him the time and resources to pursue his passion for building automobiles. In 1896, he built his first self-propelled vehicle, the Quadricycle, a four-wheeled bicycle powered by a gasoline engine. Encouraged by the success of this prototype, Ford set his sights on producing automobiles for the masses.

Founding the Ford Motor Company

After several failed ventures, including the Detroit Automobile Company, Ford established the Ford Motor Company in 1903 with the backing of a group of investors. The company's early models were relatively expensive and appealed to a niche market. However, Ford's vision was to produce an affordable car that every American family could own, revolutionizing personal transportation.

In 1908, the company introduced the Model T. Unlike its predecessors, the Model T was designed to be durable, simple to operate, and, most importantly, affordable. Ford's innovative approach to automobile manufacturing set the stage for success, but it was his next move that would change the course of industrial history.

The Assembly Line: A Game-Changing Innovation

Ford's most significant contribution to modern industry was the introduction of the assembly line in 1913. Inspired by the principles of efficiency and productivity, the assembly line drastically reduced the time it took to build a car. Before its implementation, producing a Model T took more than 12 hours. With the assembly line, production time dropped to just 90 minutes. This innovation allowed Ford to lower the cost of the Model T, eventually selling it for as little as $260, making it accessible to the average American worker.

Ford also introduced groundbreaking changes in the workplace. In 1914, he shocked the business world by doubling workers' wages to $5 per day, far above the industry standard. This move not only reduced employee turnover but also enabled his workers to afford the cars they built, further fueling demand.

Success and Legacy

By the 1920s, the Ford Motor Company was producing half of the world's automobiles. The Model T became a cultural phenomenon, symbolizing freedom, mobility, and modernity. Ford's business practices, including mass production and the $5 workday, set the standard for the industrial economy of the 20th century.

Ford's success extended beyond the automobile industry. He was a pioneer in vertical integration, owning the supply chain from raw materials to finished products. Ford also engaged in philanthropy, establishing the Ford Foundation, which would become one of the largest and most influential charitable organizations in the world.

Lessons in Innovation and Leadership

Ford's story exemplifies how a commitment to innovation, efficiency, and employee well-being can lead to transformative success. His ability to envision the future, paired with his practical approach to solving industrial challenges, solidified his place as one of the greatest entrepreneurs in history.

Although his later years were marked by challenges—including declining market share due to his reluctance to innovate beyond the Model T—Ford's influence remains undeniable. His legacy lives on in the modern automobile industry and in the principles of lean manufacturing that still shape production processes today.

Conclusion: Transforming the Way We Move

Henry Ford's journey from a farm boy in Michigan to a global industrialist reshaped the world's perception of transportation and manufacturing. His innovations empowered millions of people with personal mobility and created a blueprint for industrial success that still influences businesses today. Ford's life is a testament to the power of vision, hard work, and the belief that innovation is not just about technology—it's about improving the lives of people.

Lee Clow's Success Story: The Creative Genius Who Revolutionized Advertising

"Effective communication turns negotiations into win-win situations; it's all about making everyone feel they've gained something valuable."
— LEE CLOW, ADVERTISING LEGEND

"Creativity in advertising isn't just about standing out from the crowd; it's about creating a memorable dance that the audience can't help but join."
— LEE CLOW, LEGENDARY ADVERTISING EXECUTIVE

Lee Clow is a pioneering advertising visionary whose work transformed the way brands connect with audiences. As the mastermind behind Apple's iconic "1984" Super Bowl ad and many other groundbreaking campaigns, Clow's influence has shaped the world of modern marketing. Known for his creative spirit, rebellious approach, and deep understanding of brand storytelling, Clow helped elevate advertising to an art form.

Early Life: A Passion for Creativity

Lee Clow was born in Los Angeles, California, in 1943. From an early age, he displayed an artistic bent and a passion for creativity. After attending Santa Monica College, Clow didn't initially set out to be an advertising executive. Instead, he pursued art and design, finding joy in visual storytelling.

His creative ambitions eventually led him to the world of advertising, where he discovered that brands needed more than just slogans—they needed stories. He joined Chiat/Day (a small but daring advertising agency) as a junior art director, where his career would soon take off.

Making Waves at Chiat/Day: The Birth of Bold Advertising

Clow's early work at Chiat/Day showed his knack for disruptive ideas. Under the leadership of Jay Chiat, the agency had a culture that thrived on innovation, irreverence, and risk-taking—values that resonated with Clow. He believed that advertising shouldn't just sell products but create emotional connections with audiences.

Clow's philosophy was simple: "Great advertising isn't about selling stuff—it's about making people care." This belief became the foundation of his most famous work.

The 1984 Apple Ad: Changing Advertising Forever

Clow's big break came when Steve Jobs approached Chiat/Day in the early 1980s. Apple was about to launch the Macintosh computer, and Jobs wanted an ad campaign that would change the world. The result was the "1984" Super Bowl commercial, directed by Ridley Scott.

The ad, inspired by George Orwell's dystopian novel *1984*, depicted a heroic woman smashing a screen controlled by Big Brother, symbolizing Apple's mission to challenge conformity and empower creativity. The revolutionary tone and visual style of the ad set it apart from anything the advertising world had seen before.

The "1984" ad aired once during the Super Bowl—and that was all it needed. It became an instant cultural phenomenon, hailed as one of the greatest ads of all time, and established Apple as a brand for innovators and rebels. More importantly, it cemented Clow's reputation as an advertising legend.

A Lifelong Partnership with Apple

The partnership between Lee Clow and Steve Jobs was one of the most significant in the history of advertising. After the success of "1984," Clow continued to lead some of Apple's most memorable campaigns. His work included:

- **"Think Different" (1997):** A campaign that celebrated creative minds like Albert Einstein and Pablo Picasso, reinforcing Apple's identity as a brand for innovators.

- **iPod Silhouettes (2000s):** Vibrant ads featuring dancing silhouettes that captured the fun and freedom of music with the iPod.

- **Mac vs. PC (2006-2009):** A humorous series of commercials that positioned Apple as cool, creative, and user-friendly in contrast to traditional PCs.

These campaigns did more than sell products—they helped define Apple's brand identity and turned it into one of the most valuable companies in the world.

Leadership at TBWA\Chiat\Day

As Chiat/Day grew and merged with TBWA Worldwide, Clow took on a leadership role, becoming Chairman and Global Director of TBWA\Chiat\Day. His work influenced not only Apple but other brands like Pepsi, Nissan, and Adidas. Clow's approach was always bold and creative, encouraging brands to take risks and build emotional connections with their audiences.

Under his leadership, TBWA\Chiat\Day became known as a disruptive force in the advertising world, pioneering the idea of disruptive innovation—using bold ideas to change market dynamics and consumer perceptions.

A Legacy of Creativity and Inspiration

Clow officially retired in 2019, but his legacy lives on in the world of advertising. His campaigns have been studied and celebrated by marketers, creatives, and business leaders around the world. Clow wasn't just an ad man—he was a storyteller who believed that great advertising could inspire people and change the world.

Even after retirement, Clow's influence continues. His mantra—"Be brave. Take risks. Make people care."—remains a guiding principle for creatives everywhere.

Lessons from Lee Clow's Success

- **Take Risks:** Clow's bold ideas, like the 1984 ad, redefined advertising by taking risks that paid off.

- **Tell a Story:** He believed that advertising should make emotional connections, not just push products.

- **Build Strong Partnerships:** His collaboration with Steve Jobs shows the power of aligning creative minds with shared values.

- **Stay Disruptive:** Clow's philosophy of "disruptive innovation" reshaped how brands approach advertising and marketing.

- **Have Fun:** Known for his laid-back demeanor, Clow insisted that creativity should be fun and fulfilling—both for creators and audiences.

Conclusion: A Creative Maverick Who Shaped the Future of Advertising

Lee Clow's career is a testament to the power of bold ideas, creativity, and storytelling. From his early days at Chiat/Day to his work with Apple, Clow revolutionized advertising by making people feel something. His campaigns weren't just memorable—they shaped the way people thought about brands and connected emotionally with them.

Clow's legacy will continue to inspire creatives and marketers for generations to come. His life's work shows that great advertising isn't about selling—it's about creating connections, inspiring people, and daring to be different.

========

CHAPTER FOUR

Building Corporate Culture and Ethics

A company's culture and ethical foundation are the invisible forces that shape every decision, interaction, and outcome within an organization. Building a strong corporate culture rooted in ethics is no longer optional—it's essential for sustainable success. Culture influences employee behavior, fosters engagement, and drives innovation, while ethical principles provide a compass for navigating the complexities of modern business. This chapter explores the intertwined relationship between culture and ethics, offering strategies to create a thriving workplace where values align with actions.

Ken Robinson, an educational thought leader, emphasizes that "creativity in business comes from a diversity of perspectives and experiences." A company's culture goes beyond perks and policies; it reflects shared beliefs, attitudes, and practices that shape how employees engage with their work and each other. This chapter delves into how visionary leaders cultivate cultures that empower employees, strengthen team cohesion, and enhance productivity.

Building Corporate Culture and Ethics

At the core of culture lies trust, which must be built and maintained through consistent ethical behavior. Anna Wintour, editor-in-chief of Vogue, states, "Effective branding is about creating a sense of belonging where every product and interaction reflects the essence of your values." A brand's external reputation is deeply influenced by its internal practices, making ethics essential not only for avoiding pitfalls but for creating an identity that people admire and trust.

Effective leaders understand that corporate culture isn't static—it evolves over time. Tony Hsieh, former CEO of Zappos, explains, "Your culture is your brand." This chapter offers practical advice on fostering open communication, encouraging employee feedback, and embedding ethical decision-making at every level of the organization. Companies with strong, adaptive cultures weather change more effectively and emerge stronger from challenges.

Ethics extend to both internal operations and external relationships. Sylvia Ann Hewlett, a thought leader in gender and workplace issues, asserts, "A culture of inclusion is the cornerstone of a thriving organization." Ethics shape policies and ensure businesses engage with customers, partners, and employees fairly. This chapter provides actionable frameworks for building ethical guidelines that support transparency, integrity, and social responsibility.

Collaboration and innovation also thrive in organizations with a clear cultural identity. Ruth Bader Ginsburg, the late Supreme Court Justice, stated, "Real change, enduring change, happens one step at a time." When companies align their vision with ethical values, they not only attract talented employees but also earn the loyalty of customers and partners. This chapter highlights how culture and ethics work together to create a competitive edge in the marketplace.

Building an ethical culture requires leaders to model the behavior they wish to see. Claude Hopkins, a pioneer in advertising, advised, "The most effective way to sell is to first build trust." Leaders play a pivotal role in reinforcing ethical standards, promoting accountability, and ensuring that corporate values remain more than just words on paper.

This chapter also explores the role of diversity and inclusion in shaping a positive corporate culture. Don Norman, a design expert, points out that "good design requires a deep understanding of the people you're designing for." Companies that embrace diverse viewpoints foster innovation, drive better decision-making, and build environments where employees feel valued and motivated to contribute their best.

Organizations with strong ethical foundations enjoy long-term benefits, including increased employee retention, customer trust, and brand loyalty. The following pages draw from the experiences of industry leaders like Ken Robinson, Anna Wintour, and Tony Hsieh to provide practical insights into building corporate cultures where ethics are non-negotiable. You'll learn how to align your mission with your values, foster transparency, and create a workplace that inspires both personal and professional growth. By developing a culture rooted in ethics, companies can achieve more than just profitability—they can create a legacy of trust, innovation, and lasting impact.

Ultimately, building corporate culture and ethics is about more than following rules—it's about creating environments where people and values thrive. With strong leadership, clear principles, and a shared vision, your business can become a force for good, achieving meaningful success while making a positive difference in the world. This chapter equips you with the tools to foster a workplace where purpose, integrity, and excellence are the foundation for long-term success.

———

Ken Robinson's Success Story: The Advocate for Creativity in Education

"Creativity in branding is like electricity through wires—it powers ideas, illuminates possibilities, and transforms the mundane into something utterly magnetic." — KEN ROBINSON, AUTHOR AND EDUCATION EXPERT

Ken Robinson was a visionary educator, author, and speaker who redefined how the world views creativity and learning. Best known for his groundbreaking TED Talk *Do Schools Kill Creativity?*, Robinson challenged the status quo of traditional education systems and ignited a global conversation on the importance of fostering imagination and innovation in schools. With a background in arts education and a passion for unlocking human potential, Robinson believed that creativity should be treated as seriously as literacy. His work continues to inspire educators, policymakers, and leaders to rethink outdated teaching models and nurture students' individual talents, proving that creativity is essential not only for personal fulfillment but for the progress of society.

Early Life and Passion for Education

Ken Robinson was born in Liverpool, England, in 1950. As a child, he contracted polio, which left him with a disability, but it also gave him a unique perspective on the importance of inclusive education. Robinson's early struggles sparked a lifelong passion for education reform. Growing up in a working-class family, he was encouraged to value learning and hard work, which would become the foundation for his later achievements.

Robinson went on to study at Bretton Hall College of Education and later earned a PhD from the University of London. His academic focus was on theater and drama in education, which gave him insight into the power of creativity in the learning process. This would shape his philosophy that education should nurture creativity, not stifle it.

Shaping the Future of Arts and Education

In the 1980s and 1990s, Robinson began working with schools, governments, and cultural organizations to advocate for the integration of arts into education. He became a leading voice in the UK's education sector, where he championed the idea that creativity should be treated as seriously as literacy. He served as a professor of education at the University of Warwick, influencing educational policies and practices through his research and public speaking.

In 1998, Robinson was appointed to lead a major government inquiry into creativity, education, and the economy. The resulting report, *All Our Futures: Creativity, Culture and Education*, became a milestone in the movement to reform education systems worldwide. Robinson argued that education systems overly focused on standardized testing, limiting students' potential by discouraging creative thinking.

Global Impact: TED Talk and International Recognition

Robinson's ideas gained global recognition when he delivered a TED Talk in 2006 titled *Do Schools Kill Creativity?* His engaging storytelling, humor, and thought-provoking ideas captivated the audience, and the talk became one of the most-viewed TED Talks of all time, with millions of views worldwide. Robinson's message resonated with educators, parents, and students alike, prompting widespread discussions about the need for change in education systems.

Following the success of his TED Talk, Robinson published several influential books, including *The Element: How Finding Your Passion Changes Everything* and *Creative Schools: The Grassroots Revolution That's Transforming Education.* His work emphasized the importance of helping students discover their passions and develop their talents, urging educators to move beyond the traditional one-size-fits-all approach to learning.

Inspiring a Movement

Throughout his career, Robinson remained committed to empowering individuals to embrace creativity and innovation. He worked with governments, educational institutions, and businesses around the world, advising them on how to foster environments where creativity could thrive. His influence extended beyond education, inspiring people in various industries to rethink how they approach learning, problem-solving, and personal growth.

Robinson's legacy is not just about education reform but also about inspiring a mindset shift—one that encourages people to value imagination and innovation as essential skills for the future. His work continues to inspire educators, leaders, and changemakers across the globe, reminding them that creativity is not an optional extra but a vital part of human development.

A Lasting Legacy

Sir Ken Robinson passed away in 2020, but his ideas live on, continuing to inspire a global movement for educational change. His legacy is evident in the countless schools and organizations that have adopted more creative and personalized approaches to learning. Robinson's story is a testament to the power of visionary thinking, perseverance, and the belief that education should unlock, not limit, human potential.

Through his advocacy and teaching, Ken Robinson demonstrated that creativity is essential for personal fulfillment and societal progress, leaving an indelible mark on education worldwide.

Anna Wintour's Success Story: The Visionary Force Behind Fashion

"Defining your product brand with a signature style isn't just about how your products look; it's about embedding your brand's essence so deeply that each item becomes a tangible ambassador of your values and vision."
— ANNA WINTOUR, Editor-in-Chief

"Licensing your trademark is not just about lending your name; it's about strategically extending your brand's reach and influence while ensuring it aligns with partners who uphold its values and promise."
— ANNA WINTOUR, EDITOR-IN-CHIEF OF VOGUE

Anna Wintour, a name synonymous with fashion and influence, has shaped the global style landscape for over three decades. As the editor-in-chief of *Vogue* and the Global Chief Content Officer for Condé Nast, Wintour's visionary approach has redefined the relationship between fashion, culture, and media. Known for her sharp editorial eye, disciplined leadership, and trend-setting instincts, she has transformed *Vogue* into an iconic publication that blends high fashion with mainstream appeal. Wintour's journey from London boutiques to the heights of the fashion world showcases her relentless drive and ability to innovate, solidifying her legacy as one of the most influential figures in fashion history.

Early Life and Roots in Journalism

Anna Wintour was born on November 3, 1949, in London, England, into a family with deep ties to media and journalism. Her father, Charles Wintour, was the editor of the *London Evening Standard*, shaping her early exposure to the world of publishing. With an independent streak from a young age, Wintour dropped out of school at 16, determined to follow her passion for fashion rather than pursue formal education.

She began her career working at *Biba*, a trendy London boutique, and later took editorial roles at British publications such as *Harper's & Queen*. These early experiences honed her instincts for fashion trends, editorial strategy, and cultural movements—traits that would define her career.

A Bold Transition to American Magazines

In the 1970s, Wintour moved to New York City, seeking to make a mark on the American fashion scene. She took positions at *Harper's Bazaar* and *New York Magazine*, developing a reputation for bold, trend-setting content. It wasn't long before her daring editorial style caught the attention of Condé Nast, where she became the creative director of *Vogue* UK in 1985.

Wintour's approach was nothing short of revolutionary. She disrupted conventional magazine layouts by introducing casual models and unconventional photo shoots. This bold editorial direction, though controversial, signaled the future of fashion publishing.

The Vogue Takeover: A New Era

In 1988, Wintour was appointed editor-in-chief of *Vogue*—a position that would cement her status as a powerhouse in the fashion industry. At the time, *Vogue* was facing stiff competition from *Elle*, another rising fashion magazine. Wintour transformed the magazine with her forward-thinking approach, blending high fashion with accessible, wearable trends. She was known for putting celebrities on the cover, which at the time was a departure from the traditional practice of featuring only models. This innovation bridged the gap between fashion and pop culture, setting the stage for the *Vogue* we know today.

One of her most iconic covers featured model Michaela Bercu in a bejeweled Christian Lacroix jacket paired with blue jeans—an unconventional combination that signaled Wintour's desire to bring high fashion into everyday life.

Leadership Through Influence and Discipline

Wintour is celebrated for her meticulous attention to detail and unwavering vision. Known for her exacting standards and disciplined work ethic, she has cultivated a reputation as a demanding leader, inspiring both admiration and controversy. Her leadership style, famously depicted in *The Devil Wears Prada*, reflects her ability to make tough decisions and push boundaries. Wintour's influence extends beyond the pages of *Vogue*. Her role in organizing and chairing the annual Met Gala has elevated the event to one of the most anticipated fashion and cultural spectacles of the year.

Legacy: A Lasting Impact on Fashion

Anna Wintour's impact on the fashion world is unparalleled. Over the decades, she has mentored countless designers, models, and fashion editors, ensuring the next generation of creatives has a platform to thrive. She played a crucial role in launching the careers of designers like Marc Jacobs and Alexander McQueen, and her philanthropic efforts have supported fashion education programs around the world.

Wintour's ability to continuously reinvent *Vogue* and keep it at the forefront of culture has kept her at the top of the fashion world for over three decades. Today, she serves as the Global Chief Content Officer for Condé Nast, continuing to shape not only the future of *Vogue* but the entire publishing landscape.

Conclusion: The Power of Vision and Resilience

Anna Wintour's career is a testament to the power of bold vision and relentless dedication. From her early days working in London boutiques to leading one of the most influential fashion magazines in the world, Wintour's ability to see beyond trends and set new standards has defined her legacy. She has shown that success in any creative industry requires more than talent—it demands vision, leadership, and a fearless commitment to innovation.

Tony Hsieh's Success Story: Visionary Behind Zappos' Customer-Centered Revolution

"Creating a strong company culture isn't just good business. It's the right thing to do, and it makes your company better for all stakeholders—
employees, management, and customers."
— TONY HSIEH, FORMER CEO OF ZAPPOS

Tony Hsieh, the visionary entrepreneur behind Zappos, revolutionized not only online retail but also the way businesses think about culture, leadership, and customer service. Known for his unconventional management style and belief in the power of happiness, Hsieh built Zappos into a billion-dollar company that became synonymous with exceptional customer experience. From his early ventures—including selling his first company, LinkExchange, to Microsoft for $265 million—to transforming Zappos with a philosophy centered on delivering joy, Hsieh's journey was marked by innovation, risk-taking, and a deep commitment to meaningful work. His story continues to inspire entrepreneurs around the world to prioritize purpose over profits and to prove that business success is possible without compromising values.

Early Life and Entrepreneurial Spark
Tony Hsieh was born on December 12, 1973, in Urbana, Illinois, and raised in the San Francisco Bay Area. From an early age, he displayed a passion for entrepreneurship. As a child, he ran small ventures like a worm farm and a button-making business. This curiosity for creating new things followed him through high school and into college. Hsieh attended Harvard University, where he studied computer science. While there, he ran a pizza delivery business, which foreshadowed his future focus on customer satisfaction and convenience.

LinkExchange: First Taste of Success
After graduating from Harvard in 1995, Hsieh landed a job at Oracle. However, corporate life didn't suit him. Just five months into the job, Hsieh left to pursue his entrepreneurial passions. Along with his friend Sanjay Madan, he co-founded LinkExchange, an online advertising network. The venture quickly gained traction, and within two years, Microsoft acquired it for $265 million. This financial success gave Hsieh the freedom to explore new ventures but left him yearning for a more meaningful endeavor.

Zappos: Building a Company on Happiness
In 1999, Hsieh invested in a small online shoe retailer called ShoeSite.com, which later became Zappos. He initially saw potential in the business model but believed Zappos could be much more than just an e-commerce site. Hsieh joined the company as CEO and began transforming it with a unique vision—focusing not just on selling shoes but on delivering happiness to customers and employees.

Zappos set itself apart by offering exceptional customer service, including free shipping, a 365-day return policy, and a commitment to ensuring customers had a delightful experience. Hsieh's philosophy was simple but revolutionary: prioritize company culture, empower employees, and trust that profits would follow. His approach created a work environment that emphasized creativity, kindness, and autonomy.

The Amazon Acquisition and Expansion
Under Hsieh's leadership, Zappos grew rapidly. By 2009, it had become a major player in the online retail space. That same year, Amazon acquired Zappos for approximately $1.2 billion, with the promise that Hsieh could continue to lead Zappos independently. Hsieh's focus remained on maintaining Zappos' distinctive culture and keeping the customer at the heart of every decision.

Holacracy and Cultural Innovation
Hsieh was known not only for his business acumen but also for his unconventional approach to leadership. In 2013, he introduced "holacracy" at Zappos, a radical management system that eliminated traditional hierarchies in favor of self-managed teams. This experiment reflected Hsieh's belief that empowering employees was essential to fostering innovation and personal fulfillment within the workplace.

He also made headlines by relocating Zappos' headquarters to downtown Las Vegas, pouring millions of dollars into revitalizing the area. His Downtown Project aimed to create a thriving entrepreneurial and artistic community in the heart of the city, demonstrating Hsieh's commitment to making a positive impact beyond business.

Legacy and Impact
Tony Hsieh's influence on business went far beyond Zappos. His 2010 book, *Delivering Happiness*, became a best-seller, inspiring entrepreneurs worldwide to prioritize culture and customer experience. Hsieh's story is one of blending business success with purpose, proving that profitability and happiness can coexist. His unconventional leadership style and relentless pursuit of meaningful work made him a pioneer in the world of e-commerce and company culture.

A Tragic End
In November 2020, the world was shocked by Hsieh's sudden death at the age of 46. Despite the tragedy, his legacy continues to inspire entrepreneurs, leaders, and

employees worldwide. Zappos remains a beacon of excellent customer service, and Hsieh's philosophy of delivering happiness has become a guiding principle for countless businesses.

Tony Hsieh's journey was one of constant exploration, innovation, and kindness. His work redefined not only how companies approach customer service but also how they treat their employees. Through Zappos and beyond, Hsieh showed that business can be a force for good, leaving behind a legacy that will inspire future generations to lead with both heart and purpose.

Sylvia Ann Hewlett's Success Story: Transforming Workplaces Through Diversity and Inclusion

"Executive presence isn't just about being seen; it's about making people believe in your vision the moment you walk into the room."
— SYLVIA ANN HEWLETT, AUTHOR AND LEADERSHIP EXPERT

Sylvia Ann Hewlett is a trailblazer in the world of workplace equality, known for her pioneering research on diversity, inclusion, and the advancement of underrepresented talent. With a unique blend of academic rigor and personal insight, Hewlett has devoted her career to creating environments where people of all backgrounds can thrive. As the founder of the Center for Talent Innovation (CTI) and author of several influential books, she has shaped corporate policies and transformed the way organizations approach leadership, sponsorship, and inclusion. Her work has not only empowered individuals to navigate their careers successfully but has also provided companies with the tools to unlock the potential of a truly diverse workforce.

Early Life and Academic Foundation
Sylvia Ann Hewlett's journey began in rural Wales, where she was born into modest circumstances. She developed a passion for education early on, which led her to earn a degree from the University of Cambridge and later a Ph.D. in economics from Harvard University. Hewlett's academic background shaped her career trajectory, equipping her with the analytical tools and insights needed to

understand the dynamics of inequality and opportunity, especially for women and minorities.

A Focus on Gender and Economic Equality

Hewlett initially gained recognition as a scholar focusing on issues related to gender inequality, economic policy, and the work-family balance. Her early work, including the bestselling book *When the Bough Breaks: The Cost of Neglecting Our Children*, examined the struggles of working parents and highlighted the need for policies that support family well-being. However, it was her personal experiences—navigating a demanding career while raising children—that ignited her passion for creating systemic change in the workplace.

The Center for Talent Innovation and Influential Research

In 2004, Hewlett founded the Center for Talent Innovation (CTI), a think tank dedicated to helping organizations unlock the potential of diverse talent. Through groundbreaking research and consulting, CTI became a global authority on workforce diversity, particularly focusing on issues affecting women, LGBTQ+ individuals, and underrepresented minorities. Hewlett's work has emphasized the importance of sponsorship, leadership development, and fostering inclusive corporate cultures to drive business success.

Books that Spark Change

Hewlett has authored and co-authored several influential books, including *The Sponsor Effect: How to Be a Better Leader by Investing in Others* and *Executive Presence: The Missing Link Between Merit and Success*. These works provide actionable insights for both leaders and employees on how to build meaningful relationships and navigate organizational politics to succeed in their careers.

Global Impact and Recognition

Hewlett's research has reached some of the largest corporations and institutions worldwide, influencing policies on diversity and inclusion. She has consulted for Fortune 500 companies and advised organizations on how to leverage talent more effectively. Through her leadership at CTI, Hewlett has not only raised awareness about the challenges faced by marginalized groups but also provided organizations with data-driven strategies to promote equity and inclusion.

A Legacy of Empowerment and Advocacy

Sylvia Ann Hewlett's success lies in her ability to combine personal experiences with rigorous academic research to create meaningful change in workplaces across the globe. Her influence extends beyond academia and corporate boardrooms, inspiring individuals to advocate for themselves and others. Through her research, writing, and leadership, Hewlett has paved the way for future generations to thrive in environments that value diversity, inclusion, and opportunity.

Ruth Bader Ginsburg's Success Story: Champion of Justice and Equality

"Having a robust legal toolkit, complete with sample agreements and forms, isn't just about compliance—it's about building a foundation of trust and clarity in every business relationship." — RUTH BADER GINSBURG, ASSOCIATE JUSTICE OF THE U. S. SUPREME COURT

"As we look to the horizon, the latest trends in trademark law are shaping a landscape where intellectual property protection intersects with global commerce and digital innovation, challenging businesses to stay informed and agile." — RUTH BADER GINSBURG, ASSOCIATE JUSTICE OF THE U.S. SUPREME COURT

"Effective resolution of disputes doesn't always mean winning in the courtroom; sometimes it means knowing when to compromise and when to stand firm. That's the art of litigation." — RUTH BADER GINSBURG, U.S. SUPREME COURT JUSTICE

"Securing your work through copyright registration is not just a legal formality; it's a critical step in safeguarding your creative investments and ensuring your rights are protected in a competitive marketplace." — RUTH BADER GINSBURG, ASSOCIATE JUSTICE OF THE U. S. SUPREME COURT

Ruth Bader Ginsburg was a trailblazing legal mind and social justice advocate whose career reshaped the landscape of gender equality and civil rights in the United States. From overcoming early discrimination to becoming the second woman appointed to the U.S. Supreme Court, Ginsburg's journey was marked by relentless determination and strategic brilliance. Her ability to identify injustices, articulate them with precision, and push for lasting change not only transformed legal precedents but also inspired generations to pursue equality. Known for her sharp dissents and unwavering commitment to fairness, Ginsburg became a cultural icon whose legacy endures far beyond the courtroom.

Early Life and Education
Ruth Bader Ginsburg was born on March 15, 1933, in Brooklyn, New York, to Jewish parents Nathan and Celia Bader. From a young age, Ginsburg was inspired by her mother's emphasis on education, even though Celia herself never had the chance to pursue higher studies. Ruth excelled academically, attending Cornell University, where she met her future husband, Martin Ginsburg, and graduated at the top of her class in 1954. Her journey to legal greatness, however, was just beginning.

Overcoming Discrimination in Law
After starting law school at Harvard, Ginsburg transferred to Columbia Law School, graduating in 1959. Despite her academic brilliance, Ginsburg faced significant discrimination as a woman in a male-dominated field. Few firms were willing to hire women, and even fewer recognized their potential as equals in law. Yet, these challenges only fueled her resolve.

Ginsburg worked as a law clerk and later joined the faculty at Rutgers Law School, where she concealed her pregnancy to keep her job—an early testament to the systemic bias against women in the workplace. During her years as a professor, she began researching gender discrimination, laying the foundation for what would become her life's work.

The Legal Pioneer
In the 1970s, Ginsburg co-founded the Women's Rights Project at the American Civil Liberties Union (ACLU). She argued multiple landmark cases before the U.S. Supreme Court, not just on behalf of women but also for men discriminated

against because of gender stereotypes. Her strategy was to demonstrate that gender-based laws hurt everyone, setting new precedents for equality.

One of her most significant victories came in *Reed v. Reed* (1971), where the Supreme Court ruled for the first time that a law discriminating based on gender was unconstitutional. Through cases like these, Ginsburg became known for her meticulous legal reasoning and ability to win incremental but crucial victories for gender equality.

Supreme Court Justice and Cultural Icon

In 1993, President Bill Clinton nominated Ginsburg to the U.S. Supreme Court, where she became the second woman and the first Jewish woman to serve as a Justice. Over her 27 years on the bench, Ginsburg became a key figure in several major rulings, including cases on voting rights, same-sex marriage, and healthcare. Known for her sharp dissents, she earned the nickname "The Notorious RBG," turning into a pop culture icon who inspired generations to fight for justice.

Legacy of Resilience and Advocacy

Ginsburg's personal resilience matched her professional achievements. She battled multiple bouts of cancer while continuing to serve on the Court, never wavering in her commitment to justice. Her marriage to Martin Ginsburg was another cornerstone of her success—his unwavering support allowed her to break barriers in both law and life.

Ruth Bader Ginsburg's legacy endures through her landmark contributions to law, her advocacy for equality, and her enduring message of perseverance. Even after her passing in 2020, she remains an emblem of hope for those fighting against injustice, showing the world that change is possible when passion, intellect, and persistence converge.

———————

Claude Hopkins' Success Story: The Father of Modern Advertising and Scientific Marketing

"Mastering the legal landscape is about knowing the rules and using them to your advantage." — CLAUDE HOPKINS, ADVERTISING PIONEER

Claude C. Hopkins is often regarded as the pioneer of modern advertising and the mastermind behind scientific marketing. His innovative techniques, which emphasized testing, data, and direct response, transformed the advertising industry, setting the foundation for measurable marketing campaigns that still shape the field today. Hopkins' success is a testament to creativity grounded in practicality—an approach that made him one of the most influential figures in advertising history.

Early Life: Humble Beginnings

Claude Hopkins was born in 1866 in Michigan to a modest family. From a young age, Hopkins displayed a strong work ethic and a fascination with words and communication. He started working various jobs in his early years to support himself, but his passion for writing and persuasion eventually led him to pursue a career in advertising—which, at the time, was still in its infancy.

His early exposure to hard work gave him an appreciation for practical solutions and efficiency—qualities that would later influence his groundbreaking approach to advertising.

Breaking Into Advertising: Finding His Footing

Hopkins got his start working for small agencies and local businesses, writing ads and sales letters that promoted household products and services. He quickly realized that creative flair alone wasn't enough—advertising needed to generate measurable results. Hopkins saw advertising not as an art, but as a science, and he set out to redefine the field.

One of his earliest breakthroughs came when he developed direct response techniques for newspaper ads, encouraging readers to clip coupons or send responses to measure the effectiveness of each campaign. These early successes opened doors for Hopkins, earning him a reputation as a results-oriented copywriter.

The Scientific Approach to Advertising

In 1907, Hopkins took a pivotal role at Lord & Thomas, one of the largest ad agencies of the time. It was here that he refined his scientific advertising principles—a data-driven approach to marketing. Hopkins believed that advertising should be treated like an experiment, with results tracked and analyzed to improve future campaigns.

His campaigns became famous for using free samples, coupons, and clear calls-to-action. Hopkins tested headlines, layouts, and offers to find what resonated best with consumers. His philosophy of testing and learning was revolutionary in an era when most advertisers focused on catchy slogans and creative concepts without accountability.

Iconic Campaigns: Selling Products with Stories

Hopkins' ability to combine storytelling with practicality led to some of the most memorable campaigns in advertising history. He believed that ads should educate consumers and solve their problems. One of his landmark campaigns was for Pepsodent toothpaste in the 1920s. At a time when oral hygiene was not widely prioritized, Hopkins introduced the concept of "removing plaque film" as a key benefit.

His slogan—"You'll wonder where the yellow went when you brush your teeth with Pepsodent"—became iconic. The campaign didn't just sell toothpaste—it changed consumer behavior, leading to a nationwide increase in daily brushing habits. Pepsodent became a household name, and the campaign was credited with making toothbrushing a common habit in America.

Pioneering the Free Trial and Guarantee

Another innovation Hopkins introduced was the free trial offer, which allowed consumers to try products without risk. He believed that trust was essential in building long-term relationships with customers, and offering guarantees or free samples was a way to gain that trust.

These concepts, now standard practices in marketing, were groundbreaking at the time. Hopkins' campaigns emphasized "reason-why" copywriting, clearly explaining to customers why they should buy a product. His ads didn't rely on clever gimmicks but on simple, logical persuasion.

Writing the Bible of Advertising: *Scientific Advertising*
In 1923, Hopkins published "Scientific Advertising," a book that would become a cornerstone of modern marketing theory. The book outlined his data-driven approach to advertising and emphasized the importance of testing, tracking, and continuous improvement.

David Ogilvy, often regarded as the father of modern advertising, once said, "Nobody should be allowed to have anything to do with advertising until they have read 'Scientific Advertising' seven times." Hopkins' principles influenced generations of advertisers, including Ogilvy, and continue to be used in marketing to this day.

Later Life and Legacy
After retiring from active advertising, Hopkins wrote his autobiography, *"My Life in Advertising,"* which offered insights into his career and personal experiences. While he avoided the spotlight, his contributions left a lasting impact on the industry.

Hopkins' scientific approach to advertising paved the way for modern direct-response marketing, A/B testing, and performance marketing. His emphasis on educating consumers, offering free trials, and tracking results revolutionized advertising practices.

Lessons from Claude Hopkins' Success

- **Advertising is a science**: Treat campaigns as experiments—test, measure, and improve.

- **Focus on the consumer's needs**: Educate your audience and solve their problems with your products.

- **Build trust with offers**: Free trials and guarantees reduce risk for consumers and increase loyalty.

- **Track everything**: If you can't measure it, you can't improve it.

- **Storytelling sells**: Use narratives to connect with customers and create memorable campaigns.

Conclusion: A Legacy That Shaped Modern Marketing

Claude Hopkins didn't just create great advertising campaigns—he laid the foundation for performance marketing as we know it today. His insistence on data, testing, and consumer-focused storytelling forever changed the way businesses market their products.

Hopkins' legacy lives on in every direct-response ad, email campaign, and A/B test conducted by today's marketers. His story is a reminder that creativity paired with practicality is a powerful force—and that even the most brilliant advertising ideas must be backed by results.

Claude Hopkins' journey from humble beginnings to becoming a legend in the advertising world demonstrates the enduring power of innovation, persistence, and customer-first thinking. His contributions have made him one of the most influential figures in the history of advertising.

Don Norman's Success Story: Redesigning the World through Human-Centered Design

"Enhancing blog design is not just about aesthetic appeal; it's about creating an intuitive and seamless user experience that makes pages, posts, forms, and buttons easy to navigate and compelling to use."
— DON NORMAN, COGNITIVE SCIENTIST AND
USER EXPERIENCE ARCHITECT

Don Norman, a cognitive scientist and usability engineer, revolutionized how products are designed and experienced, introducing the world to the concept of *human-centered design.* With a unique blend of psychology, engineering, and design thinking, Norman's work reshaped the relationship between people and technology. His journey from academia to industry, and eventually to becoming one of the most influential figures in design, reveals a lifelong commitment to creating products that enhance usability, delight users, and solve real-world problems.

A Background in Psychology and Engineering

Don Norman was born in 1935, growing up at a time when technology and engineering were gaining momentum. His early interests in science and mathematics set the foundation for a career that would bridge the gap between technology and human behavior. Norman studied electrical engineering at MIT and later pursued a master's degree in the same field at the University of Pennsylvania. However, he soon realized that understanding human behavior was as essential to innovation as understanding circuits, leading him to pivot toward psychology.

In the 1960s, Norman earned a PhD in psychology from the University of Pennsylvania. This interdisciplinary background—spanning both engineering and psychology—would become the bedrock of his career in the years to come.

Discovering Design through Usability

Norman's journey into the design world began during his time as a professor of psychology and cognitive science at the University of California, San Diego (UCSD). He became deeply interested in how people interact with machines, noticing that many products, especially computers, were difficult to use. At the time, technology was evolving rapidly, but its usability was often overlooked.

Norman realized that the failure of many products was not due to poor technology but poor design. They did not consider the needs, expectations, or cognitive limitations of the people using them. This insight led to his research into user-centered design, where products are crafted with the user's experience at the forefront.

The Concept of Human-Centered Design

In the 1980s, Norman became increasingly involved with industry, consulting with companies to improve the usability of their products. His research culminated in his groundbreaking book *The Psychology of Everyday Things* (1988), later re-released as *The Design of Everyday Things*. This book became a cornerstone of design thinking, demonstrating how poorly designed objects—like doors that confuse users—result from ignoring human psychology.

Norman emphasized that good design isn't just about aesthetics; it's about making things intuitive and easy to use. He popularized concepts such as *affordances* (the perceived action possibilities of an object) and *feedback* (ensuring users know the outcome of their actions). His ideas resonated across industries, changing how designers approached product creation.

Joining Apple: A New Frontier
In the 1990s, Norman's reputation as a usability expert caught the attention of Apple, which was transforming itself into a leader in user-friendly computing. Apple hired Norman as a Vice President of Advanced Technology, where he applied his human-centered philosophy to make technology more accessible. His work at Apple solidified his belief that technology should enhance people's lives by being intuitive, delightful, and non-intrusive.

Norman's influence at Apple extended beyond products—he shaped the company's design philosophy, encouraging engineers and designers to think beyond functionality and consider the emotional impact of their products. This alignment with Norman's design principles played a role in Apple's ability to develop products that resonated with users on a personal level.

Establishing the Nielsen Norman Group
After leaving Apple, Norman co-founded the *Nielsen Norman Group* in 1998 with Jakob Nielsen, a pioneer in usability engineering. The consulting firm became a world leader in advising businesses on improving product usability and user experience (UX). Their work helped shape the digital landscape, from websites to mobile apps, ensuring products were not only functional but also pleasurable to use.

The Nielsen Norman Group's influence extended across industries, with companies relying on their expertise to create intuitive products and services. Through workshops, consulting, and research, Norman continued to spread the principles of human-centered design to thousands of professionals, embedding usability and user experience into modern design practice.

A Lasting Legacy in Design
Throughout his career, Norman authored numerous books that expanded on his design philosophy, including *Emotional Design* (2004) and *Living with*

Complexity (2010). These works explored how products affect emotions and why complexity, when properly designed, can enhance the user experience rather than detract from it. Norman's writings shaped the field of UX design and continue to influence product development in industries ranging from technology to healthcare.

Norman eventually returned to academia, serving as the director of the Design Lab at UC San Diego. There, he continued to mentor the next generation of designers, ensuring that his philosophy of human-centered design would persist for years to come.

Lessons in Human-Centered Innovation

Norman's success stems from his unwavering belief that technology should serve people—not the other way around. He showed that great design is rooted in understanding the user's needs, abilities, and limitations. His ability to merge engineering, psychology, and design into practical solutions made him one of the most influential figures in design history.

While many of his contemporaries focused on making products functional, Norman elevated the conversation to how products *feel* and how users interact with them emotionally. His legacy lies not just in the products he influenced, but in the designers and organizations he inspired to think differently about how they create.

Conclusion: The Father of User Experience Design

Today, Don Norman is widely regarded as the father of user experience (UX) design. His work has redefined the relationship between humans and technology, emphasizing that design is not just about solving problems—it's about creating meaningful, delightful experiences. Norman's journey from cognitive scientist to design pioneer exemplifies the power of interdisciplinary thinking and the importance of empathy in innovation.

Through his books, his work at Apple, and the Nielsen Norman Group, Norman has left an indelible mark on the world of design. His principles continue to shape the products we use every day, ensuring that technology works for people—not the other way around.

CHAPTER FIVE

Communication and Networking

In today's fast-paced business landscape, mastering the art of communication and building strong networks is essential for sustained success. Whether you are presenting your ideas, forming strategic partnerships, or leading a team, your ability to communicate effectively and foster meaningful connections will determine how far your business can grow. This chapter explores how intentional communication and strategic networking not only open doors to new opportunities but also cultivate long-term relationships that can elevate your business to the next level.

George Bernard Shaw famously remarked, "The single biggest problem in communication is the illusion that it has taken place." Great leaders and business professionals understand that clear, concise messaging—whether internal or external—can drive performance, enhance collaboration, and inspire action. Communication isn't just about talking; it's about listening, understanding, and engaging authentically with employees, clients, and stakeholders.

Networking plays a crucial role in expanding your business's reach and influence. Cicero, the Roman statesman and philosopher, noted, "Friendship improves happiness and abates misery, by the doubling of our joy and the dividing of our grief." Building a robust network provides access to invaluable resources, industry insights, and potential partnerships. This chapter will explore practical strategies for networking both in person and online, showing how to build connections that enhance your professional influence.

Business success also hinges on mastering various forms of communication— from public speaking to digital correspondence. Marcus Sheridan emphasizes, "The best way to sell is to help." We will cover techniques to boost your confidence and refine your messaging for meetings, presentations, and public events, equipping you to communicate with impact.

In the digital world, networking has evolved beyond business cards and events to include social media platforms and virtual communities. Ira Glass, the renowned radio personality, states, "Great stories happen to those who can tell them." This chapter provides insights into leveraging social media to grow your network and establish your personal or professional brand, turning digital interactions into meaningful connections.

The chapter also emphasizes the importance of negotiation within communication. Donald J. Trump has said, "The worst thing you can possibly do in a deal is seem desperate to make it." We'll explore how effective communicators shape dialogues to inspire trust, negotiate favorable outcomes, and foster collaboration. Understanding the nuances of verbal and non-verbal communication can elevate your ability to navigate complex business scenarios and forge lasting relationships.

Networking isn't just about collecting contacts—it's about building communities. Mike Lindell, the founder of MyPillow, encourages, "If you have a dream, you have to pursue it with everything you have." The chapter will delve into strategies for developing communities around your brand, showing how to create environments that nurture loyalty and mutual support among your network.

At the heart of communication and networking is emotional intelligence—the ability to connect with others on a meaningful level. This chapter will offer tools to enhance your emotional intelligence, helping you build stronger, more empathetic connections within your network.

Throughout this chapter, we draw from the experiences of thought leaders like Cicero, Marcus Sheridan, and George Bernard Shaw to provide practical insights into effective communication and networking. You'll discover strategies to build authentic connections, engage meaningfully with your audience, and negotiate with confidence.

In a world driven by relationships and influence, communication and networking are the currency of opportunity. With strong communication skills and a well-curated network, you can open doors to new partnerships, attract talent, and position your business for sustainable growth. This chapter equips you with the techniques needed to make every interaction count—whether you are pitching to investors, leading a team, or forming new business alliances—ensuring that your voice and connections become powerful assets in your journey from idea to empire.

―――――――

George Bernard Shaw's Success Story: The Playwright Who Used Words to Change the World

"The single biggest problem in communication is the illusion that it has taken place." — GEORGE BERNARD SHAW, PLAYWRIGHT AND CRITIC

George Bernard Shaw's journey from humble beginnings in Dublin to international acclaim as a playwright and social reformer is a testament to the power of persistence, creativity, and unorthodox thinking. Shaw was not just a master of words—he was a visionary who used humor and theater as tools to confront societal norms and inspire change. His career spanned decades, during which he produced works that merged comedy with profound social commentary. Through plays like *Pygmalion* and *Man and Superman*, Shaw questioned issues of class, identity, and morality, leaving an indelible mark on literature and culture. His life serves as a powerful reminder that art can be more than entertainment—

it can be a vehicle for change, provoking thought and encouraging action long after the final curtain falls.

Early Life: A Self-Education in Words
Born on July 26, 1856, in Dublin, Ireland, Shaw grew up in a family that struggled financially. His father was an unsuccessful merchant with a penchant for alcohol, while his mother, a singer, introduced Shaw to the world of music and performance. Despite his family's struggles, Shaw developed a deep love for books and learning—though he despised formal schooling, finding it rigid and uninspiring.

As a teenager, Shaw dropped out of school and began working in a real estate office to help support his family. But his passion for literature, art, and social issues kept growing. A lifelong autodidact, Shaw spent his free time reading novels, essays, and socialist tracts, setting the foundation for his later success.

A Bold Move to London: The Struggling Writer
In 1876, Shaw moved to London in search of greater opportunities. For nearly a decade, he faced intense rejection and poverty. He spent years living in near-destitution, relying on his mother's financial help while writing novels that nobody wanted to publish. His first five novels were all rejected by publishers, leaving Shaw frustrated but determined.

During this time, Shaw honed his writing skills by contributing to newspapers and literary reviews. He became known as a sharp-tongued critic, taking aim at the conventional values of Victorian society. His essays and book reviews, though modestly paid, began to build his reputation as an incisive thinker.

Finding His Voice: Journalism and Social Activism
In the 1880s, Shaw became deeply involved in politics, joining the Fabian Society, a group dedicated to promoting socialism through gradual reform. Shaw believed that art, politics, and ideas could change society—a belief that would shape his career as a playwright. His speeches and writings for the Fabian Society made him a well-known public intellectual, known for his debating skills and unorthodox opinions.

Though novel-writing wasn't his forte, Shaw realized that theater could be his platform for challenging societal norms. He saw the stage as more than just entertainment—it was a space to spark debate and question conventional beliefs.

Breakthrough in Theater: Plays with Purpose
Shaw's first significant theatrical work came in the form of social problem plays that challenged the norms of his time. His early plays, like "Widowers' Houses" (1892) and "Mrs. Warren's Profession" (1893), tackled controversial issues such as class inequality, prostitution, and exploitation. These plays shocked audiences but earned Shaw a reputation as a bold new voice in theater.

Shaw's early works weren't immediate commercial successes, but they gained attention for their wit, irony, and social commentary. Over time, he developed a unique style—blending comedy with serious themes, using humor as a way to confront uncomfortable truths. His plays didn't just entertain; they provoked discussion.

The Rise to Fame: Shaw's Golden Era
In the early 20th century, Shaw's reputation grew, and his plays began to receive both critical acclaim and popular success. Works like "Man and Superman" (1902), "Major Barbara" (1905), and "Pygmalion" (1913) cemented Shaw as one of the most influential playwrights of the era.

In "Pygmalion," Shaw tackled issues of class, identity, and transformation, telling the story of a flower girl transformed into a lady through the power of speech and education. The play was later adapted into the famous musical "My Fair Lady," further solidifying Shaw's legacy in popular culture.

Shaw's ability to merge humor with social criticism made his work accessible and thought-provoking. Audiences admired how he used dialogue and satire to challenge the status quo—whether it was questioning capitalism, gender roles, or religious dogma.

Winning the Nobel Prize and Leaving a Legacy
In 1925, Shaw was awarded the Nobel Prize in Literature for his contributions to drama and social thought. True to his unconventional spirit, Shaw initially declined the prize but later accepted it at the urging of friends. He donated the prize money to fund efforts to translate his works into Swedish.

Even as he aged, Shaw remained politically engaged and outspoken, supporting socialist causes and writing until the end of his life. He continued to produce thought-provoking works well into his 80s and 90s, proving that creativity and activism know no age limit.

Lessons from Shaw's Success

- **Persistence Pays Off:** Shaw faced years of rejection but never gave up on his dream of becoming a writer and playwright.

- **Art as a Tool for Change:** Shaw believed in using art to provoke thought and challenge societal norms, inspiring future generations of socially-conscious creatives.

- **Humor is Powerful:** Shaw's wit and humor made his messages more accessible, showing that even serious ideas can be communicated with charm.

- **Unconventional Thinking Wins:** Shaw's refusal to follow the norms of his time made him a leader, not a follower, in both art and politics.

Conclusion: A Life of Wit and Wisdom

George Bernard Shaw's story is one of tenacity, creativity, and fearless advocacy for change. From his humble beginnings in Dublin to becoming a world-renowned playwright and social reformer, Shaw's legacy endures not just through his plays but through the spirit of critical thinking he championed.

Shaw's life reminds us that words have power—power to entertain, to educate, and to challenge the way we see the world. His work continues to inspire artists, writers, and activists, proving that great storytelling and bold ideas can change society—one play, one joke, and one sharp-witted line at a time.

Cicero's Success Story: Master Orator and Defender of the Roman Republic

"If you wish to persuade me, you must think my thoughts, feel my feelings, and speak my words." — CICERO, ROMAN STATESMAN AND ORATOR

Marcus Tullius Cicero stands as one of the most influential figures in the history of rhetoric, politics, and philosophy. Born in 106 BCE in a modest Roman family, Cicero rose to prominence through his brilliance in public speaking and law, eventually becoming a leading voice in defense of the Roman Republic. His mastery of language not only earned him a reputation as Rome's greatest orator but also paved the way for a distinguished political career, culminating in his election as consul. Beyond politics, Cicero's writings introduced philosophical concepts to Roman society, shaping intellectual thought for centuries. Though his life was marked by personal trials, political exile, and eventual execution, Cicero's legacy endures as a testament to the power of words, ideas, and unwavering principles in the face of adversity.

Early Life: Humble Beginnings and a Passion for Learning

Marcus Tullius Cicero was born in 106 BCE in the small town of Arpinum, Italy, to a family of moderate wealth. Unlike many Roman politicians of his time, Cicero did not come from an aristocratic lineage, and his early life was defined by the pursuit of education rather than power. Recognizing his keen intellect, his father ensured Cicero studied under the finest teachers of rhetoric, philosophy, and law in Rome and Greece. His love for learning became the foundation of his remarkable career, shaping his ideals and honing the oratory skills that would later define him.

Legal Career: Finding a Voice Through Rhetoric

Cicero's first major success came as a lawyer, where his eloquence and command over language quickly distinguished him. He earned widespread recognition in 70 BCE during the prosecution of Gaius Verres, a corrupt Roman governor. Cicero's brilliant oratory and sharp arguments exposed Verres' crimes so thoroughly that the defendant fled into exile before the trial concluded. This case catapulted Cicero into the public eye, cementing his reputation as one of Rome's greatest legal minds.

Entry into Politics: The Rise of the Outsider
Despite his outsider status—having no noble lineage—Cicero pursued a career in politics. His path to power was fueled by a combination of relentless ambition and extraordinary rhetorical ability. Cicero held a series of political offices, including quaestor and aedile, steadily rising through the ranks. His skill in navigating the complex political landscape won him supporters from both the elite and the general populace.

In 63 BCE, Cicero achieved the pinnacle of Roman politics when he was elected consul, Rome's highest office, at the relatively young age of 43. His consulship was marked by a defining moment—the suppression of the Catiline Conspiracy, a plot by disgruntled aristocrats to overthrow the Republic. Cicero's speeches exposing the conspirators became legendary, demonstrating not only his mastery of rhetoric but also his commitment to the stability of the Roman Republic.

The Philosopher-Politician: Balancing Politics with Ideas
Cicero's contributions extended beyond politics. He was deeply influenced by Greek philosophy, and he sought to integrate philosophical thought into Roman society. In addition to his political career, Cicero authored numerous philosophical and rhetorical treatises, such as *On the Republic* and *On Duties*, which explored themes of ethics, justice, and governance. His writings were revolutionary for their time, helping to introduce the Roman world to Stoic, Epicurean, and Academic philosophies. Through his works, Cicero became not only a politician but also one of history's most influential thinkers.

Fall from Power: Exile and Return
Cicero's commitment to the Republic and his outspoken nature earned him both admiration and powerful enemies. After opposing Julius Caesar and aligning himself with the senatorial faction, Cicero found himself at odds with the growing power of Rome's military leaders. In 58 BCE, he was forced into exile by his political opponents. Although he returned to Rome a year later, the political landscape had shifted, and Cicero's influence was diminished.

Yet even during these turbulent years, Cicero remained dedicated to his ideals. He continued to write and speak out in defense of the Republic, maintaining his belief in the rule of law and the importance of civic virtue. His opposition to the rise of autocratic power ultimately made him a target.

Legacy and Tragic End: A Martyr for the Republic

Cicero's life came to a tragic end in 43 BCE, during the power struggles that followed Julius Caesar's assassination. Having openly criticized Mark Antony in a series of speeches known as the *Philippics*, Cicero became a marked man. The Second Triumvirate—comprising Antony, Octavian, and Lepidus—listed Cicero as an enemy of the state. He was captured and executed on Antony's orders, but even in death, Cicero's legacy endured.

Lessons from Cicero's Success

- **The Power of Rhetoric:** Cicero's ability to communicate effectively was central to his success, proving that words can wield as much power as armies.

- **Integrity in Adversity:** Despite political exile and shifting allegiances, Cicero remained steadfast in his principles, advocating for justice and the preservation of the Republic.

- **Lifelong Learning:** His passion for philosophy and education not only enriched his own life but also shaped the intellectual legacy of the Roman world.

- **Adaptability:** Cicero's ability to pivot between politics, law, and philosophy demonstrated his versatility, making him influential in multiple spheres.

Conclusion: A Legacy of Words and Principles

Cicero's story is one of ambition, intellect, and unwavering dedication to the ideals of justice and the Republic. Although he lived in an era of political turmoil and personal risk, his influence extended far beyond his lifetime. His speeches and philosophical writings became foundational texts for Western thought, inspiring generations of leaders, thinkers, and legal scholars. Cicero's life serves as a reminder that integrity, eloquence, and the pursuit of knowledge can shape history and leave a lasting impact on the world.

Donald J. Trump's Success Story: From Business Tycoon to Political Powerhouse

"Sometimes by losing a battle, you find a new way to win the war."
— DONALD J. TRUMP, MASTER OF REINVENTION
AND UNCONVENTIONAL SUCCESS

Donald J. Trump, born on June 14, 1946, in Queens, New York, became one of the most well-known figures in real estate, entertainment, and politics. His journey to success is marked by his larger-than-life personality, his ability to capitalize on opportunities, and his pursuit of branding his name into a global empire.

Early Life and Entry into Real Estate

Trump was born into a wealthy family. His father, Fred Trump, was a successful real estate developer in New York, specializing in middle-income housing in Brooklyn and Queens. From a young age, Donald was exposed to the world of real estate, learning from his father about construction and property management. After attending the New York Military Academy and then the Wharton School of the University of Pennsylvania, he joined his father's real estate business, the Trump Organization, in the late 1960s.

However, Donald Trump had bigger ambitions. Instead of focusing on affordable housing like his father, he set his sights on Manhattan and luxury properties. His first major deal came in the 1970s when he bought the financially troubled Commodore Hotel near Grand Central Terminal, which he redeveloped into the Grand Hyatt Hotel. This project, aided by significant tax abatements, marked Trump's rise in New York real estate.

Building the Trump Empire

Throughout the 1980s, Trump expanded his real estate empire, developing some of Manhattan's most iconic properties, including Trump Tower on Fifth Avenue, Trump Plaza, and Trump World Tower. His name became synonymous with luxury and opulence, and he cultivated a public persona as a brash, confident businessman.

Trump's empire wasn't limited to real estate; he ventured into casinos, owning properties in Atlantic City like Trump Taj Mahal, Trump Plaza, and Trump Marina. These high-profile deals solidified his status, but many of these ventures would later face financial difficulties.

His business also expanded into other areas, including licensing his name to various products and ventures, from Trump-branded steaks to Trump University. Despite multiple controversies, the brand name "Trump" became one of his most valuable assets.

The Apprentice and Media Success

In 2004, Trump took his brand to a new level by starring in the hit reality television show "The Apprentice." The show featured aspiring businesspeople competing for a job in Trump's organization, with the famous catchphrase "You're fired!" becoming part of pop culture. The show was a massive success, further enhancing Trump's image as a savvy businessman.

His media presence made him a household name, leading to cameo appearances in movies, TV shows, and even professional wrestling. He leveraged his fame to license his name for various developments, from hotels to golf courses around the world.

Financial Ups and Downs

Despite his immense wealth and success, Trump faced financial troubles throughout his career. His Atlantic City casinos filed for bankruptcy multiple times, and other ventures failed to take off. However, Trump was always able to bounce back, often using debt restructuring and media attention to remain in the spotlight.

While many of his ventures faced scrutiny or failed, Trump's greatest strength was his ability to market himself and turn adversity into opportunity, rebranding and relaunching projects under his name.

The Road to the Presidency

In 2015, Donald Trump announced his candidacy for the Republican nomination for president of the United States. Initially seen as an outsider with little chance of success, Trump's populist message, centered on themes of "Make America

Great Again," immigration reform, and economic nationalism, resonated with large portions of the American electorate.

Despite intense media scrutiny, controversial statements, and criticism from both political parties, Trump won the Republican nomination and went on to win the 2016 presidential election, defeating Hillary Clinton. His victory was one of the most shocking political upsets in American history, as Trump, a political novice, defied expectations and reshaped the Republican Party.

Presidency and Beyond

Trump's presidency (2017-2021) was marked by significant accomplishments, including tax cuts, deregulation, judicial appointments, and a focus on America-first policies. However, it was also a highly polarizing tenure, with frequent clashes with the media, multiple investigations, and an impeachment trial.

After losing the 2020 election to Joe Biden, Trump remains an influential figure in American politics and has hinted at a potential return to public life. Despite controversies, his name continues to carry weight in real estate, media, and politics.

Legacy

Donald Trump's story is one of ambition, resilience, and branding. From real estate mogul to reality TV star to president, Trump built his success by constantly reinventing himself and leveraging his public image. Love him or hate him, his impact on business, media, and politics is undeniable, and his journey is a unique mix of business acumen and unconventional strategies that propelled him to the highest office in the land.

His legacy as a businessman and president will be studied for years, with his influence on the modern era of celebrity culture and political disruption cementing him as a defining figure of the 21st century.

Mike Lindell's Success Story: From Addiction to Entrepreneurial Triumph

"Every adversity, every failure, every heartache carries with it the seed of an equal or greater benefit." — MIKE LINDELL, PILLOW PIONEER AND RESILIENT ENTREPRENEUR

Mike Lindell is best known as the founder and CEO of My Pillow, Inc., a company that has sold millions of pillows worldwide and made him a household name. However, his journey to success is anything but typical—it's a story of perseverance, overcoming addiction, and relentless entrepreneurial drive.

Early Life and Struggles

Mike Lindell was born in Mankato, Minnesota, and grew up in Chaska, a small town. Throughout his early years, Lindell struggled with addiction to alcohol and drugs, including crack cocaine, which plagued him for decades. His addictions affected his life in numerous ways, leading to failed businesses, divorces, and financial ruin. By the early 2000s, he had lost his home and his marriage, and his substance abuse was spiraling out of control.

The Birth of MyPillow

Despite his struggles, Lindell always had an entrepreneurial spirit. In 2004, he came up with the idea for MyPillow after experiencing sleep issues due to uncomfortable pillows. Determined to create the perfect pillow, Lindell developed a unique design that featured interlocking fill, allowing the pillow to hold its shape and offer better support.

The process of creating the product was challenging. Lindell had no background in manufacturing, and he faced multiple rejections when trying to get his pillow into stores. To get his product off the ground, he self-funded the company and began selling MyPillow products at mall kiosks, state fairs, and trade shows. His hands-on approach and belief in the product eventually helped him gain a loyal customer base.

Breakthrough and Success

The turning point for MyPillow came when Lindell decided to run infomercials in 2011. The long-format TV commercials showcased Lindell explaining the benefits of MyPillow, and they quickly proved to be a massive success. The infomercials helped MyPillow's sales explode, with the company selling over $100 million worth of pillows in the first year alone.

By focusing on direct-to-consumer sales and maintaining control over manufacturing, Lindell was able to scale MyPillow rapidly. The company soon expanded beyond just pillows, offering products like mattress toppers, bed sheets, and other sleep-related items.

Overcoming Addiction and Finding Faith

While Lindell's business was booming, his personal life was still affected by his substance abuse. In 2009, after hitting rock bottom, Lindell experienced a spiritual awakening. He credits this moment as the turning point in his life, leading him to become sober and turning to Christian faith for strength and guidance.

Since overcoming his addiction, Lindell has been open about his struggles and now uses his platform to help others facing similar challenges. He founded the Lindell Recovery Network, a nonprofit organization dedicated to helping people overcome addiction through faith-based recovery programs.

Political Involvement and Controversies

In recent years, Lindell has become known for his political involvement, particularly his support of former U.S. President Donald Trump. His public advocacy and promotion of political causes, including election fraud claims, have made him a polarizing figure. MyPillow products have faced boycotts and been dropped by several retailers, but the company has continued to thrive due to its loyal customer base and direct sales model.

Legacy and Continued Growth

Today, MyPillow is a multimillion-dollar company, and Mike Lindell has solidified himself as an entrepreneurial success story. Despite the controversies and challenges, Lindell's journey is an inspiring example of turning adversity into triumph through resilience, faith, and determination.

His rise from a struggling addict to a business mogul continues to inspire many, and he remains focused on both growing his business and giving back through charitable work.

Marcus Sheridan's Success Story: Building Trust Through Transparency and Resilience

"Great content is the best sales tool in the world." — MARCUS SHERIDAN, MARKETING AND SALES EXPERT

Marcus Sheridan's journey from a struggling small business owner to a global thought leader in marketing is a story of resilience, innovation, and the transformative power of trust. As the co-founder of River Pools and Spas, Sheridan found himself on the brink of bankruptcy during the 2008 recession. However, instead of giving up, he pioneered a radical new approach to marketing—transparency through content. By answering customers' most pressing questions openly and honestly, Sheridan not only saved his company but also created a powerful framework that businesses around the world now follow. Today, as a bestselling author, speaker, and founder of The Sales Lion and IMPACT, Sheridan has redefined success by proving that building trust is the most valuable currency in business.

Early Life and Humble Beginnings

Marcus Sheridan's journey to success began far from the polished world of corporate boardrooms. Raised in a modest home in rural Virginia, he was instilled with values of hard work and persistence. His early years were shaped by jobs that required him to work with his hands—experiences that later influenced his pragmatic, people-centered business philosophy.

In 2001, Sheridan co-founded a swimming pool installation business, River Pools and Spas, with two close friends. Their goal was simple: to build pools for local homeowners. However, they had no idea that the obstacles they would face in the coming years would lay the foundation for Sheridan's transformation from a small business owner into one of the most influential voices in modern marketing.

Facing Failure: The Turning Point

The economic recession of 2008 hit the swimming pool industry hard, leaving River Pools and Spas on the brink of collapse. With homeowners cutting back on luxury expenses, new pool installations dried up almost overnight, forcing the company into a desperate financial situation. Sheridan found himself facing potential bankruptcy, scrambling to find a way to keep his business afloat.

Rather than giving up, Sheridan realized that to survive, he needed a new approach. He asked himself a pivotal question: *What are the biggest questions our customers have, and how can we answer them better than anyone else?* This simple shift in thinking became the turning point in his career—and would later define his philosophy as a thought leader.

The Power of Transparent Content Marketing

Determined to rebuild his business, Sheridan began creating educational content addressing every possible question customers might have about swimming pools. He adopted a radical transparency model: if customers had a question, no matter how uncomfortable or difficult, he answered it honestly on the River Pools and Spas blog.

This transparency extended to even the most delicate topics, such as pricing—a subject most companies avoid. Sheridan's philosophy was that if a business didn't address customer questions upfront, the customer would simply go elsewhere to find answers. His content-driven approach focused on building trust rather than traditional sales tactics.

The results were staggering. Within a year, River Pools and Spas became one of the top-ranked swimming pool websites in the world. The company went from near bankruptcy to thriving, largely because of the online trust Sheridan had built with potential customers. His content not only generated leads but also shortened the sales cycle, allowing the business to convert inquiries into customers with greater ease.

Becoming a Thought Leader: The Sales Lion

The success of River Pools and Spas opened doors for Sheridan to share his innovative marketing approach with other businesses. Recognizing a need for companies to rethink their marketing strategies, he launched *The Sales Lion*, a consulting firm focused on teaching businesses how to use transparency and content marketing to build trust and grow revenue.

Sheridan's message resonated with audiences across industries. His philosophy— "They Ask, You Answer"—became a blueprint for companies struggling to adapt to the rapidly changing digital landscape. He emphasized the importance of listening to customers, answering their questions, and using content to establish authority.

As a sought-after keynote speaker, Sheridan delivered his insights on stages around the world, inspiring organizations to adopt a more human-centered approach to sales and marketing. His authentic style and real-world success story earned him a reputation as one of the most influential marketing strategists of the modern era.

The Evolution of Success: Author, Speaker, and Entrepreneur

In 2017, Sheridan published *They Ask, You Answer*, a book that quickly became a bestseller and solidified his status as a thought leader in the marketing world. The book offers practical advice for businesses on how to implement transparent content strategies, empowering them to earn trust and drive growth.

Beyond consulting and writing, Sheridan expanded his focus to help businesses build cultures of trust and transparency from the ground up. He emphasized that successful marketing wasn't just about tactics—it required alignment across departments, from sales to leadership. His consulting firm evolved into IMPACT, where he continues to coach companies on sustainable marketing strategies.

Legacy: A Champion of Trust in Business

Today, Marcus Sheridan's story serves as a powerful example of resilience and the transformative power of trust. What began as a pool company on the brink of collapse evolved into a thriving business and a personal brand that reshaped how companies think about sales and marketing.

His philosophy—centered on transparency, empathy, and education—remains as relevant as ever in a world where consumers demand authenticity. Sheridan's legacy is not just in the businesses he's helped save but in the mindset shift he's inspired across industries: when businesses lead with trust, they win.

———————

Cory Doctorow's Success Story: Champion of Digital Rights and Storyteller for a Changing World

"Rights reversion is about taking back control of your creative work, enabling you to rejuvenate its presence and explore new opportunities in an ever-evolving market." — CORY DOCTOROW, AUTHOR, BLOGGER, AND JOURNALIST

Cory Doctorow is a prolific author, activist, and advocate for digital freedom, known for his science fiction novels, insightful essays, and tireless work in promoting open access and internet rights. Doctorow's unique ability to blend activism with storytelling has made him a prominent figure in both the literary and technology worlds. His career reflects a commitment to creativity, social justice, and the belief that technology can empower humanity—if it remains open and fair.

Early Life and Foundation in Activism

Cory Doctorow was born on July 17, 1971, in Toronto, Canada, to politically active parents. His upbringing immersed him in discussions about human rights, activism, and social change. From an early age, Doctorow showed a keen interest in science fiction and technology, becoming an avid reader of writers like Philip K. Dick and Ursula K. Le Guin.

Doctorow was also drawn to the burgeoning digital landscape of the 1980s and 1990s, participating in early online communities. His exposure to the potential of the internet for education and collaboration laid the groundwork for his belief in open access, free software, and digital rights—principles that would become central to his career.

Merging Writing and Technology

Doctorow's early career blended his love of storytelling with a passion for technology. After attending four universities and dropping out from all of them, he decided to pursue writing full-time while staying active in technology communities. In the early 2000s, Doctorow began publishing short stories and novels that blended speculative fiction with social commentary. His work explored the intersections of technology, economics, and individual freedoms— issues that were becoming increasingly relevant in the digital age.

Doctorow's big break as a novelist came in 2003 with *Down and Out in the Magic Kingdom*, a novel released under a Creative Commons license, allowing readers to share and distribute it freely. This unconventional move was a statement of Doctorow's belief in the importance of open access. The novel received critical acclaim, not just for its story but also for its innovative distribution model, helping Doctorow gain visibility in both the literary and technology communities.

Joining Boing Boing: A Platform for Activism

In 2000, Doctorow joined *Boing Boing*, a blog dedicated to technology, culture, and digital rights, as a co-editor. Under his influence, the platform became a leading voice in discussions about copyright reform, open-source software, and online freedom. Boing Boing's witty and insightful content attracted millions of readers, amplifying Doctorow's message and cementing his status as a thought leader in the tech world.

Through his posts on Boing Boing, Doctorow not only commented on the latest developments in technology and culture but also advocated for causes such as net neutrality, privacy, and opposition to digital rights management (DRM). His ability to explain complex technical and legal issues in accessible language allowed him to reach a wide audience, from activists to everyday internet users.

Science Fiction as Social Commentary

Doctorow's novels reflect his deep understanding of technology and its impact on society. His 2008 novel, *Little Brother*, became a sensation, particularly among young adults. The book, a dystopian thriller about surveillance and resistance, struck a chord with readers at a time when debates over government surveillance and privacy were intensifying.

Little Brother not only became a bestseller but also earned numerous awards, including the Prometheus Award and the John W. Campbell Memorial Award. The novel's success demonstrated Doctorow's ability to blend gripping narratives with real-world social issues, inspiring a new generation of readers to think critically about their relationship with technology and authority.

Doctorow followed up *Little Brother* with several other influential novels, including *For the Win* (2010), a novel about online gaming and labor rights, and *Walkaway* (2017), a post-scarcity utopia that explores themes of community and technological empowerment. His works often grapple with questions of freedom, privacy, and the social implications of technological innovation.

Advocacy for Open Access and Digital Rights
Beyond his fiction, Doctorow has become one of the most outspoken advocates for internet freedom and copyright reform. He serves as a special advisor to the Electronic Frontier Foundation (EFF), a nonprofit organization focused on defending civil liberties in the digital world. Through his work with the EFF, Doctorow has fought against restrictive copyright laws and advocated for the abolition of DRM, which he views as harmful to innovation and user rights.

Doctorow's activism is driven by a belief that creators should have the freedom to share their work without fear of exploitation and that users should retain control over the technology they own. His essays and public speaking engagements often explore the dangers of corporate monopolies, surveillance capitalism, and the erosion of online privacy.

Publishing and Creative Innovation
Doctorow continues to push the boundaries of how stories are told and shared. In addition to his novels, he writes nonfiction books such as *Information Doesn't Want to Be Free* (2014), which explores the challenges and opportunities of the digital age for creators. His recent works include *Chokepoint Capitalism* (2022), co-authored with Rebecca Giblin, which addresses how corporate monopolies stifle creativity and offers strategies for reclaiming creative freedom.

In 2020, Doctorow embarked on a new experiment in publishing with his novel *Attack Surface*, releasing it alongside an audiobook read by *Little Brother* fans. This direct-to-consumer approach bypassed traditional publishing channels, allowing Doctorow to retain more control over the distribution and pricing of his work.

Doctorow has also embraced new storytelling mediums, including podcasts and serialized fiction. His willingness to experiment with formats reflects his belief that creativity and innovation should not be constrained by industry norms.

A Legacy of Creativity, Activism, and Freedom
Cory Doctorow's career exemplifies the power of combining storytelling with activism. He has used his writing to inspire readers and challenge societal norms,

while his advocacy has helped shape public policy around internet freedom and copyright reform. His ability to engage with both the literary and technology worlds has made him a unique voice in the modern landscape.

Doctorow's legacy extends beyond his novels and essays. Through his work with the EFF and Boing Boing, he has empowered countless people to understand their rights and take action to defend them. His advocacy for open access and digital freedom has influenced the way creators distribute their work and how consumers interact with technology.

Conclusion: A Storyteller for the Digital Age
Cory Doctorow's journey from a tech-savvy kid in Toronto to a globally recognized author and activist reflects a lifelong dedication to freedom, creativity, and justice. His work has reshaped how people think about technology and storytelling, reminding us that innovation should serve humanity—not control it. As the digital landscape continues to evolve, Doctorow's insights remain as relevant as ever, inspiring both creators and consumers to fight for a more open, fair, and imaginative future.

Ira Glass' Success Story: The Voice that Redefined Storytelling

"Podcasting isn't just a platform; it's a powerful conduit for storytelling that brings your message directly to listeners' ears, establishing a personal connection that other media simply cannot match."
— IRA GLASS, RADIO HOST AND PRODUCER

Ira Glass, the creator and host of *This American Life*, has redefined storytelling in modern media, blending journalism with deeply personal narratives to create stories that resonate on both intellectual and emotional levels. With his distinctive voice and conversational style, Glass transformed public radio from dry reportage into a powerful medium for human connection. His journey from an uncertain NPR intern to a pioneer in audio storytelling is a testament to persistence, curiosity, and innovation. Through groundbreaking projects like *This American*

Life and *Serial*, Glass has inspired a new generation of storytellers, shaping the podcasting landscape and proving that stories—told with honesty and empathy—have the power to connect and transform.

Ira Glass: The Voice that Redefined Storytelling

Ira Glass is a celebrated radio personality, producer, and host of the iconic program *This American Life*. Known for his distinct voice and conversational storytelling style, Glass revolutionized radio by blending journalism, narrative, and personal experiences to create deeply engaging content. His journey to becoming one of the most influential figures in modern storytelling reflects persistence, curiosity, and a relentless drive to tell stories that resonate with audiences on an emotional level.

Early Life: A Love for Storytelling in the Making

Ira Glass was born on March 3, 1959, in Baltimore, Maryland. Though he was raised in a traditional Jewish family, Glass was not particularly interested in radio or journalism as a child. He initially planned to pursue a career in film or television, unaware that radio would become his life's passion.

Glass attended Northwestern University before transferring to Brown University, where he majored in semiotics, a field that explores how meaning is created through language and signs. His interest in storytelling deepened during this time, but it wasn't until an internship at NPR that he discovered his passion for radio.

Early Career: Learning the Craft at NPR

Glass's career in radio began in 1978 when, as a college student, he landed an internship at National Public Radio (NPR). At the time, NPR was still in its early stages, providing Glass with the opportunity to learn the ropes of radio production at a pioneering organization. He spent more than 15 years working behind the scenes, taking on various roles, including production assistant, editor, newscaster, and tape cutter.

The early years were a formative period for Glass. He experimented with storytelling techniques, interviewed diverse subjects, and learned how to build narratives using sound. However, he struggled with confidence and often doubted whether radio was his true calling. Yet, over time, Glass began developing his signature approach—combining journalism with personal storytelling in a way that felt informal, intimate, and captivating.

The Birth of *This American Life*

In 1995, after years of honing his skills at NPR, Ira Glass launched *This American Life* (TAL) from WBEZ, a public radio station in Chicago. Initially called *Your Radio Playhouse*, the show was a bold experiment in storytelling, blending news, personal narratives, and humor. Each episode focused on a central theme, with different acts—sometimes essays, interviews, or fictional tales—exploring various aspects of that theme.

The show's format was unconventional for public radio. Glass's conversational style, which felt more like a friendly chat than traditional news reporting, broke new ground. *This American Life* quickly gained a loyal audience, and by the late 1990s, it became nationally syndicated. Listeners were drawn to its mix of humor, heartbreak, and insight, with stories that captured the intricacies of human experience.

Defining a New Era of Radio Storytelling

What set Glass apart from other radio hosts was his focus on storytelling as an art form. He believed that journalism could be more than just facts—it could be about emotion, human connection, and shared experience. His interviews often focused on ordinary people in extraordinary circumstances, showing how seemingly mundane events could reveal universal truths.

Glass's ability to structure stories with a beginning, middle, and end—often with surprising twists—became a hallmark of *This American Life*. He emphasized that storytelling was not just about the content but how it was told, encouraging his team to find moments of reflection and revelation within their narratives.

Breaking New Ground with Podcasting and Television

As *This American Life* grew in popularity, it became a trailblazer in the world of podcasting. When TAL episodes were made available as podcasts in the early 2000s, the show reached a global audience, long before podcasting became mainstream. The success of the TAL podcast demonstrated the power of on-demand audio storytelling and paved the way for the modern podcasting industry.

Glass also expanded into television, producing a short-lived but acclaimed TV adaptation of *This American Life* on Showtime from 2007 to 2008. Although the show only ran for two seasons, it showcased Glass's ability to translate the essence of his storytelling style into a visual format.

Collaborations and Influence on the Podcasting Landscape

Building on the success of *This American Life*, Glass and his team launched *Serial* in 2014, a spinoff podcast that revolutionized the true crime genre. Hosted by Sarah Koenig, *Serial* told the story of a real-life murder investigation over multiple episodes, captivating millions of listeners and becoming a cultural phenomenon. It was one of the first podcasts to demonstrate the potential for serialized audio storytelling, helping to fuel the podcasting boom of the 2010s.

Glass's influence extends far beyond his own work. Through his mentorship and collaborations, he has inspired a generation of storytellers, journalists, and podcast creators. Programs like *Radiolab*, *The Moth*, and *Planet Money* owe much of their narrative style to the storytelling techniques pioneered by Glass and his team.

Overcoming Challenges and Staying Relevant

Despite his success, Glass has openly discussed the challenges of creative work. He has shared his struggles with imposter syndrome and the difficulties of maintaining a high standard in storytelling. In one of his most famous talks, Glass offered advice to aspiring creators, explaining that creative work is often disappointing in its early stages, but persistence and practice are essential to closing the gap between taste and skill.

Through continuous innovation, *This American Life* has remained relevant for decades. Glass's commitment to exploring new themes, formats, and collaborations ensures that the show continues to captivate audiences. Whether tackling serious social issues or exploring quirky human experiences, Glass keeps his work fresh by staying curious and open to new ideas.

Legacy: Redefining Storytelling for the Modern Era

Ira Glass's impact on storytelling and journalism is profound. He redefined what radio could be by blending journalism with narrative storytelling, making his work feel both intimate and accessible. His belief that stories have the power to connect people, foster empathy, and reveal deeper truths has influenced not only public radio but also the broader world of media.

Under Glass's leadership, *This American Life* has received numerous awards, including Peabody Awards and the first-ever Pulitzer Prize for audio reporting. Beyond the accolades, Glass's greatest achievement is his role in shaping the way people think about storytelling—on the radio, in podcasts, and beyond.

Conclusion: A Storyteller of Empathy and Curiosity

Ira Glass's journey from a reluctant intern at NPR to one of the most influential voices in modern media reflects a lifelong dedication to storytelling. His success lies not just in talent but in persistence, experimentation, and a genuine love for stories that capture the essence of human experience.

Glass's work has inspired countless creators to pursue narrative journalism, storytelling podcasts, and innovative forms of media. As the podcasting world continues to evolve, the legacy of *This American Life* endures, reminding us that stories—told with honesty, curiosity, and empathy—can change how we see the world.

———————

CHAPTER SIX

Embracing Innovation
in Business

In the dynamic world of business, innovation is not a luxury—it is a necessity. Companies that fail to innovate risk falling behind, while those that embrace new ideas and technologies gain a competitive edge, propelling their businesses to new heights. Innovation influences every aspect of business, from operational efficiency to customer experience and market expansion. This chapter explores how business leaders can foster a culture of innovation to adapt, grow, and stay ahead in today's ever-changing landscape.

Clayton Christensen, the father of disruptive innovation, once said, "Developing your business model isn't just about laying a foundation; it's about crafting a blueprint that aligns your vision with market needs and drives sustainable success." Innovation begins with understanding your market and anticipating trends that can disrupt or transform it. This chapter delves into how companies can identify opportunities for innovation that not only solve current problems but also address future market demands.

Effective leaders recognize that technology is a strategic tool for fostering innovation. Brian Solis, a digital analyst and author, emphasizes the importance of technology in shaping the customer experience and driving business transformation. From artificial intelligence to data analytics, technology provides businesses with the tools to streamline processes, enhance customer interactions, and expand market reach. We'll explore how companies can integrate emerging technologies to remain agile and responsive to change.

Innovative thinking also involves questioning the status quo and seeking creative solutions. Dan Kennedy, a direct response marketing expert, famously noted, "The best marketing doesn't feel like marketing." Successful businesses foster a culture where employees are encouraged to experiment, challenge conventional wisdom, and think outside the box. This chapter offers strategies for building an innovative workplace culture that empowers teams to generate new ideas and implement them effectively.

At the heart of business innovation lies customer-centricity. Joanna Wiebe, the founder of Copyhackers, advises, "Great copy is the result of a deep understanding of the customer." Companies that innovate with the customer in mind build lasting relationships and brand loyalty. We'll explore real-world examples of businesses that have successfully aligned their innovations with customer needs, creating value that resonates with their target audience.

Innovation also involves navigating the challenges of change. Ann Wojcicki, co-founder of 23andMe, emphasizes, "Every great idea starts as a crazy idea." This chapter examines how businesses can develop strategies to embrace change, turn challenges into opportunities, and sustain momentum through market shifts. We'll look at companies that have successfully pivoted their strategies, transforming obstacles into catalysts for growth.

Collaboration is another essential component of innovation. Chip Kidd, a renowned book designer, points out, "Collaboration is about making connections that can lead to new ideas." We'll discuss how partnerships and cross-industry collaborations can fuel innovation by bringing together diverse perspectives and expertise. These collaborative efforts often lead to breakthrough solutions that shape industries and define the future.

Ultimately, innovation is a continuous process, not a one-time event. Gary Keller, author of *The One Thing*, notes, "To achieve extraordinary results, you must be doing one thing at a time." We'll discuss how to create a long-term innovation strategy that allows businesses to evolve, grow, and stay ahead of emerging trends.

Throughout this chapter, we draw on insights from thought leaders such as Clayton Christensen, Brian Solis, and Dan Kennedy to illustrate the power of innovation in shaping successful businesses. You'll discover actionable strategies for fostering a culture of innovation, leveraging technology, collaborating effectively, and navigating change.

Innovation is the lifeblood of sustainable growth. It enables businesses to thrive in competitive markets, create value for customers, and build a legacy that stands the test of time. As you embark on your own journey from idea to empire, embracing innovation will be essential to unlocking new opportunities and driving lasting success.

Clayton Christensen's Success Story: The Pioneer of Disruptive Innovation and Lasting Impact

"Developing your business model isn't just about laying a foundation; it's about crafting a blueprint that aligns your vision with market needs and drives sustainable success." — CLAYTON CHRISTENSEN, AUTHOR AND BUSINESS CONSULTANT

Clayton Christensen was a visionary thinker whose work reshaped the way businesses and entrepreneurs understand innovation and growth. Best known for his theory of disruptive innovation, Christensen's insights explained how small, agile companies could topple industry giants by focusing on overlooked markets and unmet needs. From humble beginnings in Salt Lake City to becoming a celebrated Harvard Business School professor, author, and mentor, Christensen's journey was marked by curiosity, persistence, and a passion for solving complex problems. His groundbreaking ideas, shared through influential books like *The*

Innovator's Dilemma, continue to influence how organizations and individuals navigate change, embrace innovation, and create lasting impact in an ever-evolving world.

Early Life and Education: Building the Foundation

Clayton Christensen was born on April 6, 1952, in Salt Lake City, Utah. Growing up in a modest household with strong values centered around faith, education, and perseverance, he learned the importance of hard work early on. Christensen excelled academically and athletically, earning a place at Brigham Young University (BYU), where he studied economics. His intellectual curiosity and passion for solving complex problems set the stage for his future achievements.

After graduating from BYU, Christensen pursued further education at Oxford University as a Rhodes Scholar, earning a degree in applied econometrics. He later attended Harvard Business School, where he earned an MBA and subsequently a Ph.D. in Business Administration. His experience at Harvard would become pivotal in shaping his revolutionary ideas.

Early Career: From Consulting to Innovation Research

Christensen started his career as a consultant with the prestigious Boston Consulting Group, gaining deep insight into how businesses strategize and grow. Later, he co-founded Ceramics Process Systems, a technology company focused on advanced materials. Although the business found modest success, the experience revealed to Christensen the importance of understanding why some innovations thrive while others falter.

Christensen then transitioned into academia, returning to Harvard Business School as a professor. It was during his tenure at Harvard that he began to develop the theories that would change the business world.

Disruptive Innovation: A New Paradigm

In 1997, Christensen published his seminal book, *The Innovator's Dilemma*, which introduced the concept of disruptive innovation. He defined disruptive innovation as the process by which smaller companies with fewer resources disrupt established businesses by offering simpler, more affordable products that meet overlooked market needs. Unlike sustaining innovations, which improve existing products, disruptive innovations create entirely new markets or reshape existing ones.

Christensen's theory provided a framework for understanding how companies like Netflix, Amazon, and Apple disrupted their industries. It also explained why successful, well-managed companies often struggle to adapt to disruptive changes—focusing too much on improving current offerings and missing emerging market shifts.

Influence and Impact: Changing the Business World
The Innovator's Dilemma quickly became a must-read in business circles, earning widespread acclaim and influencing CEOs, entrepreneurs, and policymakers. Christensen's ideas resonated across industries, inspiring companies to rethink their strategies and invest in disruptive technologies.

He followed up with several other influential books, such as *The Innovator's Solution, How Will You Measure Your Life?*, and *The Innovator's DNA*, each exploring different facets of innovation, leadership, and personal development. Christensen's ideas not only shaped the way businesses approach innovation but also provided insights into how individuals could lead more meaningful and impactful lives.

Thought Leadership and Teaching: A Lasting Legacy
Beyond his books, Christensen became a beloved teacher and mentor at Harvard Business School, where he influenced countless students and aspiring entrepreneurs. His teaching style was marked by humility, empathy, and a genuine desire to help others succeed. Christensen's work extended beyond academia, as he advised companies and governments on how to foster innovation and prepare for disruptive change.

He also co-founded the Clayton Christensen Institute for Disruptive Innovation, a non-profit think tank focused on using his theories to tackle societal challenges in areas like healthcare, education, and economic development.

Personal Challenges and Triumphs
Christensen's life wasn't without personal challenges. In 2010, he was diagnosed with cancer and later suffered a stroke, but he continued to teach, write, and inspire despite these setbacks. His resilience in the face of adversity became a

testament to his philosophy of measuring life not just by professional achievements but by the impact made on others.

Legacy: A Visionary Who Transformed Innovation
Clayton Christensen passed away in January 2020, leaving behind a profound legacy. His groundbreaking work on disruptive innovation remains a cornerstone of modern business strategy, and his teachings continue to inspire entrepreneurs, business leaders, and scholars around the world. Christensen's influence transcends industries, showing how innovation can drive progress not only in business but also in society.

Christensen's life serves as a reminder that the most enduring success comes not from protecting the status quo but from embracing change and nurturing new ideas. His journey exemplifies how intellectual curiosity, humility, and a commitment to helping others can create a lasting impact.

Brian Solis' Success Story: From Digital Disruption to Experience Guru – A Futurist's Journey

"To stay ahead in business, you need to embrace technology like it's your new best friend. Innovation isn't just about using the latest tools; it's about integrating them in ways that propel your business forward and keep you at the cutting edge. The right tech can turn today's trends into tomorrow's advantages." — BRIAN SOLIS, DIGITAL ANALYST AND AUTHOR

"In the digital age, public relations is no longer about pushing information but about engaging in a conversation that resonates across the web, turning every interaction into an opportunity for impact."
— BRIAN SOLIS, DIGITAL ANALYST AND AUTHOR

Brian Solis is a renowned digital analyst, anthropologist, and futurist, best known for his work on digital transformation, customer experience, and the impact of technology on society and business. His rise to prominence can be traced through a blend of insightful writing, thought leadership, and his ability to predict the direction of digital and technological changes.

Early Beginnings and Career

Brian Solis began his career in Silicon Valley, where he was at the forefront of the dot-com boom. He worked in marketing and public relations, helping tech companies navigate the rapidly changing digital landscape. His early work involved helping companies adapt to the internet, which was then a revolutionary space, by shaping their communication strategies and teaching them how to engage with consumers in new ways.

In the late 1990s, Solis recognized that the future of business and marketing was going to be drastically impacted by the internet, and he began to shift his focus towards digital marketing and online communication strategies. During this period, Solis established himself as an authority on social media, helping brands understand and capitalize on the emerging platforms.

Thought Leadership and Writing

Brian Solis' success is deeply tied to his thought leadership in the fields of digital transformation, technology, and user experience. His writing spans various topics, but his central theme revolves around how technology is reshaping the customer experience, business models, and human behavior.

He has authored several highly influential books, including:

- **"Engage!"** (2010): A guide to social media marketing and engagement.

- **"The End of Business as Usual"** (2011): Focused on how technology is forcing businesses to rethink their models.

- **"X: The Experience When Business Meets Design"** (2015): This book dives into how customer experience design is essential for business success in the digital age.

- **"Lifescale"** (2019): A more personal exploration of how individuals can focus and manage technology distractions in an increasingly chaotic digital world.

These books, along with his regular contributions to digital media and conferences, have cemented Solis as a key figure in understanding digital disruption.

Digital Analyst and Futurist

Solis's career has evolved beyond marketing to encompass the larger concept of digital transformation. He is often brought in by Fortune 500 companies as a consultant and speaker to advise on how businesses can not only adapt to digital trends but also leverage them for long-term growth and innovation.

He emphasizes the importance of customer experience (CX) and the need for companies to understand the changing digital behaviors of consumers. His work focuses on how businesses can redesign their strategies to be customer-first, using data, AI, and technology to create meaningful experiences.

Legacy and Influence

Today, Brian Solis is recognized as one of the leading voices in digital transformation. He continues to speak globally at conferences and to advise businesses on how to prepare for the future. His ability to translate complex technology trends into actionable insights has made him a go-to resource for companies navigating the rapidly evolving digital landscape.

Through his books, speeches, and consulting work, Solis has helped countless businesses understand the importance of adapting to the changing world, particularly as technology and customer expectations evolve.

Conclusion

Brian Solis' journey from a Silicon Valley marketer to a global thought leader in digital transformation highlights his ability to foresee and shape trends. His contributions to the understanding of how technology impacts businesses and society continue to influence leaders around the world. Solis' success is built on his passion for innovation, continuous learning, and his belief in the power of technology to transform human experiences.

———————

Dan Kennedy's Success Story: The Mastermind Behind Direct-Response Marketing

"Identify the pain point, agitate it, then solve it." — DAN KENNEDY, MARKETING CONSULTANT AND PROLIFIC AUTHOR

Dan Kennedy is a legendary figure in the world of marketing, known for revolutionizing the way businesses approach advertising and sales. With a career spanning decades, Kennedy's work has transformed countless companies through his practical, no-nonsense strategies focused on measurable results. From his early days in stand-up comedy and magic to becoming a sought-after marketing consultant, author, and speaker, Kennedy mastered the art of direct-response marketing—a method that demands every campaign drive immediate action. His candid teaching style, best-selling books, and influential seminars have made him a mentor to countless entrepreneurs. Kennedy's legacy lies not just in his groundbreaking techniques but in his relentless belief that success is about taking control, staying persistent, and focusing on what truly works.

Early Life and Career Beginnings
Born in Ohio, Dan Kennedy grew up with a passion for storytelling and entrepreneurship. From an early age, he showed an interest in communication, creativity, and business, which laid the foundation for his future career. In his early twenties, Kennedy started performing as a stand-up comedian and magician, where he quickly realized that marketing himself was essential to his success. This sparked his lifelong obsession with understanding what motivates people to take action, a skill that would later become the cornerstone of his career in direct-response marketing.

Breaking into Marketing and Consulting
Dan's turning point came when he began experimenting with direct mail and response-driven ads to market his performances. As he refined these strategies, he discovered that most small businesses and entrepreneurs struggled with the same marketing challenges. Sensing a business opportunity, Kennedy pivoted his focus from entertainment to helping others grow their businesses through powerful advertising techniques.

Kennedy immersed himself in learning everything about copywriting, sales psychology, and direct-response marketing. His expertise grew quickly, and soon he became a sought-after consultant, working with business owners across various industries. His approach was different from traditional advertising—Kennedy emphasized tangible results and measurable returns on investment (ROI), setting him apart from the competition.

Founding Magnetic Marketing

In the 1980s, Kennedy launched Magnetic Marketing, a company that provides marketing systems and strategies for small businesses. His work focused on creating practical, results-oriented marketing campaigns that business owners could implement without needing large advertising budgets. His no-nonsense, "get-rich without guilt" approach resonated with entrepreneurs who needed straightforward solutions to grow their businesses.

Kennedy's marketing philosophy was rooted in direct-response marketing—an approach that requires every campaign to generate immediate, trackable results, such as sales or leads. He became famous for his persuasive writing, using techniques that captured attention and spurred action. His strategies applied to all industries, from real estate and financial services to fitness and dentistry.

Becoming an Industry Icon and Author

Throughout his career, Kennedy wrote several influential books, including *The Ultimate Sales Letter* and *No B.S. Guide to Direct Marketing*, which have become must-reads for entrepreneurs and marketers. His practical advice and candid tone resonated with readers, turning him into one of the most influential voices in the marketing world.

In addition to his books, Kennedy became a keynote speaker and mentor to many successful marketers and business leaders. He hosted seminars and workshops, where attendees learned his direct-response techniques, and he built a reputation for delivering actionable insights with humor and blunt honesty. His teaching emphasized that success in business is not about fancy branding but about creating marketing that drives immediate results.

Challenges and Resilience
Despite his success, Kennedy's journey wasn't without challenges. He has spoken openly about battling health issues and setbacks in his career. However, these difficulties only strengthened his resolve and shaped his philosophy on persistence, hard work, and the importance of controlling your business destiny. His personal resilience became a source of inspiration for many of his followers, further cementing his legacy as both a marketing expert and a motivational figure.

Legacy and Impact
Dan Kennedy's contributions to the world of marketing are unparalleled. His teachings have influenced generations of business owners, marketers, and copywriters, many of whom credit Kennedy's strategies for transforming their businesses. His concept of direct-response marketing has become the foundation for countless businesses, and his systems continue to help entrepreneurs achieve financial freedom.

Even as he stepped away from the public eye in recent years, his influence remains strong. His books, courses, and consulting programs are still widely used, and his Magnetic Marketing system has been acquired and expanded by other marketing firms. Dan Kennedy's impact lies not only in the strategies he developed but in the mindset shift he inspired—encouraging entrepreneurs to take control of their marketing, focus on results, and never settle for mediocrity.

Lessons from Dan Kennedy's Journey

- **Action Over Perfection:** Kennedy emphasizes taking action, even if it's imperfect. Progress is made through doing, not just planning.

- **Marketing is Measurable:** Success comes from campaigns that generate immediate and trackable outcomes.

- **Persistence is Key:** Challenges are inevitable, but resilience and persistence are what separate the successful from the rest.

- **No-Nonsense Approach:** Success requires a focus on what works, not flashy trends or empty branding.

Dan Kennedy's career exemplifies the power of focused, strategic marketing combined with an entrepreneurial spirit. His teachings continue to empower business owners worldwide, proving that with the right approach, marketing can be a direct pathway to financial success and personal freedom.

———————

Gary Keller's Success Story: A Visionary Leader Who Revolutionized Real Estate

"It is not that we have too little time to do all the things we need to do, it is that we feel the need to do too many things in the time we have."
— GARY KELLER, REAL ESTATE ENTREPRENEUR
AND BESTSELLING AUTHOR

Gary Keller's journey from a small-town upbringing in Pasadena, Texas, to co-founding one of the most influential real estate companies in the world is a testament to the power of vision and innovation. As the co-founder of Keller Williams Realty, Keller reimagined the traditional real estate model by putting agents at the heart of the business, empowering them to grow their personal brands and businesses. His passion for education, coupled with his knack for developing strategic systems, has not only shaped the real estate industry but also influenced entrepreneurs and professionals across industries. With best-selling books like *The Millionaire Real Estate Agent* and *The ONE Thing*, Keller's legacy extends beyond real estate, inspiring others to achieve success through focus, discipline, and innovation. His story is one of bold ambition, continuous learning, and a commitment to creating opportunities for others.

Early Life and Passion for Real Estate
Gary Keller was born in Pasadena, Texas, and grew up in a working-class family. From an early age, Keller had a strong sense of ambition and a desire to make a difference. He attended Baylor University, where he earned a degree in real estate and marketing. His time at Baylor ignited his passion for real estate, and after graduation, Keller moved to Austin, Texas, to pursue a career in the industry.

Founding Keller Williams Realty
In the early 1980s, Keller gained experience working for various real estate firms, quickly rising through the ranks thanks to his natural leadership abilities and keen

business acumen. However, he grew frustrated with the way traditional real estate companies operated, particularly their lack of focus on agent empowerment. Determined to change the industry, Keller co-founded Keller Williams Realty in 1983 with the mission of building a firm that prioritized the success of agents.

Innovating with a New Business Model

Keller's vision was to create a real estate company that operated differently—one where agents would be treated as business partners, with more control over their commissions and the freedom to build their own brands. This agent-centric model became the foundation for Keller Williams' success, allowing it to attract top talent across the country. Keller also introduced innovative training programs and tools to help agents grow their businesses, setting a new standard in the industry.

Overcoming Challenges and Achieving Growth

In its early years, Keller Williams faced stiff competition from established real estate firms, but Keller's focus on empowering agents began to pay off. The company grew steadily, and by the 1990s, it had expanded beyond Texas. Despite market downturns and challenges, Keller's leadership kept the company on a path of continuous growth, always emphasizing education, teamwork, and adaptability.

Writing the Playbook for Success: "The Millionaire Real Estate Agent"

In 2004, Gary Keller co-authored *The Millionaire Real Estate Agent*, a best-selling book that outlined proven strategies for building a thriving real estate business. The book became a go-to resource for agents and entrepreneurs, cementing Keller's reputation as both a thought leader and mentor. His other works, including *The ONE Thing*, focused on the power of prioritization and have been embraced by a broader audience seeking personal and professional success.

Building a Lasting Legacy

Under Keller's leadership, Keller Williams grew into the largest real estate franchise in the world by agent count. The company's commitment to education, innovation, and agent empowerment has made it a leader in the industry. Beyond real estate, Keller's influence extends to leadership and personal development, with his books inspiring individuals across various fields.

Lessons from Gary Keller's Success

Gary Keller's journey offers powerful lessons about the importance of vision, innovation, and focusing on people. He believed in challenging the status quo, creating opportunities for others, and building a business culture rooted in empowerment and trust. His emphasis on continuous learning and strategic thinking has made him an icon in the real estate industry and beyond.

Today, Keller's influence continues through his leadership at Keller Williams and his ongoing contributions to personal development. His story serves as an inspiration for entrepreneurs who aspire to create meaningful change in their industries while empowering those around them to achieve their own success.

———

Joanna Wiebe's Success Story: Pioneer of Conversion Copywriting and Marketing Innovation

"Risk management is like having a business safety net—it's not about dodging every challenge but about preparing to tackle them with agility. The real power comes from anticipating potential issues and having strategies that keep your business resilient and ready to thrive."

— JOANNA WIEBE, FOUNDER OF COPYHACKERS

Joanna Wiebe is known as one of the leading voices in the world of copywriting and conversion copywriting, a field where effective, compelling writing is used to drive user action, like sales or sign-ups. Wiebe's journey to success is rooted in her ability to blend creativity with data-driven results, making her one of the most sought-after experts in digital marketing and copywriting today. Here's how she started and became so successful.

Early Career and Beginnings

Joanna Wiebe started her career in technical writing, working for companies like Intuit and Conversion Rate Experts. During her time at Intuit, she honed her skills in crafting clear, concise, and engaging copy for software products. Her work required translating complex ideas into simple, user-friendly language, which laid the foundation for her future career in copywriting.

However, she soon realized that copywriting, particularly conversion-focused copy, was where her true passion lay. Unlike technical writing, conversion copywriting focuses on persuasion and the psychological triggers that motivate users to take action. This shift in her career led her to explore how copy can influence everything from website conversions to email marketing.

Founding Copyhackers

In 2011, Joanna founded Copyhackers, a platform and community dedicated to helping marketers, startups, and copywriters write better content that converts. Copyhackers quickly became a go-to resource for copywriters looking to sharpen their skills and businesses seeking to improve their conversion rates. Joanna's deep knowledge of copywriting, combined with her ability to distill complex principles into actionable advice, made her a trusted authority in the space.

Her blog posts, courses, and workshops focused on a blend of data-driven insights and storytelling techniques, offering readers practical strategies they could apply to their own copy. Copyhackers became known for its focus on A/B testing, user psychology, and crafting messages that resonate with target audiences.

Revolutionizing Conversion Copywriting

Joanna Wiebe is credited with coining the term "conversion copywriting," which puts a heavy emphasis on using copy to convert visitors into customers. She taught her readers that copywriting should be treated as an evolving craft, where understanding customer behavior, running tests, and iterating copy based on results are key elements to success.

Her "problem-first" approach to copywriting, where the copy focuses on solving a user's problem rather than simply selling a product, revolutionized how marketers and businesses approached writing for conversion. Joanna's techniques moved away from the traditional, often "hype-heavy" advertising copy toward copy that builds trust, empathy, and relatability with the reader.

Speaking and Training

As Copyhackers grew in popularity, Joanna's influence expanded beyond the written word. She became a sought-after speaker, delivering keynote addresses and workshops at major marketing conferences like ConConf, Unbounce's Call to Action Conference, and ConversionXL Live. Her energetic, no-nonsense style made her talks incredibly popular, further solidifying her position as a leader in the copywriting world.

Joanna also launched various copywriting courses, mentoring thousands of students around the world on how to write high-converting copy. Her programs, like The 10x Launches and The Copy School, focus on everything from landing page optimization to writing compelling emails, helping businesses grow through the power of effective copy.

Collaborations and Continued Success
Over the years, Joanna has worked with leading tech companies, including Shopify, Crazy Egg, SEMrush, and Wistia, to help optimize their messaging and increase conversions. Her strategic approach and focus on writing copy backed by data and psychology have helped her clients see significant improvements in user engagement and revenue growth.

Legacy and Influence
Joanna Wiebe's impact on the world of copywriting goes beyond just writing tips and templates. She has empowered a new generation of marketers and entrepreneurs to see copy as one of the most valuable tools in their business toolkit. Her work has transformed how people view digital marketing, making copywriting a science of persuasion rather than just an art of words.

Today, Joanna continues to lead Copyhackers, offering new insights into copywriting while expanding her influence through speaking engagements and ongoing training programs.

Conclusion
Joanna Wiebe's success is a testament to her ability to innovate, educate, and continually evolve in a fast-changing industry. Her contribution to conversion copywriting has made her a pioneer, and her platform, Copyhackers, remains a cornerstone for those looking to use the power of words to drive business growth. From technical writer to one of the most influential voices in the world of digital marketing, Joanna Wiebe's story is one of passion, innovation, and mastery of her craft.

Anne Wojcicki's Success Story: Pioneering the Future of Person Genomics

"Maintaining vigilance over your trademarks is akin to guarding the crown jewels; it's essential for ensuring your brand's legacy and authority in the marketplace remain intact."
— ANNE WOJCICKI, CEO OF 23ANDME

"Managing licensing agreements is like conducting an orchestra; each contract plays a different instrument, and it's your job to ensure they all harmonize to create a symphony of success." — ANNE WOJCICKI, CO-FOUNDER AND CEO OF 23ANDME

Anne Wojcicki, co-founder and CEO of 23andMe, revolutionized personal health by making genetic testing accessible to millions. Her vision for democratizing access to DNA data has transformed how individuals understand their ancestry and health, empowering people to take control of their well-being. Wojcicki's success reflects her ability to combine scientific innovation with entrepreneurial spirit, navigating challenges in healthcare, regulation, and technology to build one of the most influential companies in biotechnology.

Early Life and Educational Foundation

Anne Wojcicki was born on July 28, 1973, in Palo Alto, California, into a family that valued education and curiosity. Her mother, Esther Wojcicki, was an esteemed educator, and her father, Stanley Wojcicki, was a Stanford professor of physics. Growing up in Silicon Valley alongside her sisters Susan and Janet— who would also become influential leaders—Anne was immersed in an environment that fostered innovation.

Wojcicki studied biology at Yale University, where she developed a deep interest in molecular biology and genetics. While at Yale, she also honed her love for competitive sports as a member of the university's varsity ice hockey team. This combination of scientific rigor and athletic determination would later play a crucial role in her entrepreneurial journey.

Starting a Career in Finance and Pivoting to Science

After graduating from Yale, Wojcicki initially pursued a career in finance. She worked as an analyst on Wall Street, focusing on healthcare investments. During this time, Wojcicki gained insight into the complexities of the healthcare system and saw firsthand how traditional healthcare models often failed to empower patients.

Although she was successful in finance, Wojcicki became increasingly frustrated with the industry's focus on profits over patient outcomes. She realized that the key to changing healthcare lay not in incremental improvements but in giving individuals greater access to their own health information. In 2006, with this goal in mind, she left her lucrative finance career to pursue her passion for biology and genetics.

Founding 23andMe: Democratizing DNA Data

Wojcicki co-founded 23andMe in 2006 with Linda Avey and Paul Cusenza, aiming to create a direct-to-consumer genetic testing service. At a time when genetic testing was primarily available through specialized clinics, Wojcicki envisioned a future where individuals could access their DNA information at home. The name "23andMe" reflects the 23 pairs of chromosomes in the human genome, emphasizing the company's mission to help people understand their genetic blueprint.

The company's first product, a saliva-based DNA test, launched in 2007. It provided users with insights into their ancestry, genetic traits, and predispositions to certain health conditions. 23andMe's mission was ambitious: to create a new kind of healthcare experience, one where consumers had greater knowledge and agency over their own genetics.

Challenges with Regulation and Market Expansion

Despite its innovative model, 23andMe faced significant challenges. In 2013, the U.S. Food and Drug Administration (FDA) ordered the company to halt marketing its health-related genetic tests, citing concerns about accuracy and the potential for misinterpreting results. The setback forced 23andMe to temporarily scale back its offerings and work closely with regulators to ensure compliance.

Rather than giving up, Wojcicki took the challenge as an opportunity to improve the company's scientific processes and rebuild trust with the FDA. In 2015, 23andMe became the first direct-to-consumer genetics company to receive FDA approval for a genetic test that provides health-related insights, marking a significant milestone for both the company and the personal genomics industry.

Transforming Healthcare through Genetic Research
In addition to consumer services, Wojcicki expanded 23andMe's focus to include scientific research. With millions of customers consenting to share their data anonymously, 23andMe built one of the largest genetic databases in the world. This data has been used for groundbreaking research in genetics, disease prevention, and drug development.

The company's research collaborations with universities, pharmaceutical companies, and nonprofit organizations have led to important discoveries in conditions like Parkinson's disease and cancer. 23andMe has also ventured into drug development, leveraging its genetic insights to create more targeted therapies.

Empowering Individuals and Shaping the Future of Genomics
Wojcicki's work at 23andMe reflects her belief in empowering individuals through information. She advocates for patient access to genetic data, arguing that people have a right to understand their own DNA without gatekeeping from traditional healthcare systems. This philosophy has reshaped the way consumers engage with their health, enabling them to make more informed decisions.

The success of 23andMe has also changed societal attitudes toward personal genetics, making it a common tool for exploring ancestry and understanding health risks. Wojcicki has positioned the company at the intersection of technology, science, and consumer empowerment, helping people unlock the mysteries of their DNA.

Personal Life and Public Influence
Wojcicki's personal life has also drawn public attention. From 2007 to 2015, she was married to Sergey Brin, co-founder of Google, with whom she has two children. Although their marriage ended, Wojcicki and Brin remain close collaborators, sharing a commitment to innovation and philanthropy.

Wojcicki's ability to balance public scrutiny with her professional responsibilities reflects her resilience and determination. She remains active in advocating for women's leadership in business and STEM fields, inspiring future generations of female entrepreneurs.

Legacy: A Visionary in Personal Genomics

Anne Wojcicki's journey from biology student to Wall Street analyst to genomics pioneer exemplifies the power of combining scientific expertise with entrepreneurial vision. Her leadership at 23andMe has not only transformed how people think about genetics but also redefined the relationship between consumers and healthcare.

Wojcicki's success lies in her ability to overcome challenges, navigate regulatory hurdles, and maintain a clear focus on the company's mission to empower individuals through information. Through 23andMe, she has made DNA testing accessible to millions, contributing to advances in personalized medicine and genetic research.

Conclusion: Paving the Way for a New Era of Health and Science

Anne Wojcicki's work with 23andMe has opened new frontiers in healthcare, demonstrating the potential of personal genomics to transform lives. Her relentless focus on empowering individuals with knowledge reflects a belief that healthcare should be transparent, accessible, and personal. As the fields of genetics and personalized medicine continue to evolve, Wojcicki's influence will undoubtedly remain central to the future of science and consumer health, inspiring others to challenge the status quo and pursue innovation that benefits humanity.

Chip Kidd's Success Story: The Mastermind Behind Iconic Book Covers

"A great book cover is like a portal, visually compelling enough to draw readers into the story before they even turn the first page."
— CHIP KIDD, RENOWNED BOOK DESIGNER

"The art of book manufacturing and binding is a meticulous craft where precision meets legacy, transforming mere words into timeless treasures."
— CHIP KIDD, GRAPHIC DESIGNER AND BOOK COVER ARTIST

Chip Kidd is an American graphic designer, author, and editor renowned for revolutionizing the art of book cover design. With a career spanning over three decades, Kidd's work has become synonymous with visually striking and thought-provoking covers that tell stories before readers even open a book. His innovative designs have made him a pivotal figure in the publishing world, bridging the gap between literature and visual art, and redefining how readers connect with books.

Early Life: A Love for Comics and Art
Chip Kidd was born on September 12, 1964, in Shillington, Pennsylvania. Growing up, he was captivated by comics, particularly Batman, which sparked his fascination with visual storytelling. His early interest in the relationship between imagery and narrative would later shape his career as a book cover designer.

Kidd went on to study graphic design at Penn State University, where he honed his artistic skills. During this time, he became increasingly drawn to how visual elements can convey meaning and emotion, laying the foundation for his future success in book design.

The Big Break: Joining Knopf Publishing
After graduating from Penn State in 1986, Kidd moved to New York City, where he landed a job at Alfred A. Knopf, one of the most prestigious publishing houses. What began as an entry-level role soon transformed into a groundbreaking career. Kidd's talent for blending typography, imagery, and symbolism caught the attention of authors and publishers alike. His first designs demonstrated a keen understanding that a book cover is not merely packaging but a crucial part of the reader's experience.

Kidd's big break came in 1990 when he designed the now-iconic cover for *Jurassic Park* by Michael Crichton. The skeletal T-rex silhouette, both bold and minimalist, captured the essence of the story and became instantly recognizable. The design was so powerful that it was adapted for the film's promotional materials, cementing Kidd's reputation as a visionary.

Revolutionizing Book Design
Kidd's success with *Jurassic Park* set the tone for the rest of his career. He continued to produce covers that pushed the boundaries of traditional design,

133

employing a variety of styles—minimalist, surreal, abstract, and playful. His designs often hinted at the book's themes without revealing too much, inviting readers to explore the narrative within. This philosophy has become his trademark: designing covers that complement the content while sparking curiosity.

Throughout the 1990s and 2000s, Kidd became a go-to designer for literary giants, including Haruki Murakami, James Ellroy, and Cormac McCarthy. He worked closely with these authors, understanding their vision and translating it into visual form. His ability to interpret stories visually, combined with his knack for innovation, elevated book cover design to an art form.

A Legacy of Innovation and Impact
Beyond his work at Knopf, Kidd has had a profound influence on the field of graphic design. His work has been featured in exhibitions at the Cooper Hewitt Smithsonian Design Museum and the Museum of Modern Art (MoMA). Kidd has also authored several books about design, including *Chip Kidd: Book One* and *Judge This*, which explore his creative process and offer insights into the world of book design.

Kidd's influence extends beyond the publishing industry into academia and popular culture. He has delivered talks at TED, inspiring audiences with his unique approach to creativity and storytelling. In his TED Talk, *Designing Books Is No Laughing Matter. OK, It Is*, Kidd emphasizes the importance of humor, surprise, and emotional connection in design, revealing how small details can make a big impact.

Writing and Personal Projects
In addition to his work as a designer, Kidd has pursued his passion for storytelling by writing novels and graphic novels. His first novel, *The Cheese Monkeys* (2001), is a semi-autobiographical story set in the 1950s, following a young art student navigating the complexities of design education. The novel, like Kidd's designs, is filled with humor and thought-provoking moments.

Kidd also co-wrote *Batman: Death by Design*, a graphic novel that pays homage to his childhood love for Batman and explores themes of architecture, art, and heroism. His personal projects reflect his belief that design and storytelling are interconnected, each enriching the other.

Challenges and Perseverance in a Changing Industry
Despite his success, Kidd has navigated challenges in the evolving publishing landscape. The rise of e-books and digital media has shifted how readers interact with books, placing new demands on designers to create covers that stand out both in print and online. However, Kidd has embraced these changes, continuing to innovate and adapt his style to meet new challenges.

He has also spoken about the importance of balancing creativity with commercial demands. As a designer working within the constraints of publishing deadlines and marketing goals, Kidd has learned to navigate the fine line between artistic expression and practicality.

Conclusion: A Legacy of Storytelling through Design
Chip Kidd's career exemplifies how design can shape the way we experience stories, turning book covers into powerful works of art. His ability to blend creativity, humor, and insight has redefined the role of the book designer, proving that a well-crafted cover is more than just a visual element—it is a vital part of the storytelling process.

From *Jurassic Park* to literary classics, Kidd's covers have captivated readers, inviting them into the world of the narrative with a single glance. His work continues to inspire designers, authors, and readers alike, leaving a lasting legacy in the fields of graphic design and publishing. As Kidd himself once said, "A book cover is a distillation. It is a haiku of the story." And through his designs, Chip Kidd has mastered the art of saying everything with just a few strokes of genius.

CHAPTER SEVEN

The Role of Technology in Growth

In today's fast-paced business landscape, technology is not merely a support system—it is a driving force behind growth and innovation. Companies that harness the power of technology are better equipped to streamline operations, engage with customers, scale efficiently, and outpace their competitors. This chapter explores how adopting the right technologies can be pivotal to business expansion and sustained success, offering insights into integrating technology into every layer of the business framework.

Nate Silver, renowned statistician and author, asserts, "Big Data isn't just about having vast amounts of information; it's about making vast improvements in how we understand our market." Businesses that successfully incorporate technology unlock new ways to automate processes, reduce operational costs, and respond rapidly to market shifts. In this chapter, we'll examine how technology-driven companies have optimized their workflows and boosted profitability through strategic technological adoption.

The growth enabled by technology extends beyond operations into customer engagement. Tim Cook, CEO of Apple, emphasizes, "Planning your operations is like setting gears in motion: the right synchronization ensures efficiency and drives your business engine forward." Companies that leverage e-commerce platforms, AI-driven personalization, and customer management tools not only expand their reach but also offer exceptional customer experiences. We'll explore stories of businesses that have mastered digital strategies to attract and retain customers through technology.

In the digital age, data is a goldmine for informed decision-making. This chapter will discuss how companies use data analytics to uncover patterns, predict trends, and make data-informed decisions that drive growth. By turning raw data into actionable strategies for expansion, businesses can effectively navigate the complexities of their markets.

Stewart Butterfield, co-founder of Slack, explains, "The best technology is the one that makes you forget you're using technology." This chapter will illustrate how companies implement scalable technologies to manage growth effectively, ensuring their operations run smoothly even as demand increases. We'll explore examples of businesses that have successfully expanded into new markets by leveraging scalable technologies.

However, integrating technology into a business comes with challenges, including cybersecurity risks. Michael Hyatt, an expert in productivity and leadership, emphasizes the importance of building robust systems to protect sensitive data and infrastructure. We'll examine how companies create cybersecurity frameworks to safeguard their digital assets, maintain customer trust, and ensure business continuity.

Technological growth also requires adaptability. Michael Bloomberg, entrepreneur and former mayor of New York City, stresses, "In business, you need to be willing to adapt and evolve." Businesses must remain agile, constantly adjusting their technology strategies to stay relevant. We'll look at companies that have pivoted their technology approach to remain competitive in changing markets.

Collaboration between technology and business is essential for innovation. Laszlo Bock, former Senior Vice President of People Operations at Google, observes, "Scaling new heights in business requires not just vision but also a robust strategy that includes scalability from the start." This chapter explores how businesses foster collaboration between technology teams and other departments to drive growth, foster creativity, and solve complex challenges.

Throughout this chapter, you will discover practical strategies for integrating technology into your business to fuel growth. By embracing innovation, data analytics, and effective communication tools, businesses can unlock new opportunities and navigate the challenges of expansion with confidence. Technology is not just a tool; it is the foundation upon which modern businesses build sustainable growth, ensuring they stay competitive in an increasingly digital world.

Nate Silver's Success Story: Transforming Forecasting with Data and Probabilistic Thinking

"The key to making a good forecast is not in limiting yourself to quantitative information. Rather, it's in knowing where the boundaries between the two lie." — NATE SILVER, DATA-DRIVEN VISIONARY OF PREDICTIVE ANALYTICS

Nate Silver is a data scientist, statistician, and journalist whose innovative approach to forecasting has reshaped fields ranging from sports analytics to political predictions. Known for his groundbreaking work with PECOTA in baseball and for founding FiveThirtyEight, a site renowned for its election forecasts, Silver has built a career at the intersection of data, media, and storytelling. By making complex statistics accessible to the public, he has inspired a cultural shift toward probabilistic thinking, encouraging people to embrace uncertainty and data-based decision-making. Silver's journey from sports enthusiast to one of the world's most influential forecasters exemplifies how curiosity, resilience, and analytical rigor can revolutionize traditional industries and reshape how we understand the world.

Early Life and Education: A Passion for Numbers

Nate Silver was born on January 13, 1978, in East Lansing, Michigan, where his early curiosity about data and statistics was nurtured. Fascinated by math, sports, and games, Silver developed a love for forecasting and patterns at a young age. He went on to study economics at the University of Chicago, earning his degree in 2000. During his time in college, Silver's analytical mindset was further refined, leading to his first attempts at developing predictive models.

The Start: Sports Analytics and PECOTA

Silver's career began outside politics—in the world of sports. As a baseball enthusiast, he created PECOTA (Player Empirical Comparison and Optimization Test Algorithm) in 2003, a statistical system designed to predict player performance. PECOTA became a breakthrough tool for baseball forecasting and was later acquired by *Baseball Prospectus*, solidifying Silver's reputation as a leading figure in sports analytics.

While working at *Baseball Prospectus*, Silver built a foundation in using data to challenge conventional wisdom. His approach of mixing rigorous statistical analysis with creative thinking paved the way for his future endeavors in politics and journalism.

Transition to Politics: The Birth of FiveThirtyEight

In 2008, Silver shifted his focus to political forecasting, launching the website FiveThirtyEight. The site, named after the number of electors in the U.S. Electoral College, aimed to apply statistical models to predict election outcomes. Silver's predictions for the 2008 presidential election were remarkably accurate—he correctly forecasted the winner in 49 of 50 states. His work was praised for its transparency and innovative use of polling data, quickly setting FiveThirtyEight apart from traditional punditry.

Silver's success continued with the 2012 presidential election, where he correctly predicted the outcomes in all 50 states. His approach of aggregating and weighting polls, alongside data-driven analysis, transformed how political forecasts were conducted. Silver became a household name, recognized for using data to demystify elections in an increasingly polarized media landscape.

Expanding Influence: Journalism and Beyond

In 2013, Silver moved FiveThirtyEight to *ESPN*, expanding the site's scope to cover not only politics and sports but also economics, science, and popular culture. FiveThirtyEight combined in-depth analysis with accessible storytelling, making complex data relatable to the public. Under Silver's leadership, the site grew into a respected voice in journalism, known for its analytical rigor and commitment to evidence-based reporting.

Silver's approach wasn't without controversy—particularly when his predictions diverged from conventional narratives. During the 2016 election, FiveThirtyEight gave Donald Trump higher odds of winning than many media outlets, prompting debates about the limits of data and forecasting. Silver embraced these challenges, advocating for humility in predictions and emphasizing the importance of probability rather than certainty.

Books and Public Impact

In 2012, Silver published *The Signal and the Noise: Why So Many Predictions Fail—But Some Don't*, which became a best-seller. The book explores the challenges of making predictions in various fields, from weather forecasting to financial markets. It solidified Silver's reputation not just as a forecaster but as a thought leader in understanding uncertainty and separating meaningful signals from noise.

Through his writing, public speaking, and work with FiveThirtyEight, Silver has encouraged a broader cultural shift toward data literacy. His advocacy for probabilistic thinking—understanding the world through probabilities rather than absolutes—has influenced both professionals and the general public.

Legacy: Redefining Forecasting in the Digital Age

Nate Silver's career is a testament to the power of data, innovation, and intellectual curiosity. From baseball analytics to political forecasting, Silver has consistently pushed the boundaries of what data can achieve. He has redefined how predictions are made and communicated, inspiring a new generation of data scientists, journalists, and analysts.

Silver's ability to turn raw data into meaningful insights has made him one of the most influential voices in modern forecasting. His journey demonstrates that success often lies at the intersection of passion, discipline, and a willingness to challenge assumptions. As FiveThirtyEight continues to evolve, Silver's impact on journalism, analytics, and public discourse will undoubtedly endure.

Tim Cook's Success Story: From Quiet Operator to Visionary CEO of Apple

"Every delay is a chance to refine and rethink. It's not about when you arrive but how well-prepared you are when you do."
— TIM COOK, CEO OF APPLE

"Protecting your work is not about building barriers; it's about ensuring that your creativity can thrive safely in a world full of opportunities—and threats." — TIM COOK, CEO OF APPLE

"Checklists turn overwhelming challenges into practical actions. They provide a visible path to success and a measure of how far you've come and What's left to tackle." — TIM COOK, CEO OF APPLE

"Securing a trademark is not merely a formality; it's a declaration of your brand's uniqueness in the marketplace. Handle it with the same attention to detail as you would any major business initiative." — TIM COOK, CEO OF APPLE

"Planning your operations is like setting gears in motion: the right synchronization ensures efficiency and drives your business engine forward." — TIM COOK, CEO OF APPLE INC.

Tim Cook's journey from a modest upbringing in Robertsdale, Alabama, to becoming the CEO of Apple is a story of perseverance, precision, and purposeful leadership. Known for his quiet demeanor and exceptional operational expertise, Cook took the reins of Apple in 2011 during a pivotal moment, following the visionary Steve Jobs. While many doubted whether he could maintain Apple's innovative momentum, Cook not only steered the company to new heights but also expanded its legacy through a commitment to sustainability, privacy, and social responsibility. His success demonstrates that leadership is not just about vision, but about building processes, driving execution, and leading with integrity in a way that aligns business goals with human values.

Early Life and Education

Born on November 1, 1960, in Robertsdale, Alabama, Tim Cook grew up in a modest, hard-working family. His father was a shipyard worker, and his mother managed a pharmacy. Cook excelled academically and earned a degree in Industrial Engineering from Auburn University in 1982. He later obtained an MBA from Duke University's Fuqua School of Business, where he was recognized as a Fuqua Scholar, placing him among the top of his class.

Career Beginnings: Building Operational Expertise

Cook's early career was marked by his interest in operations and manufacturing efficiency. He began working at IBM, where he spent over a decade climbing the corporate ladder. His expertise in supply chain management and manufacturing optimization became his hallmark. After IBM, Cook joined Compaq as Vice President of Corporate Materials, but his tenure there was short-lived. Fate soon brought him into contact with Steve Jobs.

Joining Apple: A Crucial Turning Point

In 1998, Steve Jobs, who had just returned to Apple and was working to revive the company, recruited Cook. Although Apple was struggling at the time, Cook saw an opportunity in Jobs' vision. He took a leap of faith, despite reservations about the company's uncertain future.

As Apple's Senior Vice President of Worldwide Operations, Cook transformed the company's supply chain. He closed inefficient factories, outsourced manufacturing to reliable partners, and implemented just-in-time inventory practices. His operational brilliance reduced costs and prepared Apple to scale effectively, laying the foundation for its explosive growth in the 2000s.

Ascending to the Role of CEO

Tim Cook's steady rise within Apple continued over the years, earning him the roles of Chief Operating Officer and eventually CEO. In 2011, Steve Jobs, facing health issues, officially stepped down and entrusted Cook with Apple's future. Stepping into Jobs' shoes was no small task—critics questioned whether Cook could maintain Apple's innovative edge.

However, Cook's leadership was markedly different but equally effective. He focused on refining existing products, expanding Apple's global reach, and cultivating a culture of inclusivity. Under his guidance, Apple introduced new product lines, including the Apple Watch, AirPods, and services like Apple Music and Apple TV+. Cook's steady hand and strategic decisions helped Apple navigate competitive pressures while maintaining its identity.

Championing Social Responsibility and Sustainability
Tim Cook has also been a leading advocate for corporate responsibility. He made diversity, privacy, and environmental sustainability key pillars of Apple's strategy. Under his leadership, Apple committed to carbon neutrality and expanded efforts to ensure worker protections in its global supply chain. Cook's emphasis on privacy set Apple apart from competitors, reinforcing trust with its customers.

In addition to these initiatives, Cook has been vocal about social justice, human rights, and equality, using Apple's influence to promote positive change. This commitment to values-driven leadership has further defined Cook's legacy.

Apple's Unprecedented Growth
During Cook's tenure, Apple became the first U.S. company to reach a $1 trillion market valuation, followed by $2 trillion shortly thereafter. Under his guidance, Apple has become not just a technology leader but one of the most valuable and influential companies in the world.

A Legacy of Leadership
Tim Cook's journey from a small-town upbringing in Alabama to leading one of the world's largest companies is a testament to the power of discipline, operational excellence, and values-based leadership. While Cook is not known for the charismatic flair of his predecessor, his quiet strength and commitment to purpose have cemented his legacy as one of the most influential CEOs of the 21st century.

His story proves that success is not just about vision but also about execution, integrity, and the willingness to lead with purpose in an ever-evolving world.

Stewart Butterfield's Success Story: The Accidental Entrepreneur Behind Flickr and Slack

"The best technology is the one that makes you forget you're using technology."
— STEWART BUTTERFIELD, CO-FOUNDER OF SLACK

Stewart Butterfield's journey to success is a story of creativity, resilience, and the art of pivoting. As the co-founder of two groundbreaking companies—Flickr and Slack—Butterfield didn't set out with traditional business plans, but instead embraced unexpected opportunities born from failure. With a background in philosophy, his unique perspective shaped how he approached problem-solving, allowing him to spot hidden potential where others might see only setbacks. His ability to transition from failed gaming projects into transformative technology platforms revolutionized both photo-sharing and workplace communication. Butterfield's career is a testament to the power of adaptability, proving that innovation often emerges from the most unexpected places.

Early Life and Education

Born in 1973 in Lund, British Columbia, Stewart Butterfield grew up in an unconventional environment. His parents lived off the grid for the early years of his childhood, instilling in him a sense of curiosity and resourcefulness. Butterfield's passion for technology began at a young age, with early access to computers sparking his interest. He went on to study philosophy, earning a bachelor's degree from the University of Victoria and later a master's degree in philosophy from the University of Cambridge. His philosophical background gave him a unique perspective on problem-solving—something that would define his career.

The First Pivot: From Gaming to Flickr

Butterfield's first major entrepreneurial venture started with a game. In the early 2000s, he co-founded Ludicorp with his then-wife, Caterina Fake. The goal was to develop an online multiplayer game called "Game Neverending." However, as development progressed, they realized that one of the game's features—an innovative photo-sharing capability—had far greater potential. Recognizing the opportunity, Butterfield pivoted the company's focus and launched Flickr in 2004, an early and innovative photo-sharing platform.

Flickr was a hit, attracting users with its user-friendly interface and community-oriented features. Its success caught the attention of Yahoo!, which acquired the platform in 2005 for approximately $25 million. Although Flickr grew under Yahoo!, Butterfield grew frustrated with corporate bureaucracy, eventually leaving the company in 2008. His experience with Flickr taught him invaluable lessons about product development and navigating the challenges of growth.

The Birth of Slack: A Second Pivot
In 2009, Butterfield co-founded a new gaming company, Tiny Speck, aiming to create another ambitious online game called "Glitch." Despite high hopes, the game struggled to find traction, leading the team to shut it down in 2012. While the game failed, the internal communication tool the team had built to collaborate efficiently became the seed of something far bigger.

Recognizing the potential of the messaging platform they had developed, Butterfield pivoted again—this time toward enterprise software. In 2013, the tool was rebranded as Slack, a communication platform designed to streamline team collaboration. Slack launched publicly in 2014 and quickly became a runaway success, revolutionizing the way businesses communicated internally. With its sleek design, integrations, and focus on user experience, Slack transformed workplace productivity.

Rapid Growth and Acquisition by Salesforce
Slack's growth was explosive. By 2019, the company had over 10 million daily active users and had become essential to countless organizations worldwide. Slack's success attracted investors and eventually led to an initial public offering (IPO) in 2019. The company's focus on collaboration and customer-centricity resonated in an increasingly remote workforce environment.

In 2020, Salesforce acquired Slack in a deal valued at $27.7 billion, marking one of the largest technology acquisitions in history. Butterfield continued to lead Slack as part of Salesforce, helping to integrate the platform into Salesforce's broader ecosystem of enterprise solutions.

Lessons in Leadership and Innovation
Stewart Butterfield's entrepreneurial journey is a testament to the power of adaptability and perseverance. Both of his most successful ventures—Flickr and

Slack—emerged from failed projects. His ability to pivot quickly and recognize the value hidden in setbacks allowed him to create two transformative products. Butterfield is also known for his emphasis on creating positive work environments and fostering innovation, believing that the way people work together matters just as much as the product itself.

Legacy and Impact

Butterfield's success story underscores the importance of being open to change and embracing failure as part of the entrepreneurial journey. By focusing on solving real problems and leveraging technology to improve communication, he has left an indelible mark on both the consumer and enterprise technology landscapes. Today, Slack continues to thrive under his leadership, embodying the philosophy that great products are often born from unexpected beginnings.

Michael Hyatt's Success Story: From Publisher to Personal Growth Pioneer

"Launch day is the author's grand finale of preparation and the exciting beginning of a new chapter. It's about making such a splash that the ripples turn into waves of ongoing success." — MICHAEL HYATT, AUTHOR AND BUSINESS COACH

"Setting the right price for your book is not just about covering costs; it's about understanding the perceived value, and how it fits into the broader market. Get it right, and you not only gain readers, you gain fans willing to pay what your work is truly worth." — MICHAEL HYATT, AUTHOR AND BUSINESS COACH

Michael Hyatt is an inspiring example of how strategic leadership, perseverance, and a focus on personal growth can transform a career and impact millions. His journey from the corporate publishing world to becoming a best-selling author, thought leader, and productivity expert illustrates how embracing change and focusing on personal goals can lead to incredible success.

Early Career and Breakthrough in Publishing

Michael Hyatt began his career in the publishing industry—an early passion that would shape his path. He initially worked as a literary agent and later held leadership roles at several publishing houses, including Thomas Nelson Publishers, one of the largest Christian publishing companies in the world. Hyatt's talent for identifying impactful books and his deep understanding of market trends quickly became evident.

In 2005, Hyatt became the CEO of Thomas Nelson, leading the company through a turbulent time when the publishing industry was transitioning due to the rise of digital platforms. Under his leadership, Thomas Nelson flourished, and Hyatt helped the company focus on innovative publishing strategies and digital expansion, laying the foundation for future growth. The company was eventually acquired by HarperCollins in 2011, marking the end of Hyatt's corporate tenure—but also the beginning of a new chapter in his life.

Starting Over: Building a Personal Brand

After stepping down as CEO, Hyatt felt called to reinvent himself. Recognizing that the internet provided limitless opportunities for thought leaders, he focused on building a personal brand around leadership, productivity, and personal development.

Hyatt launched his blog and started sharing insights on time management, goal-setting, and leadership principles, drawing from his years of experience. His blog quickly gained traction, resonating with entrepreneurs, leaders, and professionals seeking practical advice for both their careers and personal lives.

He also began podcasting, expanding his audience and offering more in-depth content. His podcast, *Lead to Win*, became a popular resource for anyone looking to grow as a leader while maintaining a work-life balance.

Best-Selling Books and the 5 Days to Your Best Year Ever Program

In 2012, Hyatt published "Platform: Get Noticed in a Noisy World," which became an instant best-seller. The book offered practical advice on how individuals and businesses can build platforms in the digital age to promote their ideas, products, or services. Hyatt's personal story of starting from scratch and growing an audience resonated with readers, solidifying his reputation as a leading voice in the world of personal branding and entrepreneurship.

He followed the success of *Platform* by creating online courses and coaching programs, including "5 Days to Your Best Year Ever," which focused on setting and achieving meaningful goals. This course became a cornerstone of his offerings, empowering people to create clarity, purpose, and accountability around their personal and professional goals. Hyatt's work struck a chord, particularly with individuals who struggled to maintain momentum and direction throughout the year.

The Birth of Full Focus and Scaling Success

In 2017, Hyatt took his passion for productivity to the next level by launching the Full Focus Planner, a physical product designed to help people structure their days and focus on what matters most. The planner integrates the principles Hyatt had been teaching for years—goal-setting, prioritization, and reflection—into a systemized tool for daily use. It quickly became a best-seller and gained a cult following among business leaders, entrepreneurs, and professionals.

The success of the Full Focus Planner led Hyatt to create Full Focus Co., a company dedicated to helping people achieve more with less stress. He expanded his offerings to include leadership coaching programs, conferences, and online courses, all focused on personal growth, productivity, and achieving work-life balance.

Transitioning from Hustle to Restful Productivity

While Hyatt initially emphasized hard work and building platforms, his philosophy evolved over time. He began advocating for a balanced approach to success, encouraging people to pursue their goals without sacrificing their health or personal relationships. Hyatt coined the term "restful productivity," which promotes the idea that sustainable success requires intentional rest, time with family, and personal reflection.

This philosophy came to life in his books, including "Free to Focus" and "The Vision-Driven Leader." These works explore how leaders can clarify their vision, set boundaries, and structure their lives for long-term impact.

Hyatt's Leadership Legacy and Personal Impact

Throughout his career, Hyatt has mentored countless entrepreneurs and leaders, sharing wisdom from his own journey through books, podcasts, and coaching programs. His Lead to Win podcast and speaking engagements continue to inspire leaders around the world to strive for meaningful success.

In addition to his business achievements, Hyatt remains a family-oriented individual, often speaking about the importance of family life and spiritual growth. He is a passionate advocate for balancing work and life in a way that aligns with one's core values and priorities.

Key Lessons from Michael Hyatt's Success

1. **Start Small and Scale Gradually:** Hyatt's blog was the foundation for his business, proving that consistent, focused effort leads to growth.

2. **Reinvent Yourself When Necessary:** Leaving Thomas Nelson was a turning point for Hyatt, allowing him to redefine his purpose and goals.

3. **Systems Create Freedom:** Hyatt's emphasis on productivity tools like the Full Focus Planner shows how the right systems lead to more personal and professional freedom.

4. **Success is a Journey, Not a Destination:** Hyatt's philosophy shifted over time, embracing restful productivity and encouraging others to enjoy the journey, not just the destination.

5. **Prioritize Family and Faith:** Hyatt's success story demonstrates that family and faith are essential components of a meaningful life.

Conclusion: A Life of Purpose and Influence

Michael Hyatt's journey from publishing executive to personal growth pioneer is a testament to the power of reinvention, focus, and intentional living. Through his books, planners, and coaching programs, Hyatt has empowered millions to pursue their dreams while maintaining balance in their lives. His ability to adapt, inspire, and innovate has not only brought him personal success but also helped shape a new generation of leaders who seek purpose and fulfillment beyond traditional definitions of achievement.

Today, Hyatt's legacy is marked by his commitment to sustainable success—a life driven by clear goals, meaningful relationships, and intentional rest. His story is a reminder that success is not about working harder but about working smarter, staying true to your values, and enjoying the journey along the way.

=========

Michael Bloomberg's Success Story: A Visionary Leader Across Business, Politics, and Philanthropy

"Effective record keeping is a cornerstone of corporate success. It's not just about staying organized; it's about ensuring the integrity of your business for decisions that shape its future." — MICHAEL BLOOMBERG, FOUNDER OF BLOOMBERG L.P.

"Understanding and exercising your audit rights isn't about mistrust; it's about due diligence and ensuring the accuracy that your hard work merits." — MICHAEL BLOOMBERG, BUSINESSMAN AND FORMER MAYOR OF NEW YORK CITY

Michael Bloomberg's journey from Wall Street to global prominence is a story of resilience, strategic vision, and relentless innovation. Born into a modest family, Bloomberg developed a deep appreciation for education and hard work, values that became the foundation of his success. After a promising career in finance, a sudden setback inspired him to launch Bloomberg LP, a company that revolutionized financial data and analytics. Beyond business, Bloomberg's influence extended into politics, where he served three terms as mayor of New York City, transforming the city through data-driven policies. Today, Bloomberg continues to make an impact through his business, political involvement, and extensive philanthropic efforts, demonstrating how one individual can leave a lasting mark across multiple spheres.

Early Life and Education
Michael Bloomberg was born on February 14, 1942, in Boston, Massachusetts, into a middle-class family. His parents emphasized the importance of hard work and education, values that shaped his ambitious nature. Bloomberg attended Johns

150

Hopkins University, where he earned a degree in electrical engineering, followed by an MBA from Harvard Business School. Armed with both technical expertise and business acumen, he set his sights on a career in finance.

A Rise Through Wall Street

Bloomberg began his career at Salomon Brothers, a prestigious investment bank, in 1966. Starting out in an entry-level position, he quickly rose through the ranks due to his analytical skills and work ethic. By the 1970s, he was leading Salomon's equity trading department, where he developed a deep understanding of market data and technology. However, in 1981, when Salomon Brothers merged with another firm, Bloomberg was unexpectedly let go.

Turning Setbacks into Opportunities

Rather than seeing his dismissal as a defeat, Bloomberg viewed it as a new opportunity. Using his $10 million severance package, he launched his own company, Bloomberg LP, in 1981. He recognized that Wall Street traders lacked easy access to timely financial data and analytics, so he set out to create a product that could fill that gap. The result was the Bloomberg Terminal—a groundbreaking computer system that offered real-time financial data to investors.

Building a Global Information Empire

Bloomberg LP quickly became a success, revolutionizing the way financial professionals accessed data. The Bloomberg Terminal's user-friendly design and powerful analytics tools attracted clients from across the finance industry. Over time, the company expanded its offerings, adding news services, media platforms, and financial software, establishing Bloomberg LP as a leader in financial information and technology.

From Business to Politics

In 2001, Bloomberg made a surprising pivot from business to politics, running for mayor of New York City. He won the election and went on to serve three terms, from 2002 to 2013. During his tenure, he focused on public health, education, and economic development, earning a reputation as a data-driven leader. Under his leadership, the city implemented significant reforms, including a smoking ban, bike lanes, and sustainability initiatives.

Philanthropy and Global Influence

After leaving office, Bloomberg returned to Bloomberg LP but also became deeply involved in philanthropy. He has donated billions to causes like public health, climate change, education, and the arts. Through his organization, Bloomberg Philanthropies, he continues to support innovative solutions to global challenges.

Legacy and Ongoing Impact

Michael Bloomberg's journey from Wall Street to politics and philanthropy exemplifies how resilience, innovation, and a commitment to public service can lead to extraordinary achievements. Today, he is recognized not only as one of the wealthiest individuals in the world but also as a global leader in business, politics, and philanthropy. His legacy serves as a testament to the power of strategic thinking and the impact one individual can have across multiple industries and sectors.

Alan Kay's Success Story: The Pioneer of Personal Computing and Modern Interfaces

"The best way to predict the future is to invent it."
— ALAN KAY, COMPUTER SCIENTIST

Alan Kay is an American computer scientist, visionary, and inventor whose groundbreaking ideas have shaped the foundations of personal computing, graphical user interfaces (GUIs), and object-oriented programming. Known for his belief that "the best way to predict the future is to invent it," Kay's innovative work laid the groundwork for many technologies that have become integral to modern computing. From his early research to his role at Xerox PARC and beyond, Kay's journey reflects a passion for education, creativity, and transforming ideas into practical technology.

Early Life: A Love for Science and Learning

Alan Kay was born on May 17, 1940, in Springfield, Massachusetts, but grew up in various parts of the U.S. His parents fostered an environment of curiosity, and

Kay developed a love for learning at an early age. As a child, he taught himself to read by the age of three and later developed a passion for music, math, and science. His eclectic interests in multiple fields, from literature to technology, would define his interdisciplinary approach to innovation.

Kay's early experience with computing began in high school, where he encountered one of the earliest computers. This sparked a fascination with the potential of technology to enhance learning and creativity, a theme that would shape the rest of his career.

Education and Early Career in Computing
Kay pursued a degree in mathematics and molecular biology at the University of Colorado Boulder, where he also played jazz guitar, blending his scientific and artistic passions. After graduation, he served briefly in the U.S. Air Force, where he was introduced to computing systems and worked as a programmer on early IBM computers.

Realizing that computing held the key to a more interactive and creative form of education, Kay enrolled at the University of Utah, one of the leading centers for computer science research at the time. There, he completed his Ph.D. under the guidance of computing pioneers such as Ivan Sutherland and Dave Evans. His work on graphical interfaces and programming languages began to solidify his belief that computers should be accessible to everyone, not just specialists.

The Vision of Personal Computing: Xerox PARC
In 1970, Kay joined Xerox's Palo Alto Research Center (PARC), a think tank known for groundbreaking research in computing. At Xerox PARC, Kay became a central figure in the development of many technologies that would later become standard in personal computing. It was here that Kay developed his vision of the **Dynabook**, an early concept of a laptop or tablet computer designed for children. Though the Dynabook never became a physical product during Kay's time, it inspired the development of personal computing devices for decades.

Kay played a key role in developing the **Alto**, the first computer to feature a graphical user interface (GUI). This innovation—using windows, icons, and a mouse to interact with the system—laid the foundation for the operating systems we use today. Although Xerox PARC never capitalized on the Alto commercially, it inspired companies like Apple and Microsoft to bring the GUI to mainstream computing.

Object-Oriented Programming: A New Way to Build Software
In addition to his work on GUIs, Kay was instrumental in the development of object-oriented programming (OOP), a revolutionary approach to software design. Kay and his team at Xerox PARC developed the programming language Smalltalk, which treated software components as "objects" that could communicate with one another. This modular way of building software simplified complex systems and became a standard in modern programming.

OOP has had a profound influence on the software industry, serving as the foundation for many modern programming languages, including Java, Python, and C++. Kay's contributions to OOP not only changed how programmers develop software but also helped create systems that are easier to use, maintain, and extend.

Collaboration with Apple and Influence on Modern Technology
After leaving Xerox PARC in the 1980s, Kay joined Apple as a fellow, where he continued to pursue his vision of personal computing. His work at Apple involved exploring new ways to integrate education and technology, with a focus on making computers more accessible to children and non-experts.

Kay's influence on companies like Apple was significant. Steve Jobs, inspired by the work at Xerox PARC, adapted many of the concepts developed there—such as the GUI—into the Apple Macintosh. Kay's belief that computers should enhance creativity and learning aligned closely with Apple's mission to make technology intuitive and empowering for users.

Later Career: Advancing Education and Computing
Throughout his career, Kay has been committed to using technology to improve education. In the 2000s, he became involved with the One Laptop Per Child (OLPC) initiative, which aimed to provide affordable laptops to children in developing countries. The OLPC laptops reflected many of the ideas from Kay's original Dynabook concept, demonstrating how his early vision of personal computing continued to influence the field.

Kay also founded the Viewpoints Research Institute, an organization dedicated to advancing computing and education. Through research and teaching, Kay has continued to explore new ways to combine computing with pedagogy, empowering future generations to learn through creativity and experimentation.

Legacy: Shaping the Future of Technology

Alan Kay's work has had a profound impact on how we interact with technology today. His vision of personal computing, graphical interfaces, and object-oriented programming transformed not only the field of computer science but also the way people live and work. Technologies we now take for granted—such as laptops, tablets, smartphones, and intuitive software interfaces—owe much of their existence to Kay's groundbreaking ideas.

Kay has received numerous accolades for his contributions, including the Turing Award in 2003, often regarded as the Nobel Prize of computing. His acceptance speech emphasized the importance of creativity, learning, and interdisciplinary thinking in technological innovation.

Conclusion: A Visionary Who Saw the Future of Computing

Alan Kay's story exemplifies the power of imagination, curiosity, and persistence in shaping the future. From the early days at Xerox PARC to his continuing work in education, Kay has remained a passionate advocate for making technology accessible, intuitive, and empowering for all. His innovations in graphical interfaces and programming continue to influence modern computing, proving that technology can be a tool not just for efficiency but for creativity and learning.

Kay's legacy endures in the countless devices, software systems, and educational initiatives that draw from his pioneering work. As the world of technology evolves, Kay's vision of personal computing as a tool for empowerment and exploration remains as relevant as ever, reminding us that the best way to shape the future is, indeed, to invent it.

Laszlo Bock's Success Story: Redefining People Management in the Corporate World

"True talent management is not just about placing the right person in the right role; it's about creating an environment where people are empowered, engaged, and energized to reach their full potential."

— LASZLO BOCK, FORMER SVP OF PEOPLE OPERATIONS AT GOOGLE

Laszlo Bock, former Senior Vice President of People Operations at Google and co-founder of Humu, transformed the way organizations think about employee management and workplace culture. His innovative strategies at Google revolutionized HR practices, shifting the focus from traditional management to data-driven approaches that prioritize employee well-being, productivity, and happiness. Bock's story is one of persistence, creativity, and a commitment to making work better for people, ultimately influencing how companies across the globe manage and empower their talent.

Early Life and Education: A Foundation in Curiosity and Ambition

Laszlo Bock was born in 1971 in Romania. At a young age, his family immigrated to the United States, seeking better opportunities. Growing up as an immigrant in the U.S. gave Bock a unique perspective on hard work, resilience, and the importance of community. His upbringing cultivated in him a deep curiosity about people and how they thrive in different environments.

Bock pursued a bachelor's degree in international relations from Pomona College and later earned an MBA from the Yale School of Management. His educational background gave him a solid foundation in leadership, human behavior, and organizational strategy, which would later define his career.

Early Career: Navigating the Corporate World

Before joining Google, Bock held several roles in consulting and HR management. He worked at McKinsey & Company, where he gained valuable experience advising companies on strategy and operations. He later held executive positions at General Electric (GE), learning firsthand the complexities of managing talent in large, traditional organizations.

While these early roles gave him insights into management, Bock also observed the limitations of conventional HR practices. He noticed that many companies failed to fully understand their employees' potential and well-being, treating people as resources rather than partners in the success of the business. These observations inspired Bock to seek new ways of managing talent.

Transforming HR at Google: The Rise of People Operations

In 2006, Bock joined Google as Senior Vice President of People Operations, marking the beginning of a transformative era in human resource management. At the time, Google was rapidly growing, and its leadership sought to create a work environment that could attract and retain the best talent in the world. Bock's mission was not only to recruit top performers but also to build a workplace where employees could thrive.

Bock's approach to HR was revolutionary. Instead of relying on traditional HR practices, he implemented data-driven decision-making to understand what employees needed to succeed. His team used analytics to measure everything— from hiring processes to employee satisfaction—to make informed decisions about how to improve the workplace. This new, data-backed approach to HR became known as People Operations.

Innovations in Workplace Culture

Under Bock's leadership, Google introduced several groundbreaking initiatives aimed at fostering employee happiness and productivity. Some of his most notable innovations included:

1. **Hiring Algorithms and Structured Interviews**: Bock restructured Google's hiring process by introducing data-based assessments and structured interviews. He reduced the emphasis on traditional résumés and credentials, focusing instead on candidates' problem-solving abilities and potential.

2. **Employee Benefits and Perks**: Recognizing that employee well-being directly impacts productivity, Bock introduced comprehensive benefits, including free meals, on-site healthcare, generous parental leave, and time for creative projects. Google's famous perks became a benchmark for other companies seeking to attract top talent.

3. **Project Oxygen**: Bock led **Project Oxygen**, an internal study that identified the qualities of effective managers at Google. The findings challenged the stereotype that technical skills are the most important aspect of management, highlighting the value of empathy, coaching, and communication skills.

4. **Workplace Transparency and Employee Voice**: Bock promoted transparency within the organization by encouraging open communication between employees and leadership. Google regularly surveyed employees and used their feedback to make meaningful changes.

The Book that Shaped HR: "Work Rules!"

In 2015, Bock published *Work Rules!: Insights from Inside Google That Will Transform How You Live and Lead*. The book provides a deep dive into Google's HR practices, offering lessons on how to create a workplace culture that fosters innovation, well-being, and collaboration.

Work Rules! became a bestseller, resonating with leaders across industries. Bock emphasized that a great workplace is built on trust, autonomy, and meaningful work, challenging traditional management norms. The book's insights continue to influence how organizations design their employee experiences and manage talent.

Founding Humu: Using Nudges to Improve Workplace Happiness

After a decade at Google, Bock co-founded **Humu** in 2017 with two former Google colleagues. Humu is a human resources technology company that leverages **behavioral science** and **nudging** to improve employee engagement and performance. The concept of nudging—small, actionable suggestions designed to encourage positive behavior—was inspired by research in behavioral economics.

Humu's platform uses data to identify areas where employees or managers might need support and sends personalized nudges to help them improve. For example, a manager might receive a nudge reminding them to recognize their team's efforts, or an employee might be encouraged to take breaks to avoid burnout. Humu aims to make workplaces more productive and enjoyable by helping people make small changes that lead to big improvements over time.

Impact and Legacy: Redefining People Management

Bock's work at Google and Humu has reshaped how companies approach HR and workplace culture. His data-driven, employee-centric strategies have set new standards in the field of people management, inspiring organizations worldwide to prioritize well-being, autonomy, and purpose.

Bock's legacy is evident in the growing emphasis on employee experience in the corporate world. Many companies now recognize that happy employees are more productive, innovative, and committed. His influence can be seen in the rise of people analytics, the adoption of flexible work policies, and the focus on creating workplaces that are not just profitable but also meaningful.

Conclusion: A Visionary in the Future of Work

Laszlo Bock's journey from an immigrant upbringing to becoming one of the most influential figures in HR and workplace culture exemplifies the power of innovation, empathy, and leadership. Through his work at Google, Bock demonstrated that managing people is not just about policies—it's about building environments where individuals can thrive.

With Humu, Bock continues to push the boundaries of what is possible in workplace culture, proving that even small changes can have a profound impact on employee happiness and performance. His story is a reminder that the future of work is not just about technology but about people—and the belief that every organization can become a place where individuals flourish.

CHAPTER EIGHT

Digital Marketing and SEO Strategies

In an era where digital presence defines business success, mastering digital marketing and search engine optimization (SEO) is essential for driving visibility, engagement, and growth. As businesses transition from traditional methods to online strategies, they must adopt techniques that elevate their brand above the noise. This chapter delves into the fundamentals of digital marketing and SEO, offering insights into how businesses can leverage these tools to capture audiences, build relationships, and convert interest into profit.

David Newman, a leading expert in marketing strategy, emphasizes, "The key to successful digital marketing is to focus on creating value and connection with your audience." SEO serves as the backbone of online visibility, ensuring that your audience discovers your brand through targeted search queries. This chapter explores how businesses can optimize their websites and content to climb search rankings and attract organic traffic that drives meaningful engagement.

Another vital element is storytelling within content marketing. Donald Miller, author of *Building a StoryBrand*, states, "People don't buy the best products; they buy the story behind them." High-quality content acts as the bridge between a brand and its audience, helping to build trust, inform, and encourage action. We'll highlight stories of businesses that have mastered the art of creating compelling narratives to connect with their customers.

Email marketing is equally critical for nurturing relationships. Larry Kim, an expert in PPC and digital marketing, describes it as "creating valuable, personal touches—at scale." In this chapter, we explore how businesses craft compelling email strategies that engage their audience regularly, building trust and driving sales.

Social media also plays a cornerstone role in digital marketing success. Reed Hastings, co-founder of Netflix, asserts, "The key to innovation is creating a culture where everyone feels free to contribute." This chapter dives into the ways businesses leverage social platforms to connect with audiences, develop brand loyalty, and generate leads.

Digital advertising, from Google Ads to Pay-Per-Click (PPC) campaigns, amplifies online reach significantly. Nation Norris, a digital advertising strategist, notes, "PPC is not just about the bid; it's about understanding the value of your investment in reaching the right audience." This chapter showcases strategies that businesses use to invest in digital advertising effectively, transforming campaigns into conversion engines.

Local SEO and customer reviews are crucial in the digital space as well. Claire Jenkins, a local marketing expert, explains, "Building a local presence is about engaging with your community and being visible where it matters most." We'll explore how businesses cultivate loyal audiences and use reviews as valuable social proof to enhance credibility.

As we navigate through real-world examples, including insights from Ian Schafer, a leader in digital marketing and social media, we will cover advanced SEO tactics, including mobile optimization and voice search. This chapter also emphasizes that SEO is not just about algorithms; it's about understanding user intent and creating a seamless experience.

Throughout this chapter, you will discover actionable steps for optimizing digital marketing efforts. Whether through targeted keywords, engaging social media campaigns, or compelling email marketing strategies, businesses can unlock the full potential of the digital realm. With SEO as a foundation, companies not only increase visibility but also build meaningful relationships that fuel long-term growth.

By the end of this chapter, you will learn how to craft a robust digital marketing strategy that aligns with your business goals. From mastering the intricacies of SEO to leveraging analytics tools, digital marketing offers an array of opportunities to grow your brand, attract the right customers, and stay relevant in an ever-evolving online marketplace.

David Newman's Success Story: The Marketing Maven Who Empowers

"Email has an ability many channels don't: creating valuable, personal touches—at scale." — DAVID NEWMAN, MARKETING EXPERT AND SPEAKER

David Newman is a marketing strategist, speaker, and author known for transforming the way experts, speakers, and consultants grow their businesses. With a passion for communication and a talent for simplifying complex marketing strategies, Newman built a thriving career by helping professionals embrace their unique value and market themselves effectively. As the founder of *Do It! Marketing* and author of the best-selling book by the same name, Newman has empowered countless individuals to turn their expertise into successful enterprises. His blend of humor, actionable advice, and authentic connection has made him a sought-after thought leader in the entrepreneurial world. Newman's story exemplifies the power of aligning passion with purpose to create lasting impact.

Early Life and Background

David Newman's journey began with a passion for communication, creativity, and helping others succeed. From an early age, Newman showed an interest in public speaking and marketing, which later shaped his career. After earning a degree in communication, he explored various roles in marketing, sales, and consulting, gaining hands-on experience that would become invaluable in his entrepreneurial journey.

The Shift to Thought Leadership

Newman discovered his passion for empowering experts and professionals while working in corporate settings. He realized that many brilliant individuals, such as coaches, consultants, and speakers, struggled with marketing themselves effectively. Motivated by a desire to bridge this gap, Newman pivoted toward entrepreneurial ventures, launching his own consulting business to help experts grow their influence and revenue.

Building Do It! Marketing

In 2009, Newman founded *Do It! Marketing*, a platform offering marketing advice, strategy sessions, and resources for thought leaders. He also authored the book *Do It! Marketing: 77 Instant-Action Ideas to Boost Sales, Maximize Profits, and Crush Your Competition*, which became a best-seller. The book's actionable tips and humorous, no-nonsense style resonated with readers, establishing Newman as a go-to expert in the marketing field.

Success Through Authenticity and Service

What set Newman apart was his genuine approach to helping clients. Rather than pushing generic marketing tactics, he focused on building authentic connections and leveraging individual strengths. His approach helped clients not only grow their businesses but also align their work with their passions. Newman's workshops, coaching programs, and speaking engagements soon attracted a loyal following, earning him recognition in the industry.

Expanding Influence and Impact

Newman's success led to opportunities as a keynote speaker, podcast guest, and marketing coach for top industry professionals. His programs, including the *Do It! MBA* and *Speaker Profit Formula*, provided step-by-step strategies to help entrepreneurs and experts build sustainable businesses. Newman's ability to simplify complex marketing concepts made him a favorite among professionals seeking practical, actionable advice.

Legacy of Empowerment
David Newman's impact goes beyond business growth; he's inspired countless individuals to embrace their potential, market themselves with confidence, and turn their expertise into thriving enterprises. With his books, coaching programs, and speaking engagements, Newman continues to equip entrepreneurs and experts with the tools they need to succeed. His story is a testament to the power of combining passion with strategy—and the difference one person can make by helping others shine.

Larry Kim's Success Story: From Bootstrapped Startup to Digital Marketing Visionary

"Pay-Per-Click advertising is like a high-stakes poker game—every bid you place and every keyword you choose needs to be strategic, calculated, and aimed at outsmarting the competition to win big."
— LARRY KIM, PPC Expert

Larry Kim's entrepreneurial journey is a testament to the power of curiosity, resilience, and forward-thinking. From his humble beginnings as a self-taught SEO consultant to founding WordStream and later MobileMonkey, Kim has consistently identified emerging trends and transformed them into thriving businesses. With a knack for simplifying complex challenges in digital marketing, Kim has become a trusted thought leader, inspiring entrepreneurs and marketers alike. His story demonstrates how a passion for technology, combined with a relentless drive to innovate, can turn a small idea into a multimillion-dollar success.

Early Life and Education
Larry Kim grew up in Ontario, Canada, where his curiosity for technology developed early. He pursued electrical engineering at the University of Waterloo, though his passion for entrepreneurship soon pulled him toward business. He

began to experiment with web development and search engine optimization (SEO), laying the groundwork for his future ventures in the digital marketing space.

The Birth of WordStream

In 2007, Larry founded WordStream, a digital marketing software company that began as a side project. Initially, he bootstrapped the business, starting with SEO consulting services. While juggling multiple freelance projects, Kim noticed that companies struggled with pay-per-click (PPC) advertising and needed tools to manage and optimize their campaigns more effectively. Recognizing this gap, Kim pivoted WordStream into a comprehensive software platform focused on simplifying online advertising for small businesses.

Scaling the Business

Kim's innovative approach to PPC advertising positioned WordStream as a leader in the digital marketing space. The company offered tools to help businesses of all sizes maximize their advertising budgets on platforms like Google Ads and Facebook. WordStream's success was driven by Kim's strategic focus on creating data-driven content, including blog posts, webinars, and studies that provided valuable insights to marketers. His unique blend of technical expertise and marketing know-how allowed WordStream to gain visibility and trust among both small businesses and industry professionals.

Acquisition and the Start of MobileMonkey

After more than a decade of rapid growth, WordStream was acquired by Gannett, the media giant behind *USA Today*, for $150 million in 2018. Following the sale, Kim was eager to explore new opportunities in the rapidly evolving world of digital marketing. He identified conversational marketing, specifically chatbots and messaging automation, as the next frontier.

In 2018, Kim founded MobileMonkey, a platform designed to help businesses automate customer interactions using chatbots across platforms like Facebook Messenger, Instagram, and web chat. With MobileMonkey, Kim sought to revolutionize how businesses engage with their customers, emphasizing real-time, personalized communication at scale.

Thought Leadership and Ongoing Impact

Beyond his entrepreneurial ventures, Larry Kim is recognized as a thought leader in digital marketing. His blogs and articles on topics like content marketing, paid search strategies, and artificial intelligence are widely read by marketers worldwide. Known for coining the term "unicorn content," he emphasizes the importance of creating standout content that drives extraordinary results.

Kim's ability to identify emerging trends and turn them into actionable strategies has made him a sought-after speaker at industry events. He continues to mentor and advise startups, sharing his journey of bootstrapping, scaling, and selling a business with aspiring entrepreneurs.

Legacy of Innovation

Larry Kim's journey from freelancer to multi-million-dollar entrepreneur highlights the importance of identifying gaps in the market and acting decisively. His story reflects a relentless pursuit of innovation, from PPC software to chat-based marketing solutions. Kim's ability to stay ahead of trends, paired with his passion for simplifying complex challenges, has left a lasting mark on the digital marketing landscape. His ventures inspire businesses to embrace change, harness technology, and engage customers in meaningful ways.

Donald Miller's Success Story: From Memoirist to Marketing Maestro and Business Guru

"When you clarify your message, your company begins to grow."
— DONALD MILLER, AUTHOR AND BUSINESS
STORYTELLING EXPERT

Donald Miller is a bestselling author, business coach, and the founder of StoryBrand, a company that has revolutionized the way businesses communicate with their customers. Miller's journey from personal memoir writer to marketing expert and entrepreneur is a story of reinvention, creativity, and a passion for storytelling. Along the way, he discovered the power of narrative—not just for writing books, but for helping businesses clarify their message, grow, and succeed.

Early Life and the Memoir That Put Him on the Map

Born in Houston, Texas, Miller didn't always know he wanted to be an entrepreneur. His first foray into writing came through personal reflection and faith exploration. In 2003, he published "Blue Like Jazz," a spiritual memoir that was both introspective and witty, tackling faith and personal growth in a way that resonated with readers.

"Blue Like Jazz" became a bestseller, earning a spot on the New York Times list and gaining a cult following. The success of the book established Miller as an insightful storyteller and led to speaking engagements and media appearances. For a while, Miller continued to explore themes of faith, personal growth, and identity through more books like "A Million Miles in a Thousand Years" and "Through Painted Deserts."

Transitioning from Author to Business Leader

Though Miller found success as a writer, he began to feel restless. He wanted to do more than just tell personal stories—he wanted to help others succeed. As he spoke with entrepreneurs and businesses, he realized that many of them struggled with the same problem: their messaging was confusing and didn't resonate with customers.

That's when Miller had an "aha!" moment: the principles of storytelling he had mastered as a writer could be applied to business communication. Every brand, he realized, could craft its message as a story, with the customer as the hero and the company as the guide. This insight laid the foundation for what would become StoryBrand.

Founding StoryBrand: Simplifying Business Messaging

In 2010, Miller founded StoryBrand, a company that helps businesses clarify their message using a simple, seven-part storytelling framework. Miller's formula is based on the idea that every business can structure its message like a story:

1. The hero (your customer) has a problem.

2. The hero meets a guide (your brand) who offers a solution.

3. The guide provides a plan and a call to action.

4. The story ends in success or avoids failure.

Miller began offering workshops and consulting services, teaching businesses how to use this framework to attract more customers by making their message clearer and more compelling. StoryBrand quickly became a must-know tool for marketers, entrepreneurs, and business leaders looking to grow their companies.

Writing "Building a StoryBrand"
In 2017, Miller published "Building a StoryBrand," a book that distilled his storytelling framework into a practical guide for business leaders. The book became a bestseller, solidifying Miller's reputation as a marketing guru. It offered step-by-step instructions for crafting effective business messaging and resonated with companies of all sizes, from small startups to Fortune 500 corporations.

"Building a StoryBrand" has been praised for demystifying marketing and providing a clear path to growth. It introduced the idea that clarity beats cleverness when it comes to messaging—a principle that has since been embraced by thousands of companies worldwide.

Scaling His Impact with Business Made Simple
In addition to StoryBrand, Miller expanded his vision to help entrepreneurs and business leaders grow in all areas of their business. He launched Business Made Simple, an online education platform offering courses on leadership, productivity, marketing, and personal development. Through Business Made Simple, Miller teaches practical business skills in a no-nonsense, accessible way, emphasizing that success is within everyone's reach if they have the right tools and mindset.

Miller also published "Business Made Simple: 60 Days to Master Leadership, Sales, Marketing, Execution, and More," offering bite-sized lessons on essential business topics. His ability to simplify complex concepts has made him a favorite among busy entrepreneurs looking for actionable advice without fluff.

Public Speaking, Podcasting, and Influence
Miller's influence extends beyond books and courses. He is a sought-after public speaker, delivering keynote talks at business conferences and corporate events. He also hosts the popular Business Made Simple podcast, where he shares insights

on leadership, productivity, and marketing, often interviewing industry leaders and experts.

Through his podcast and public appearances, Miller has become known for his engaging, practical style. He avoids jargon and focuses on real-world strategies that can drive immediate results. His goal is always to equip entrepreneurs with the tools they need to succeed and grow.

Building a Legacy of Empowering Businesses
Today, Donald Miller is more than an author—he's a thought leader, entrepreneur, and educator. Through StoryBrand and Business Made Simple, he has helped thousands of companies communicate more effectively, grow their revenue, and achieve their goals. His storytelling framework has become a cornerstone of modern marketing, and his simple, actionable advice has empowered countless business leaders to reach new heights.

Conclusion
Donald Miller's journey from memoirist to marketing guru is a story of reinvention, resilience, and impact. He discovered that stories have the power to transform not just lives but businesses, and he's dedicated his career to helping others find success through clarity and purpose. Whether through books, podcasts, or online courses, Miller's message is clear: anyone can grow their business if they can simplify their message and tell their story well. His legacy will be one of empowering businesses to thrive by embracing the power of storytelling.

Reed Hastings' Success Story: From DVD Rentals to Streaming Giant

"In the digital age, your work can travel faster and further than ever before. It's essential to understand international copyright laws to ensure your creations are respected worldwide." — REED HASTINGS, CO-FOUNDER AND CEO OF NETFLIX

Netflix, the world's leading streaming service, didn't start out as the entertainment powerhouse we know today. Its success story is a tale of bold innovation, strategic pivots, and a deep understanding of the shifting landscape in technology and media.

The Beginning: DVD Rentals by Mail

Netflix was founded in 1997 by Reed Hastings and Marc Randolph in Scotts Valley, California. The original idea came when Hastings, frustrated by a late fee from Blockbuster for a rented movie, thought there had to be a better way to rent films. Instead of traditional rental stores, Hastings and Randolph envisioned a service where people could rent DVDs online and receive them by mail.

The company's DVD-by-mail model was innovative because it eliminated late fees and offered a subscription plan that allowed customers to rent DVDs for as long as they wanted. In the late 1990s, Netflix launched its website with a vast selection of DVDs, shipping movies to customers all over the U.S.

The subscription model became a game-changer. Rather than paying per rental, subscribers paid a flat fee for unlimited rentals, a concept that made Netflix stand out from its competitors like Blockbuster and Hollywood Video.

Transition to Streaming

Although Netflix started with physical DVD rentals, the company was always forward-thinking. Hastings and Randolph anticipated that the future of entertainment would move beyond physical media, and Netflix began investing in streaming technology.

In 2007, Netflix introduced video streaming, allowing subscribers to watch movies and TV shows directly on their computers. This move marked the beginning of the company's transformation into the streaming giant it is today. By offering on-demand streaming, Netflix disrupted the traditional video rental industry and laid the foundation for the streaming revolution.

As the demand for streaming increased, Netflix continued to expand its library of licensed content. The company worked to make its platform available across multiple devices, including smart TVs, gaming consoles, and smartphones, making streaming accessible to a wider audience.

The Shift to Original Content

One of Netflix's most significant strategic moves was its decision to start producing original content. In 2013, the company launched its first original series, "House of Cards," which quickly became a hit and earned critical acclaim. This was followed by other original series like "Orange is the New Black" and "Stranger Things." Netflix's ability to invest heavily in high-quality original programming helped differentiate it from competitors.

By 2016, Netflix had doubled down on original content, with Hastings stating that Netflix was aiming to become a global TV network. The company's success in creating its own content meant that it no longer had to rely solely on licensing deals with studios. As a result, Netflix rapidly expanded its content library, producing films, documentaries, and stand-up specials across different genres and languages.

International Expansion

One of the key factors behind Netflix's success has been its aggressive international expansion. In 2010, Netflix started expanding beyond the U.S., first into Canada and then into other regions such as Latin America and Europe. By 2016, Netflix was available in over 190 countries, becoming a truly global platform.

To cater to diverse audiences around the world, Netflix invested in local-language programming and began producing original series and films in various regions. Shows like "Money Heist" (Spain), "Dark" (Germany), and "Sacred Games" (India) became international hits, proving that global audiences were eager for content from around the world.

Data and Algorithms

Another major factor in Netflix's success is its use of data and algorithms to improve user experience. Netflix has always been a tech-driven company, using data analytics to track viewing habits and make personalized recommendations. This personalized approach helps keep subscribers engaged by suggesting content they're likely to enjoy, reducing churn and increasing overall satisfaction.

Netflix also uses data to make decisions about which new shows or movies to produce. By analyzing the viewing habits of its vast global audience, the company can identify trends and predict what types of content are likely to succeed, ensuring that its original productions have a higher chance of resonating with audiences.

Overcoming Challenges

Despite its success, Netflix has faced challenges along the way. With the rise of competitors like Amazon Prime Video, Disney+, HBO Max, and others, Netflix has had to navigate an increasingly crowded streaming landscape. However, by continuing to innovate and invest in original content, Netflix has maintained its position as the dominant player in the market.

The company has also navigated shifting licensing agreements. As other studios and networks started to pull their content off Netflix to launch their own streaming platforms (e.g., Disney pulling Marvel and Star Wars content), Netflix accelerated its move towards original programming to ensure it had a robust library of exclusive content.

Financial Success and Market Dominance

As of 2024, Netflix remains one of the largest entertainment companies in the world, with over 230 million subscribers globally. The company's market value has soared, and it has become a dominant force in both the tech and entertainment industries.

With its vast content library, commitment to producing groundbreaking original programming, and ability to stay ahead of technological trends, Netflix has firmly established itself as a pioneer in digital entertainment.

Conclusion: The Future of Netflix

Netflix's journey from a DVD rental service to a streaming giant is a testament to innovation, adaptability, and forward-thinking leadership. Under the vision of Reed Hastings and his team, Netflix has revolutionized the way the world consumes entertainment, and its influence continues to grow.

With ongoing investments in technology, content creation, and global expansion, Netflix is well-positioned to remain a key player in the entertainment industry for years to come, despite growing competition. The company's ability to adapt to changing consumer behaviors and technological advancements has solidified its place as a cultural and entertainment powerhouse.

Nitin Nohria's Success Story: Shaping the Future of Leadership at Harvard Business School

"Effective communication is the bridge between confusion and clarity, transforming the essence of a leader's vision into a palpable force that moves people to action." — NITIN NOHRIA, FORMER DEAN OF HARVARD BUSINESS SCHOOL

Nitin Nohria is a renowned academic, leadership expert, and former Dean of Harvard Business School (HBS), celebrated for his contributions to management education and his ability to shape the future of leadership. His journey from India to one of the most prestigious academic institutions in the world is a story of hard work, intellectual rigor, and visionary leadership.

Early Life and Education: A Foundation in Curiosity
Born in Nandurbar, India, in 1962, Nitin Nohria grew up in a family that placed a high value on education and learning. His father, Kewal Nohria, was an executive at Indian engineering giant Crompton Greaves, which exposed Nitin to the world of business from a young age. Inspired by his father's work ethic and leadership, Nitin developed a passion for business, leadership, and management.

Nohria earned his bachelor's degree in chemical engineering from the Indian Institute of Technology (IIT), Bombay—one of the most prestigious engineering schools in India. Despite his technical background, his curiosity about organizational behavior and leadership principles grew, motivating him to pursue graduate studies in the United States.

A New Chapter: Graduate Studies and Academic Excellence
Nohria moved to the U.S. to attend the Massachusetts Institute of Technology (MIT) Sloan School of Management, where he earned his Ph.D. in management. His research focused on corporate leadership and the behaviors that define effective managers.

Early in his academic career, Nohria displayed an ability to connect theory with real-world practice, making his insights not only relevant to scholars but also applicable to business leaders. His work on the dynamics of leadership and organizational behavior began garnering attention, setting the stage for an illustrious academic career.

Joining Harvard Business School: A Rising Star in Academia

Nohria joined Harvard Business School (HBS) in 1988 as a faculty member, specializing in leadership and organizational behavior. He quickly earned a reputation for being an engaging professor who challenged students to think deeply about the principles of leadership and ethical management.

Throughout the 1990s and early 2000s, Nohria co-authored several influential books on leadership, including:

- **"The Arc of Ambition"** (with James Champy), which explores how ambition drives individuals and organizations to achieve greatness.

- **"What Really Works"** (with William Joyce and Bruce Roberson), based on a study of business success factors over a decade.

- **"Paths to Power,"** which examines how individuals achieve and wield influence within organizations.

His research was widely recognized for being evidence-based and offering practical strategies for business leaders.

Becoming Dean of Harvard Business School

In 2010, Nitin Nohria was appointed Dean of Harvard Business School, becoming the first Indian-American to hold the position. His tenure as dean was marked by innovation, inclusivity, and bold leadership initiatives. Nohria focused on adapting the HBS curriculum to the challenges of the 21st century, emphasizing the importance of global leadership, ethical behavior, and entrepreneurship.

During his decade-long leadership, Nohria:

- Introduced the Field Immersion Experiences for Leadership Development (FIELD) program, providing students with real-world business challenges.

- Expanded the focus on entrepreneurship, making HBS a hub for future founders and business innovators.

- Launched the Gender Initiative to foster a more inclusive environment, addressing gender equity among faculty, students, and alumni.

- Raised over $1 billion in a capital campaign, securing resources to sustain HBS's leadership in business education for future generations.

Nohria's tenure saw HBS solidify its reputation as a global leader in business education, and he earned widespread respect for his collaborative leadership style and dedication to diversity and ethics.

Navigating Challenges and Leading Through Crises

Nohria's leadership was tested during critical moments, including the #MeToo movement and the COVID-19 pandemic. In response to the pandemic, Nohria led HBS through a rapid transition to virtual learning, ensuring that students continued to receive world-class education despite the challenges.

His ability to navigate complex social issues and respond swiftly to unforeseen crises further highlighted his calm, adaptive leadership. Nohria's leadership during these challenges earned him respect not only within HBS but across the global business community.

Stepping Down and Legacy

After 10 years as dean, Nohria stepped down from his role in 2020. His tenure is remembered for transforming HBS's approach to leadership education, focusing not just on profitability and success but also on responsibility, ethics, and diversity.

Even after leaving the dean's position, Nohria remains actively engaged with HBS and global leadership initiatives. He continues to mentor students, advise organizations, and contribute to thought leadership through lectures, writing, and consulting.

Lessons from Nitin Nohria's Success

- **Adaptability is key**: Nohria's ability to pivot during crises like the COVID-19 pandemic shows the importance of flexibility in leadership.

- **Values matter**: His emphasis on ethics, diversity, and inclusion demonstrates that long-term success requires more than just financial performance.

- **Lifelong learning is essential**: Nohria's career exemplifies the importance of continuous personal and professional growth.

- **Mentorship creates impact**: His dedication to teaching and mentoring reflects the belief that great leaders help others succeed.

Conclusion: A Legacy of Leadership and Learning

Nitin Nohria's journey from India to Harvard Business School is a story of intellectual excellence, transformative leadership, and a commitment to shaping future leaders. His work has left an indelible mark on management education, ensuring that leadership in the 21st century is grounded in ethics, responsibility, and global perspective.

Nohria's story is not just about personal success—it's about empowering others to lead with purpose and integrity. His impact will continue to shape leaders, organizations, and industries for years to come, proving that great leadership is about more than power—it's about making a positive difference.

━━━━━━━━

Claire Jenkins' Success Story: Transforming Veterinary Care with VetChat

"A well-crafted press release is your book's first conversation with the world; make it so compelling that the media can't help but spread the word."
— CLAIRE JENKINS, MEDIA RELATIONS EXPERT

Claire Jenkins, a veterinary professional turned entrepreneur, co-founded VetChat to bridge the gap between traditional pet care and modern technology. Jenkins identified a growing need for accessible veterinary advice, especially for pet owners facing challenges in obtaining timely consultations. Her passion for animal health, combined with an understanding of evolving consumer needs, led to the creation of VetChat—a telehealth platform that offers real-time, remote consultations with veterinarians.

Jenkins' approach reflects her mission to make veterinary care more efficient, responsive, and available from the comfort of home. With VetChat, pet owners can now receive expert advice quickly, addressing minor issues before they escalate, saving time and stress for both pets and their owners. The platform also reduces the strain on traditional veterinary clinics by filtering non-urgent cases through online consultations.

Claire Jenkins' success is driven by her ability to innovate within the veterinary field, utilizing digital tools to create practical solutions. VetChat has become a significant advancement in telemedicine, transforming how pet care is delivered and ensuring that animals receive the care they need, no matter where their owners are. Jenkins' journey exemplifies the power of blending expertise with technology to solve real-world problems in an evolving landscape.

———————

Ian Schafer's Success Story: A Visionary in Digital Marketing and Branded Entertainment

"Innovation needs to be part of your culture. Consumers are transforming faster than we are, and if we don't catch up, we're in trouble."
— IAN SCHAFER, DIGITAL MARKETING EXPERT

Ian Schafer is a visionary entrepreneur in the digital marketing industry, known for transforming the way brands engage with audiences through creative media strategies. His journey began at Miramax Films, where he served as Vice President of New Media. This early experience gave him deep insights into the entertainment industry and digital storytelling, which would later fuel his entrepreneurial success. In 2002, Schafer founded Deep Focus, a digital marketing agency that quickly gained recognition for its innovative approach to branded content and social media engagement.

Building Deep Focus: A Digital Pioneer
Schafer's vision for Deep Focus was to help brands create meaningful connections with consumers in the digital age. At a time when many agencies were still adapting to the shift toward online marketing, Schafer saw an opportunity to leverage emerging social media platforms to engage audiences in new ways. Deep Focus became known for executing cutting-edge campaigns for major brands, including PepsiCo, Nestlé, and AMC's Mad Men. The agency's work, such as the

award-winning "MadMenYourself" campaign, became iconic, showcasing the power of interactive, shareable content.

Through Schafer's leadership, Deep Focus distinguished itself not only for its creative execution but also for its use of consumer insights and real-time media strategies. The agency earned numerous industry accolades, including Webby Awards and a prestigious Cannes Gold Lion, positioning it at the forefront of the digital advertising world.

Recognition and Industry Influence

Schafer's contributions to digital marketing have earned him several notable recognitions. In 2007, Advertising Age named him a "Media Maven," highlighting his role as a thought leader in the industry. In 2015, he was inducted into the Advertising Hall of Achievement, an honor recognizing his influence on the future of advertising. Schafer also earned recognition for his ability to engage with audiences directly—he was named "Best CEO Social Media Presence" by the Shorty Awards for his use of platforms like Twitter to build authentic connections with followers.

Beyond his work at Deep Focus, Schafer has served on the boards of various industry organizations, including the Social Media Advertising Consortium and the Global Advisory Board for Social Media Week. His involvement in these initiatives reflects his commitment to advancing the field of digital marketing and fostering collaboration between brands, agencies, and tech innovators.

Expanding Horizons with Kindred

After more than a decade leading Deep Focus, Schafer shifted his focus toward a new venture aimed at aligning business with social responsibility. He co-founded Kindred, an organization that helps companies integrate purpose-driven practices into their operations. Kindred's mission reflects Schafer's belief that businesses have a responsibility to contribute positively to society, especially in a world where consumers expect brands to take meaningful action on social and environmental issues.

Schafer's work with Kindred builds on the principles that defined his career at Deep Focus—creating authentic connections between brands and their audiences while addressing pressing global challenges. Through Kindred, Schafer continues to push the boundaries of what marketing and business can achieve when aligned with values and purpose.

A Legacy of Innovation and Impact

Ian Schafer's career exemplifies the power of combining creativity, strategy, and technology to shape the future of advertising. His ability to anticipate trends and embrace new platforms has made him a leader in the digital marketing space. From MadMenYourself to Kindred's purpose-driven initiatives, Schafer has shown that brands can do more than sell products—they can foster meaningful relationships and drive positive change.

His journey from Miramax to Deep Focus, and now to Kindred, reflects a commitment to continuous innovation and adaptation. Schafer's legacy lies not only in the campaigns he's led but in the impact he's had on the broader marketing industry, inspiring a new generation of entrepreneurs and marketers to think creatively and act with purpose.

CHAPTER NINE

Legal and Financial
Foundations

A business without solid legal and financial foundations is like a house built on sand—it may appear stable at first, but it's vulnerable to collapse at the slightest challenge. Establishing these pillars early ensures that your business can weather uncertainties, remain compliant, and thrive in competitive markets. This chapter dives deep into the essential legal structures, financial planning strategies, and risk management practices required to create a sustainable, well-governed business.

Jean Chatzky, a leading financial journalist, emphasizes, "Understanding your financial landscape is crucial for entrepreneurial success. It's not just about making money; it's about making informed decisions that lead to lasting prosperity." Financial planning goes beyond budgeting; it involves forecasting revenues, controlling costs, and managing cash flow to ensure long-term solvency. In this chapter, we examine case studies where robust financial management practices paved the way for sustainable growth and expansion.

Naomi Klein, a prominent author and activist, highlights the importance of ethical considerations in business, stating, "In today's marketplace, your values are your brand." Building a business that aligns with ethical principles not only strengthens reputation but also fosters customer loyalty. This chapter explores how entrepreneurs integrate ethics into their financial and legal frameworks, ensuring that their business practices reflect their values.

Robert Kiyosaki, author of *Rich Dad Poor Dad*, adds, "The rich invest in time, energy, and knowledge—learning the rules of money and business is essential." Entrepreneurs must prioritize financial literacy to navigate the complexities of business operations effectively. This chapter offers practical advice on managing business accounts, securing funding, and developing financial dashboards that help entrepreneurs monitor progress and make data-driven decisions.

Sue Roman, a financial consultant, emphasizes, "The legal framework of your business is as critical as its financial health." This chapter delves into the various business structures—sole proprietorships, partnerships, LLCs, and corporations—and how each impacts liability, taxes, and governance. By aligning their vision with the right structure, entrepreneurs can create legally sound operations adaptable to growth.

Alan Dershowitz, a renowned legal scholar, notes, "Having a robust legal toolkit isn't just about compliance; it's about establishing clarity in every business relationship." Contracts and agreements are critical tools for setting clear terms with partners, vendors, and employees. We provide insights into how businesses have used carefully crafted legal documents to minimize disputes and protect their interests.

Jamie Dimon, CEO of JPMorgan Chase, reminds us that "a solid financial foundation is essential for a company's longevity." This chapter explores the importance of risk management strategies, including insurance policies and contingency planning, to safeguard operations from unforeseen challenges. Effective risk management empowers businesses to focus on growth while protecting their assets.

Nell Minor, a respected strategist in corporate governance, emphasizes, "Effective record-keeping is a cornerstone of corporate success." Accurate financial records ensure transparency and compliance, facilitating audits and informed decision-making. We explore the tools and systems businesses use to maintain organized, error-free financial documentation.

By the end of this chapter, readers will understand how to lay the legal and financial groundwork necessary for success. From choosing the right business structure to navigating compliance challenges, managing risks, and mastering financial literacy, this chapter equips entrepreneurs with the tools needed to build a strong, resilient foundation. With insights from thought leaders such as Jean Chatzky, Robert Kiyosaki, and Jamie Dimon, it underscores the importance of legal and financial diligence in creating businesses that can thrive in today's complex marketplace.

Jean Chatzky's Success Story: From Aspiring Journalist to Personal Finance Powerhouse

"Great CFOs don't just manage a company's finances; they forecast futures, strategize sustainability, and translate numbers into narratives that guide corporate journeys." — JEAN CHATZKY, FINANCIAL JOURNALIST AND AUTHOR

Jean Chatzky is a leading voice in personal finance, known for her ability to demystify money and make financial literacy accessible to millions. Her journey from an aspiring journalist to a respected author, speaker, and media personality is a story of persistence, adaptability, and passion for helping people achieve financial well-being. Let's dive into how Chatzky built her empire in the world of personal finance education.

Early Life and Education

Jean Chatzky grew up in Wisconsin with a deep curiosity about the world and an ambition to become a journalist. She attended The University of Pennsylvania, where she majored in English, hoping to pursue a career in writing and media. After graduation, Chatzky initially landed a job in publishing, working in the editorial department at Working Woman magazine. However, she soon discovered that her true passion lay in the intersection of storytelling and finance.

Finding Her Niche in Personal Finance

In the early 1990s, Chatzky pivoted into financial journalism, recognizing the need for simple, relatable financial advice in an era when the topic was often overwhelming for everyday people. She joined Forbes magazine as a researcher and began learning the ropes of finance and investing. It was here that she honed her ability to translate complex financial concepts into clear, actionable advice.

Chatzky then moved on to Dow Jones/I.D.G, where she wrote about money management and personal finance trends. But her big break came when she joined SmartMoney magazine, where she rose through the ranks to become a senior editor. This role put her on the path to becoming a trusted voice in personal finance journalism.

Breaking into Television and Building a Brand

Chatzky's knack for explaining financial topics in a relatable way soon caught the attention of media outlets. She became a financial editor and contributor for the Today Show on NBC, a position that allowed her to reach millions of viewers and build her reputation as a personal finance expert.

Through her frequent television appearances, Chatzky became known for her ability to break down financial jargon, offering viewers practical steps to manage debt, budgeting, and investing. Her approachable style and empathetic tone made her a favorite among audiences who felt overwhelmed by the world of personal finance.

Authoring Bestselling Books

Chatzky's desire to help people manage their money extended beyond television. She began writing bestselling books on personal finance, including:

- **"Pay It Down!"** (2004): A guide to eliminating debt, which became a New York Times bestseller.

- **"Make Money, Not Excuses"** (2006): Aimed at empowering women to take control of their finances.

- **"Age Proof"** (2017): Co-authored with Dr. Michael Roizen, it offers insights into financial health and longevity.

Her books have resonated with readers because they focus on practical, actionable advice. Chatzky's writing style combines financial expertise with personal storytelling, making even the most intimidating topics feel approachable.

Expanding Her Influence with HerMoney

In 2018, Chatzky launched HerMoney Media, a digital platform and podcast focused on helping women achieve financial independence. Through HerMoney.com and the HerMoney podcast, Chatzky provides insights into money management, investing, and career growth, all with a focus on empowering women to take charge of their financial futures.

Her podcast has become a hit, featuring interviews with finance experts, entrepreneurs, and thought leaders. The HerMoney platform reflects Chatzky's mission to create a safe space for financial conversations, offering advice that is both encouraging and realistic.

Public Speaking and Education

Chatzky is also a sought-after public speaker, delivering keynotes at conferences and corporate events on topics ranging from retirement planning to financial literacy for families. She has partnered with organizations like AARP and Fidelity to promote financial education and has become a leading advocate for improving financial literacy across the United States.

Her work extends to schools and non-profits, where she collaborates on initiatives to teach kids and young adults the basics of personal finance. Chatzky believes that early financial education is key to creating a generation that is more confident and capable with money.

A Legacy of Empowering Financial Wellness

Jean Chatzky's success lies not only in her expertise but in her genuine desire to help others. Over the years, she has built a trusted brand that emphasizes transparency, empathy, and action. Whether through books, podcasts, or TV appearances, her goal has always been the same: to make people feel more comfortable and confident managing their money.

Her message is that financial well-being isn't just for the wealthy—it's achievable for anyone with the right tools and mindset. She has shown that financial empowerment begins with small, consistent actions and that knowledge is the key to long-term success.

Conclusion

Jean Chatzky's journey from aspiring journalist to personal finance icon is a testament to following your passion, adapting to change, and helping others along the way. Through her books, media platforms, and public speaking, she has empowered millions to take control of their finances and create a more secure future. Her legacy is one of education and empowerment, proving that anyone can achieve financial success with the right guidance—and that it's never too late to start.

Naomi Klein's Success Story: An Advocate for Justice Through Investigative Journalism

"Managing your rights post-publishing is crucial for maintaining control over your work's future, ensuring you can continue to benefit from it under changing circumstances." — NAOMI KLEIN, AUTHOR, SOCIAL ACTIVIST, AND FILMMAKER

Naomi Klein has built an illustrious career at the intersection of journalism, activism, and social commentary, becoming one of the most influential thinkers of her generation. Known for her fearless critiques of corporate power, neoliberal economics, and environmental exploitation, Klein's work resonates with those seeking systemic change. From her debut with *No Logo*, which dissected the hidden costs of globalization, to *The Shock Doctrine* and *This Changes Everything*, Klein's books have sparked global conversations about the intersections of capitalism, inequality, and climate change. Her ability to challenge the status quo with clarity and urgency has made her a powerful voice in both activist movements and public discourse, inspiring people to think critically about the structures shaping our world.

Early Life and Education

Naomi Klein was born in Montreal, Canada, in 1970, to politically active parents who instilled in her a deep awareness of social justice. Klein's mother was a feminist documentary filmmaker, and her father, a physician, had moved the family to Canada in protest against the Vietnam War. Growing up, Klein was immersed in discussions about politics, activism, and human rights, which set the foundation for her future career. She studied at the University of Toronto, initially focused on literature and philosophy, but found herself increasingly drawn toward activism and journalism.

Breakthrough with *No Logo*

Klein's rise to prominence began with her groundbreaking book *No Logo*, published in 1999. Written during the height of globalization, the book explores how corporate branding has evolved beyond products, infiltrating culture and identity. Klein criticized multinational corporations for exploiting labor in developing countries and dissected the rise of anti-globalization movements. *No Logo* became an international bestseller and a manifesto for activists around the world, cementing Klein as a powerful voice in the global justice movement.

Expanding Influence: *The Shock Doctrine*

In 2007, Klein published *The Shock Doctrine: The Rise of Disaster Capitalism*, a meticulously researched book that examined how governments and corporations exploit crises—such as natural disasters and political upheaval—to implement neoliberal policies. This work elevated her reputation as one of the leading intellectuals critiquing capitalism and corporate power. It was praised for its depth and insight, sparking debates across political and economic spheres. The book's impact extended beyond readers, influencing activists, academics, and policymakers.

Climate Activism and *This Changes Everything*

Klein's advocacy evolved further with the release of *This Changes Everything: Capitalism vs. The Climate* in 2014. The book argues that addressing climate change requires a fundamental shift away from neoliberal capitalism, which prioritizes profit over sustainability. Klein's ability to blend investigative journalism with economic theory and environmental activism made the book both compelling and influential, inspiring a new wave of environmental movements.

She became a prominent advocate for the Green New Deal and has been deeply involved in environmental organizations, including 350.org.

Ongoing Impact and Legacy

Klein continues to use her platform to challenge the status quo, contributing articles to major publications like *The Guardian* and *The Intercept* while engaging in public speaking and activism. She has also taken on academic roles, including a faculty position at Rutgers University, where she helps shape the next generation of thinkers and activists.

Lessons from Klein's Journey

- **Courage to Critique Power:** Klein's success comes from her willingness to confront corporate and political power head-on, even when her views are controversial.

- **Interdisciplinary Thinking:** Her ability to weave economics, politics, and environmental science into compelling narratives makes her work resonate across different audiences.

- **Using Crisis as a Catalyst:** Rather than waiting for change, Klein's work demonstrates how crises can be opportunities for meaningful transformation.

Naomi Klein's career exemplifies how journalism, activism, and thoughtful critique can spark global conversations. Through her books, articles, and advocacy, she has inspired countless individuals to rethink the role of corporations, governments, and citizens in building a more just and sustainable world.

Robert Kiyosaki's Success Story: The Entrepreneur Who Redefined Financial Education

"Negotiating financial terms is more than a skill—it's an art that ensures the value of your work is fully recognized and rewarded in every contract."

— ROBERT KIYOSAKI, AUTHOR AND BUSINESSMAN,

FAMOUS FOR HIS BOOK "RICH DAD POOR DAD"

Robert Kiyosaki, the author of the wildly popular book "Rich Dad Poor Dad," is a renowned entrepreneur, investor, and financial education advocate. His journey to success, much like the lessons in his book, is about breaking away from conventional financial thinking and embracing a new mindset focused on financial independence and entrepreneurship.

Early Life and the Two Dads

Kiyosaki was born in Hilo, Hawaii, in 1947, to a family of educators. His father, whom he refers to as the "Poor Dad" in his book, was a highly educated man who worked as the Head of Education for the State of Hawaii. Despite his prestigious position and academic success, Kiyosaki's father struggled financially. He followed the traditional path of education, job security, and working for a paycheck but never achieved financial freedom.

In contrast, Kiyosaki's "Rich Dad" was the father of his best friend, who had little formal education but was a successful entrepreneur and businessman. Rich Dad mentored Kiyosaki from a young age, teaching him the principles of wealth-building, investing, and entrepreneurship. These contrasting experiences gave Kiyosaki a unique perspective on money and success, which would later form the foundation of his teachings.

Military Service and Early Career

Before finding success in finance, Kiyosaki served in the U.S. Marine Corps during the Vietnam War, where he worked as a helicopter gunship pilot. This experience taught him discipline, leadership, and risk management—skills that he would later apply to his business ventures.

After leaving the military, Kiyosaki dabbled in various careers, including working as a salesman for Xerox and trying his hand at entrepreneurship. His first two businesses—a nylon and Velcro wallet company and a t-shirt business—both failed, leaving him in financial ruin. But these failures didn't deter him. Instead, they fueled his desire to learn from his mistakes and find a path to true financial independence.

The Breakthrough: Rich Dad Poor Dad

In 1997, Kiyosaki self-published "Rich Dad Poor Dad," a book that would eventually become one of the most successful personal finance books of all time.

The book presents financial lessons through the lens of his "two dads"—his educated but financially struggling Poor Dad and his wealthy, street-smart Rich Dad.

The book challenges conventional ideas about money, particularly the belief that a good education and steady job are the keys to financial success. Instead, Kiyosaki advocates for financial literacy, investing in assets, and building passive income streams. He emphasizes that the rich don't work for money; instead, they make money work for them.

At first, Rich Dad Poor Dad didn't gain much traction. However, through grassroots marketing, word-of-mouth, and Kiyosaki's relentless promotion efforts (including seminars and workshops), the book gradually gained popularity. It eventually became a bestseller, remaining on The New York Times Best Seller list for over six years.

Expanding the Empire
Following the success of "Rich Dad Poor Dad," Kiyosaki built an entire brand around financial education. He authored numerous follow-up books, including "Cashflow Quadrant," "The Real Book of Real Estate," and "The Business of the 21st Century," further expanding on his philosophies of wealth-building and entrepreneurship.

He also developed the Rich Dad Company, which offers financial education through seminars, games, and online courses. His Cashflow board game is designed to teach players the principles of investing, cash flow, and financial independence in a fun, interactive way.

Kiyosaki has continued to spread his message of financial freedom through various media, including speaking engagements, webinars, and appearances on talk shows. His ability to break down complex financial concepts into simple, digestible lessons has made him one of the most influential voices in personal finance.

Controversy and Criticism
Despite his success, Kiyosaki has also faced criticism. Some financial experts question the practicality of his advice, particularly his strong emphasis on real estate investing and the stock market as the primary means of wealth-building.

Others have criticized the high costs of some of his Rich Dad seminars and courses.

Nevertheless, Kiyosaki's core message—that financial education is crucial and that traditional paths to wealth may not work for everyone—continues to resonate with millions of readers worldwide.

Legacy and Continued Influence

Today, Robert Kiyosaki is regarded as one of the leading voices in financial education. His work has inspired countless individuals to rethink their approach to money, wealth, and work. His concept of making money work for you rather than working for money has empowered people to take control of their financial futures.

Despite the controversies, Kiyosaki's teachings have left a lasting impact, changing the way people think about earning, investing, and achieving financial freedom. Through his Rich Dad brand, he has built an empire that continues to educate, challenge, and inspire future generations to pursue their financial dreams.

Suze Orman's Success Story: The Financial Guru Who Empowered Millions

"Effective accounting and diligent tracking of your income are not just about financial management; they're crucial for maintaining the fiscal health and sustainability of your business." — SUZE ORMAN, FINANCIAL ADVISOR AND AUTHOR

Suze Orman, one of the world's most influential personal finance experts, is known for her practical advice, engaging personality, and passion for financial empowerment. Her journey from humble beginnings to becoming a best-selling author, television personality, and financial educator demonstrates the power of perseverance, self-education, and determination. Orman's mission has always been to help people achieve financial security and live life on their own terms, earning her the title of a "financial guru."

Early Life and Challenges

Suze Orman was born on June 5, 1951, in Chicago, Illinois, to a working-class Jewish family. She faced financial struggles early in life, which deeply shaped her future views on money. Orman's mother worked as a secretary, and her father owned a deli that later burned down, leaving the family with almost nothing. This experience taught Orman valuable lessons about the fragility of financial security and the importance of planning for the unexpected.

Despite her modest upbringing, Orman dreamed of becoming successful and living life free from financial worries. She attended the University of Illinois Urbana-Champaign, earning a degree in Social Work. After graduation, Orman moved to California, where she spent years working as a waitress in Berkeley. These were difficult years for Orman, marked by uncertainty about her career and financial future.

An Entrepreneurial Spark and a Big Mistake

In her late 20s, Orman decided to pursue her dream of opening her own restaurant. With little financial knowledge, she asked regular customers at the restaurant where she worked for financial help. In an act of trust and generosity, they lent her $50,000 to start her business.

However, when Orman entrusted a stockbroker at Merrill Lynch to invest the loan, she lost all the money due to poor financial advice. The experience was devastating, but it also sparked her determination to understand the world of finance. Rather than dwell on her loss, Orman decided to learn everything she could about money and investing, determined to never be financially vulnerable again.

From Waitress to Financial Advisor

In a bold move, Orman took a job as a trainee at Merrill Lynch, the same firm where she had lost her savings. She excelled quickly, realizing that many people had the same lack of financial literacy that she once had. Her ability to translate complex financial concepts into practical, easy-to-understand advice made her popular with clients and set her apart from other advisors.

In 1983, Orman left Merrill Lynch to join Prudential Bache Securities, where she became one of the company's top-producing financial advisors. After gaining enough experience, she decided to start her own financial firm, the Suze Orman Financial Group, in 1987. Her hands-on experience managing money and investments gave her invaluable insights into the financial challenges faced by everyday people.

The Rise of a Financial Guru: Writing and Television Success

In the mid-1990s, Orman decided to share her financial knowledge with a wider audience by writing books. Her first book, "You've Earned It, Don't Lose It," was published in 1994 and became a bestseller. But it was her 1997 breakthrough book, "The 9 Steps to Financial Freedom," that made her a household name. The book resonated with readers by offering not only financial advice but also emotional insights into people's relationships with money.

Orman's engaging and no-nonsense style caught the attention of television producers. She began appearing on PBS specials, which further expanded her audience. In 2002, she launched "The Suze Orman Show" on CNBC, where she provided real-time financial advice to callers and viewers. The show was a massive hit, running for over a decade, and Orman became known for her signature phrases, such as "People first, then money, then things" and "Denied!"

Key Messages and Philosophy

Throughout her career, Orman's financial philosophy has been centered on empowering people to take control of their money and make decisions based on long-term financial health. Some of her core messages include:

- **"Live below your means but within your needs."**
- **Save first, spend later.**
- **Create an emergency fund** to protect against unexpected expenses.
- **Avoid bad debt,** such as credit card debt, which can hinder financial progress.
- **Plan for the future** with retirement accounts, insurance, and smart investments.

Orman's unique approach has always emphasized the emotional relationship people have with money. She teaches that self-worth and net worth are deeply connected, encouraging individuals to develop healthy financial habits rooted in self-discipline and self-love.

Best-Selling Books and Other Media Ventures
Orman became a prolific author, publishing numerous bestselling books that offered practical advice on saving, investing, and retirement planning. Some of her most notable works include:

- **"The 9 Steps to Financial Freedom" (1997)**

- **"The Courage to Be Rich" (1999)**

- **"The Road to Wealth" (2001)**

- **"Women & Money: Owning the Power to Control Your Destiny" (2007)**

- **"The Ultimate Retirement Guide for 50+" (2020)**

These books have sold millions of copies and been translated into multiple languages, making Orman one of the most successful personal finance authors in the world. In addition to her books, she has launched podcasts, online courses, and financial tools designed to help individuals and families manage their finances.

Helping Women Achieve Financial Empowerment
One of Orman's most impactful initiatives has been her advocacy for women's financial empowerment. She has consistently emphasized the importance of women taking control of their financial futures, citing societal pressures that often leave women financially dependent or unprepared for retirement.

In her book "Women & Money," Orman addresses the unique financial challenges women face, such as the gender pay gap, longer life expectancy, and caregiving responsibilities. She encourages women to invest in themselves, build emergency savings, and plan for retirement early.

Challenges and Controversies
Orman's outspoken style and high-profile career have not been without criticism. Some financial experts have questioned her investment advice and expressed concern over the marketing tactics used in some of her products and partnerships.

Additionally, her prepaid debit card venture, the Suze Orman Approved Card, faced backlash for high fees and was eventually discontinued.

Despite the controversies, Orman remains unapologetically committed to her mission of helping people take control of their financial lives. She often reminds her critics that her advice is rooted in experience and intended to help people build financial security, especially those who lack access to traditional financial education.

Philanthropy and Retirement Focus

In 2015, Orman announced that she was stepping back from television to focus on philanthropy and personal projects. She and her wife, Kathy Travis, moved to a small island in the Bahamas, where they now enjoy a quiet life focused on health and well-being. However, Orman has not fully retired—she continues to write, host a popular podcast, and appear as a guest on various financial programs.

Her recent work has focused heavily on retirement planning and helping people over 50 prepare for their financial future. In 2020, she published "The Ultimate Retirement Guide for 50+," addressing the specific needs of older adults as they transition into retirement.

Key Lessons from Suze Orman's Success

1. **Control Your Money, Control Your Life:** Financial independence gives people the freedom to live on their own terms.

2. **Start Small, Think Big:** Even small financial habits, like saving $1 a day, can lead to long-term success.

3. **Prepare for the Unexpected:** Life is unpredictable—building an emergency fund is essential.

4. **Invest in Yourself:** Orman emphasizes that self-love and financial success are interconnected.

5. **Empowerment through Knowledge:** Financial education is the key to building confidence and wealth.

Conclusion: A Legacy of Financial Empowerment

Suze Orman's story is one of overcoming personal challenges and turning setbacks into opportunities for growth and learning. From her early struggles as a waitress to becoming a global financial expert, Orman has used her platform to educate and inspire millions to take control of their finances. Her straightforward advice, engaging personality, and commitment to empowering women have made her one of the most trusted voices in personal finance.

Through her books, television appearances, and ongoing work, Suze Orman continues to transform lives by teaching people how to achieve financial freedom. Her legacy lies not only in her financial advice but in her ability to inspire confidence, self-worth, and hope for a better financial future.

Alan Dershowitz's Success Story: The Rise of a Legal Icon

"Navigating the complex legal labyrinths of trademark challenges requires not just knowledge of the law but strategic thinking to protect your brand's identity and leverage your intellectual property effectively."
— ALAN DERSHOWITZ, LAWYER AND LEGAL SCHOLAR

Alan Dershowitz is one of the most renowned and controversial lawyers in the world. Known for his sharp intellect, groundbreaking legal work, and high-profile cases, Dershowitz's career spans decades in the fields of criminal law, civil liberties, and constitutional law. From his early days as a Harvard law professor to becoming a defender of the most polarizing figures, Dershowitz's journey exemplifies how fearless advocacy and intellectual rigor can lead to both success and notoriety.

Early Life and Education: Shaping a Passion for Justice

Alan Morton Dershowitz was born on September 1, 1938, in Brooklyn, New York, to an Orthodox Jewish family. Growing up in a working-class neighborhood, Dershowitz attended Yeshiva schools, where he developed a deep appreciation for debate, argumentation, and intellectual exploration. He often described himself as a "troublemaker" in school, not out of rebellion but because he loved challenging ideas and authority—a trait that would later define his legal career.

Dershowitz went on to attend Brooklyn College, where he earned his bachelor's degree in 1959. He later pursued his law degree at Yale Law School, graduating at the top of his class. At Yale, Dershowitz distinguished himself as a brilliant legal thinker and skilled debater, laying the foundation for his future success.

Becoming the Youngest Professor at Harvard Law School

After graduating from Yale, Dershowitz clerked for Justice Arthur Goldberg on the U.S. Supreme Court, an experience that exposed him to the complexities of constitutional law. In 1964, at the age of just 25, Dershowitz was offered a position at Harvard Law School, becoming the youngest full professor in the school's history.

Dershowitz's time at Harvard marked the beginning of his lifelong focus on civil liberties, criminal justice reform, and constitutional issues. He quickly earned a reputation as a dynamic and provocative teacher, challenging his students to think critically about the tension between law and justice. Dershowitz's legal scholarship often focused on the rights of the accused and the importance of free speech, placing him at the forefront of public debates about civil liberties.

High-Profile Cases and Legal Triumphs

While teaching at Harvard, Dershowitz began taking on high-profile criminal cases, cementing his reputation as one of the most formidable defense attorneys in the United States. Over the years, he represented a diverse array of clients, ranging from celebrity figures to controversial public figures, often drawing intense media scrutiny.

Some of his most famous cases include:

1. **Claus von Bülow (1984):** Dershowitz successfully appealed the conviction of von Bülow, who had been accused of attempting to murder his wife, Sunny von Bülow. This case was later depicted in the film "Reversal of Fortune."

2. **O.J. Simpson (1995):** Dershowitz was part of Simpson's defense team during his murder trial, advising on legal strategy and contributing to

Simpson's acquittal in one of the most publicized cases in American history.

3. **Jeffrey Epstein (2008):** Dershowitz represented Epstein during his controversial plea deal involving sex trafficking charges, a case that would resurface years later, bringing renewed public scrutiny.

4. **Jonathan Pollard:** Dershowitz fought for the release of Pollard, a U.S. intelligence analyst convicted of spying for Israel, citing excessive sentencing.

These cases established Dershowitz as one of the most effective and controversial defense attorneys in the legal world. His ability to construct compelling legal arguments—even for unpopular clients—earned him both praise and criticism.

Championing Civil Liberties and Free Speech
Throughout his career, Dershowitz has been a vocal advocate for civil liberties, emphasizing the importance of the First Amendment and the right to a fair trial, even for those accused of heinous crimes. He has long argued that the law must protect the rights of all individuals, regardless of public opinion or the nature of the accusations against them.

Dershowitz's legal philosophy reflects his belief in the presumption of innocence and the idea that everyone deserves the best defense possible. His views often placed him at odds with mainstream opinion, but he remained committed to defending unpopular causes in the name of justice and constitutional principles.

Author, Public Intellectual, and Media Personality
In addition to his legal work, Dershowitz is a prolific author and public speaker. He has written more than 30 books on topics ranging from criminal law and constitutional rights to Israel and the Middle East conflict. Some of his most notable works include:

- **"The Case for Israel"**
- **"The Case for Peace"**
- **"The Best Defense"**
- **"Chutzpah"**

- **"Guilt by Accusation"**

Dershowitz's books reflect his interest in both legal theory and current political issues, offering insights into civil liberties, criminal defense, and geopolitics. His outspokenness and ability to translate complex legal concepts for the general public made him a frequent media commentator and guest on news programs.

In recent years, Dershowitz's willingness to defend controversial figures and speak out on divisive issues has kept him in the public eye, often drawing criticism from those who disagree with his stances. Nevertheless, he has remained unapologetically committed to his principles, believing that intellectual debate and legal rigor are essential to a healthy democracy.

Controversies and Criticism

Dershowitz's career has not been without controversy. His involvement in the defense of clients like Jeffrey Epstein and O.J. Simpson has attracted significant backlash, with critics accusing him of using his legal skills to shield powerful individuals from justice. In response, Dershowitz has consistently argued that everyone—no matter how reviled—deserves a robust legal defense, a principle he believes is essential to the rule of law.

Additionally, Dershowitz has faced criticism for his outspoken support of Israel and his critiques of anti-Israel sentiment in academia and politics. While some admire his advocacy, others have accused him of being overly defensive of Israeli policies.

Legacy and Influence

Despite the controversies, Alan Dershowitz remains one of the most influential legal minds of his time. His contributions to criminal law, constitutional theory, and civil liberties have shaped public discourse and legal education in profound ways. At Harvard Law School, where he taught for over 50 years, Dershowitz influenced generations of lawyers, judges, and policymakers, many of whom went on to become leaders in their fields.

Beyond his legal victories, Dershowitz's work serves as a reminder of the importance of due process, free speech, and the presumption of innocence, even in the most contentious cases. His career embodies the idea that justice is not about popularity but about ensuring that the rule of law applies to everyone equally.

Key Lessons from Alan Dershowitz's Success

1. **Defend Principles, Not Popularity:** Dershowitz's career shows the importance of upholding legal principles even in the face of public criticism.

2. **Embrace Debate:** His lifelong commitment to intellectual debate demonstrates the value of challenging ideas and engaging with opposing viewpoints.

3. **Stand Up for Civil Liberties:** Dershowitz's advocacy for free speech and the rights of the accused underscores the importance of individual rights in a democracy.

4. **Never Stop Learning:** As a teacher, author, and lawyer, Dershowitz's career exemplifies the importance of continuous learning and critical thinking.

5. **Separate the Person from the Case:** Dershowitz's ability to defend controversial figures without endorsing their actions reflects the legal principle that everyone deserves a fair defense.

Conclusion: A Life of Legal Mastery and Public Debate

Alan Dershowitz's career is a testament to the power of legal advocacy, intellectual rigor, and fearless debate. From defending controversial clients to shaping public discourse on civil liberties, Dershowitz has left an indelible mark on the legal profession. His unwavering commitment to the principles of justice, free speech, and the rule of law continues to inspire both admiration and criticism, making him one of the most complex and fascinating figures in the modern legal landscape.

Through his work as a lawyer, scholar, and public intellectual, Dershowitz has demonstrated that law is not just a profession—it is a calling to protect the rights of all individuals, even when it is unpopular to do so. His legacy will be remembered as one of legal brilliance, bold advocacy, and relentless pursuit of justice.

Jamie Dimon's Success Story: From Wall Street Trainee to Banking Titan

"Understanding equity and stock ownership complexities is crucial for navigating the corporate landscape effectively and ensuring all stakeholders thrive." — JAMIE DIMON, CEO OF JPMORGAN CHASE

Jamie Dimon, the long-time Chairman and CEO of JPMorgan Chase, has risen to become one of the most influential figures in global finance. Born on March 13, 1956, in New York City to Greek-American parents, Dimon's early interest in business was nurtured by family conversations around finance—his grandfather and father both worked as stockbrokers. This upbringing, combined with his natural curiosity, set the foundation for his future success.

Education: Building a Strong Foundation in Economics and Business

Dimon's academic journey began with a degree in economics and psychology from Tufts University. His passion for understanding complex financial systems led him to pursue an MBA from Harvard Business School. While at Harvard, Dimon made a connection that would shape the trajectory of his career—meeting Sandy Weill, a prominent Wall Street figure. Dimon's decision to work with Weill instead of pursuing a role at Goldman Sachs marked the start of a powerful mentorship and business partnership.

Early Career: Climbing the Corporate Ladder

After graduating from Harvard in 1982, Dimon joined American Express, working directly under Sandy Weill. There, he gained hands-on experience in financial operations and leadership, serving as assistant to the chairman. When Weill left American Express in 1985, Dimon followed him to Commercial Credit, a struggling financial firm. At Commercial Credit, Dimon played a key role in turning the company around, refining his skills in leadership and corporate restructuring.

Over the next decade, Dimon and Weill orchestrated a series of mergers and acquisitions, transforming Commercial Credit into Travelers Group and later merging it with Citicorp in 1998 to form Citigroup. Despite his contributions to building one of the largest financial institutions in the world, Dimon's tenure at

Citigroup ended abruptly when he was forced out due to tensions with Weill. The setback, however, became a turning point in Dimon's career.

Revitalizing Bank One: A Bold Comeback

In 2000, Dimon was named CEO of Bank One, a major U.S. bank struggling with poor performance. Dimon quickly implemented changes, cutting costs, streamlining operations, and instilling a performance-driven culture. Under his leadership, Bank One returned to profitability, earning Dimon a reputation as a dynamic and effective leader.

Dimon's successful turnaround of Bank One attracted the attention of JPMorgan Chase, which acquired the bank in 2004. Following the merger, Dimon became the company's president and later succeeded William Harrison as CEO in 2005.

Leading JPMorgan Chase: Navigating Crisis and Innovation

As CEO of JPMorgan Chase, Dimon led the bank through significant transformations and challenges, including the 2008 financial crisis. While other banks struggled or required government bailouts, Dimon's focus on risk management and sound financial practices allowed JPMorgan to weather the storm. The bank emerged from the crisis stronger than many of its peers, earning Dimon praise for his leadership and foresight.

Dimon's strategy emphasized balancing innovation with risk management. Under his tenure, JPMorgan Chase expanded its retail banking operations, invested heavily in technology, and strengthened its global presence. Dimon prioritized integrating advanced digital platforms and AI-driven solutions to keep the bank competitive in a rapidly evolving financial landscape.

Challenges and Leadership Philosophy

Despite his many successes, Dimon's tenure at JPMorgan Chase has not been without controversy. The bank has faced regulatory fines and legal challenges, including the infamous "London Whale" trading scandal in 2012, which resulted in significant losses. However, Dimon's willingness to take responsibility and implement reforms helped restore confidence in the bank.

Dimon's leadership style is marked by directness, decisiveness, and resilience. He is known for his hands-on approach, often meeting with employees at all levels to stay connected to the day-to-day operations. Dimon also champions diversity and inclusion, emphasizing the importance of building a workforce that reflects the global community JPMorgan serves.

Health Challenges and Personal Resilience
In 2014, Dimon was diagnosed with **throat cancer**, a personal challenge that tested his resilience. Despite undergoing treatment, he continued to lead JPMorgan Chase, demonstrating his commitment to both the company and its employees. Dimon's recovery and return to full-time leadership further solidified his reputation as a determined and dedicated leader.

Legacy and Impact: A Titan of Global Finance
Today, Jamie Dimon is widely regarded as one of the most influential figures in banking. Under his leadership, JPMorgan Chase has become the largest bank in the U.S. by assets and one of the most respected financial institutions globally. Dimon's ability to balance growth with discipline has set a standard for modern banking, influencing both peers and competitors.

Beyond his role at JPMorgan, Dimon serves as a trusted voice in public policy and economics. He frequently provides insights on global financial issues, advocating for regulatory reforms and economic growth policies. His impact extends beyond the boardroom, as he works to address inequality and education through philanthropic initiatives.

Conclusion: A Visionary Leader for the Modern Era
Jamie Dimon's journey from a young economist to the CEO of one of the world's largest banks reflects a career built on resilience, strategic thinking, and innovation. His ability to navigate setbacks and crises, while maintaining a focus on long-term growth, has defined his legacy in global finance. As JPMorgan Chase continues to evolve, Dimon's influence will undoubtedly shape the future of banking, inspiring future leaders to combine bold ambition with sound management.

Nell Minow's Success Story: A Leader in Corporate Governance and Film Criticism

"In the realm of corporate governance, the goal is not merely to play by the rules but to set a gold standard that integrates ethical practices with strategic business objectives." — NELL MINOW, CORPORATE GOVERNANCE EXPERT

Nell Minow has built a multifaceted career as a corporate governance expert and film critic, blending her legal expertise with a passion for storytelling. Often referred to as the "Queen of Good Corporate Governance," Minow has been recognized for her work in shareholder activism, corporate ethics, and leadership, influencing companies to improve their governance practices and align with shareholder interests.

Early Career: Law and Government Work
Minow's career began in public service, working as an attorney at the U.S. Environmental Protection Agency, the Department of Justice, and the Office of Management and Budget. This experience gave her critical insights into regulatory frameworks and systemic inefficiencies, which later shaped her governance philosophy.

Lens and Shareholder Activism: Investing with a Purpose
In the 1990s, Minow served as a principal at Lens Investment Management, a $100 million fund dedicated to shareholder activism. Lens focused on buying stakes in underperforming companies and working with management to unlock shareholder value. Minow and her team often engaged in direct dialogue with boards to push for transparency and accountability. Her efforts helped define modern shareholder activism as a powerful tool for improving corporate performance.

The Corporate Library and GMI Ratings: Holding Companies Accountable
Building on her work at Lens, Minow co-founded The Corporate Library in 2000. The organization provided independent research and analysis of corporate governance practices, becoming a trusted resource for investors, insurers, and regulators. Later, it merged with Governance Metrics International to form GMI Ratings, which further expanded its influence by rating companies based on

governance risk factors. These initiatives reflected Minow's belief in holding companies accountable and using governance metrics to protect shareholders and investors.

Leadership at ValueEdge Advisors

Today, Minow serves as the Vice Chair of ValueEdge Advisors, continuing her focus on governance and shareholder activism. Her work involves advising institutional investors on managing governance risks and using their voting power effectively. She remains a vocal advocate for better corporate governance practices, diversity on boards, and responsible executive compensation.

A Passion for Film: The Movie Mom

In addition to her work in corporate governance, Minow is also known as The Movie Mom, writing reviews and columns focused on family films. Her passion for movies has provided a creative outlet alongside her more technical governance work. As a contributing editor at RogerEbert.com, she shares thoughtful critiques on film and media, demonstrating her unique ability to bridge the worlds of business and culture.

Recognition and Impact

Throughout her career, Minow has received numerous accolades, including being named one of the 20 most influential people in corporate governance. She was also honored by the International Corporate Governance Network with a lifetime achievement award in 2008 for her contributions to the field. Her books, co-authored with Robert A.G. Monks, such as the textbook *Corporate Governance*, have become essential readings in the field.

Conclusion: A Life of Advocacy and Insight

Nell Minow's career reflects a rare combination of expertise in corporate governance and a deep appreciation for storytelling through film. Whether advocating for shareholder rights, writing about boardroom practices, or reviewing movies, Minow has shown a commitment to improving systems and fostering accountability. Her influence extends across industries, serving as a model for how one person can make meaningful change through both business acumen and creative expression.

Minow's journey is an example of how passion and professionalism can coexist, leaving a lasting impact in both governance and media circles.

———————

CHAPTER TEN

Creating a Lasting Legacy

B uilding a business is more than just achieving success in the present—it's about laying the groundwork for a lasting legacy. A business legacy is not merely measured in profits but in the enduring impact it leaves on customers, employees, and the broader community. This chapter explores how entrepreneurs can craft legacies that endure long after they step away, aligning purpose, passion, and vision into something that stands the test of time.

Bill Gates emphasizes, "Effective philanthropy requires a commitment not just of resources, but of vision and intent." This chapter highlights how business leaders can forge alliances that extend their influence and create lasting value beyond individual success, showing that giving back can be integral to building a strong legacy.

J. K. Rowling reminds us, "The greatest gift you can give your children is a good life, full of values and opportunities." This sentiment resonates deeply in the business world, where thoughtful succession planning and vision alignment play crucial roles. We examine how companies that prioritize succession planning ensure smooth leadership transitions that maintain the integrity of the organization's mission.

James Patterson, a master storyteller, notes that "the best stories come from the heart." This chapter emphasizes the role of values and ethics in creating a sustainable legacy, illustrating how businesses that prioritize integrity become trusted institutions in their industries and communities. We explore real-world examples where corporate culture has evolved into a powerful force for lasting change.

Zig Ziglar, a renowned motivational speaker, states, "You don't have to be great to start, but you have to start to be great." A lasting legacy is shaped by the meaningful contributions a company makes to its community and the world. We discuss how businesses align their operations with core values, ensuring that every decision reflects a commitment to positive impact.

David Ogilvy, the father of advertising, underscores the importance of long-term thinking when he says, "The consumer isn't a moron, she is your wife." Legacy-building requires not just planning but the flexibility to adapt to changing landscapes. This chapter explores how businesses that remain resilient and innovative continue to shape their industries for decades.

Walter Wriston emphasizes the power of relationships, stating, "Good business is not just about the product, but about the people." Similarly, for businesses, legacy is not built in a single moment—it is cultivated over time through sustained engagement, innovation, and meaningful interactions. We examine how leaders create ecosystems around their brands that continue to grow, evolve, and inspire.

Philanthropy often becomes a key component of a business legacy. Sloan Wilson reflects, "True success is measured by the lives you touch and the hearts you inspire." Many businesses create enduring legacies by giving back to their communities and investing in causes that reflect their values, leaving behind more than financial wealth—leaving a legacy of impact.

In this chapter, readers will discover the importance of aligning purpose with action to create a legacy that transcends the individual and becomes an integral part of the broader world. Through the insights of Bill Gates, J. K. Rowling, James Patterson, and others, this chapter offers practical guidance on leadership, ethics, and giving back—ensuring that readers are equipped to build not just businesses but legacies that inspire generations to come.

Bill Gates' Success Story: From Software Pioneer to Global Philanthropist

"The first rule of any technology used in a business is that automation applied to an efficient operation will magnify the efficiency. The second is that automation applied to an inefficient operation will magnify the inefficiency." — BILL GATES, CO-FOUNDER OF MICROSOFT

Bill Gates, co-founder of Microsoft, is widely recognized as one of the most influential figures in modern technology and business. His journey from a curious teenager with a passion for computers to the architect of a software empire revolutionized the way people interact with technology. Gates didn't just shape the personal computing industry—he also transformed himself into one of the world's leading philanthropists. With Microsoft's success behind him, Gates channeled his energy into global health, education, and poverty alleviation through the Bill & Melinda Gates Foundation. His story is one of innovation, strategic vision, and a commitment to using wealth and influence to create lasting change.

Early Life: A Love for Technology

Born on October 28, 1955, in Seattle, Washington, Bill Gates grew up in a family that valued education and competition. His father was a prominent lawyer, and his mother served on charitable boards. From an early age, Gates displayed an intense curiosity and love for learning. At just 13, he wrote his first computer program on a school teletype machine—a simple game of tic-tac-toe. It was at Lakeside School where Gates first encountered computers, igniting his passion for programming and software.

While most teenagers spent their time on sports or hobbies, Gates and his close friend Paul Allen dove deep into coding. The pair spent countless hours exploring the potential of computers, gaining early experience that would shape their future careers.

The Founding of Microsoft: A Leap of Faith

In 1975, Gates and Allen saw a golden opportunity when the Altair 8800 microcomputer was released. Recognizing that personal computers could become the next big thing, the duo dropped out of their respective universities—Gates from Harvard and Allen from Washington State University—and founded Microsoft. Their goal was to develop software that would make computers accessible and functional for everyday users.

The breakthrough came when Microsoft created a version of the BASIC programming language for the Altair. This marked the start of their mission to provide software solutions to the emerging personal computer industry. Gates' leadership and business acumen quickly became evident, as he negotiated strategic deals that would place Microsoft at the center of the rapidly growing tech world.

Dominating the PC Market: The Rise of Windows

In 1980, Microsoft secured a game-changing deal with IBM to provide the operating system for its first personal computer. Gates and Allen licensed MS-DOS to IBM, but wisely retained the rights to sell the software to other manufacturers. This decision proved to be pivotal, enabling Microsoft to dominate the software market as more companies adopted MS-DOS for their PCs.

Building on this momentum, Microsoft introduced Windows in 1985, a graphical user interface that revolutionized personal computing. Windows became the standard operating system for PCs worldwide, catapulting Microsoft to the forefront of the software industry. Gates' relentless focus on innovation and strategic partnerships helped solidify Microsoft's dominance, transforming it into a global powerhouse.

Challenges, Success, and Controversy

While Microsoft soared to success, Gates faced challenges and controversies along the way. In the late 1990s, the U.S. government launched an antitrust investigation, accusing Microsoft of monopolistic practices. The legal battle resulted in a settlement, but it marked a turning point in Gates' career. Though he remained chairman of Microsoft, he began to shift his focus toward philanthropy.

Despite the legal challenges, Gates' vision for software innovation had forever changed the world. By the early 2000s, Microsoft was a multi-billion-dollar company, and Gates was recognized as one of the wealthiest people on the planet.

The Bill & Melinda Gates Foundation: A New Chapter

In 2000, Gates and his then-wife, Melinda, launched the Bill & Melinda Gates Foundation, one of the largest private charitable foundations in the world. The foundation focuses on global health, education, and poverty alleviation, with significant investments in combating diseases like malaria and supporting public health initiatives.

Gates officially stepped down from his day-to-day role at Microsoft in 2008 to devote more time to philanthropy. In 2020, he left Microsoft's board entirely, marking the end of an era in technology but the continuation of his impact through charitable work.

Legacy and Continued Influence

Bill Gates' story is a testament to the power of vision, innovation, and strategic thinking. His ability to see the potential of personal computing and act on it early on shaped the digital landscape we know today. But Gates' legacy goes beyond software; his philanthropic efforts have redefined how the world approaches global health and education challenges.

Whether as a tech visionary or a philanthropist, Gates has consistently focused on solving complex problems. His journey from a young coder to the founder of Microsoft, and now a global humanitarian, continues to inspire future generations to think big, embrace technology, and give back to the world.

J. K. Rowling's Success Story: From Rejection to Global Phenomenon: The Magic of Harry Potter

"Crafting a book without a plan is like navigating without a map. Planning is the compass that guides you through the writing process, ensuring every chapter leads you closer to your destination of success." — J. K. ROWLING, AUTHOR OF THE HARRY POTTER SERIES

"Merchandising isn't just about selling products; it's about enriching the story world you've created and inviting readers to bring a piece of it into their everyday lives." — J. K. ROWLING, AUTHOR

"Copyright doesn't cover everything, but understanding its boundaries can transform how effectively you protect and leverage your creative works." — J. K. ROWLING, AUTHOR

"Mastering your publishing rights isn't just about understanding the fine print—it's about crafting the passport for your book's global journey." — J. K. ROWLING, AUTHOR

The Harry Potter series, created by J. K. Rowling, is one of the most successful and beloved book franchises in the world, captivating readers of all ages with its rich storytelling, magical universe, and unforgettable characters. However, its journey to global success wasn't an easy one—it is a story filled with perseverance, creativity, and the transformative power of imagination.

The Humble Beginnings of J. K. Rowling

Before Harry Potter became a household name, J. K. Rowling (born Joanne Rowling) was a single mother living in Edinburgh, Scotland, struggling to make ends meet. The idea for Harry Potter came to her during a train ride from Manchester to London in 1990, when she imagined a young boy who discovers he is a wizard. The idea captured her imagination, and she immediately began developing the story.

Rowling spent the next several years working on the manuscript for Harry Potter and the Philosopher's Stone (titled Harry Potter and the Sorcerer's Stone in the U.S.), writing mostly in coffee shops. She worked on the manuscript while facing significant personal challenges, including the death of her mother and financial hardships. However, Rowling's belief in her story kept her going.

Rejection and Determination

Despite her hard work, Rowling faced numerous rejections from publishers. After completing the manuscript, she submitted it to 12 different publishers, all of whom rejected it. The constant rejection could have deterred many aspiring writers, but Rowling refused to give up on her dream. Her persistence finally paid off when Bloomsbury Publishing, a small British publishing house, agreed to publish the book after the daughter of the company's chairman loved the story.

In 1997, Harry Potter and the Philosopher's Stone was published in the UK, with an initial print run of just 500 copies. Even with such modest beginnings, the book quickly gained traction. Word-of-mouth recommendations from readers, along with rave reviews from critics, helped propel the book's popularity.

Breakthrough Success

The success of the first book led to Rowling securing a U.S. deal with Scholastic for a $105,000 advance, an unprecedented amount for a children's book. Renamed Harry Potter and the Sorcerer's Stone for the U.S. audience, the book was released in 1998 and became a bestseller almost immediately. Rowling's magical world began to take the world by storm.

With the publication of each new book in the series, the popularity of Harry Potter only grew. Readers of all ages were drawn into the enchanting world of Hogwarts School of Witchcraft and Wizardry, as they followed the adventures of Harry, Hermione Granger, and Ron Weasley as they faced challenges, friendships, and the dark forces led by Lord Voldemort.

The seven-book series went on to sell over 500 million copies worldwide, translated into over 80 languages, and became one of the best-selling book series in history.

The Impact of the Harry Potter Films

The success of the book series soon attracted attention from Hollywood. In 2001, Warner Bros. released the first Harry Potter film, Harry Potter and the Sorcerer's Stone, directed by Chris Columbus. The film was a massive box office success, launching what would become one of the most successful film franchises in cinematic history.

The Harry Potter films continued to dominate box offices globally, with the final film, Harry Potter and the Deathly Hallows – Part 2, becoming the highest-grossing film of 2011. The movies introduced Harry Potter to an even broader audience, cementing the characters, magical creatures, and the world of Hogwarts into popular culture.

Cultural Phenomenon and Legacy

Beyond the books and films, Harry Potter became a cultural phenomenon. The series inspired merchandise, video games, and theme park attractions, such as The Wizarding World of Harry Potter in Universal Studios. The fanbase has remained passionate and engaged through fan conventions, fan fiction, and Pottermore, the interactive website that expands on Rowling's magical universe.

Rowling herself became one of the wealthiest and most successful authors in history, but her impact goes far beyond financial success. Harry Potter has touched the lives of millions, inspiring generations of readers and creating a deep, emotional connection with its audience. Rowling's story is also an inspiration for aspiring writers and creatives—an example of how persistence, belief in your vision, and resilience can turn a dream into a global success story.

Key Factors in Harry Potter's Success:

- **Relatable Characters**: Harry Potter, though a wizard, deals with issues of friendship, identity, and courage, making him relatable to readers of all ages.

- **Rich World-Building**: The detailed and immersive world of Hogwarts, with its own rules, history, and culture, captivated readers and allowed them to escape into a fully realized universe.

- **Timeless Themes**: The series addresses themes like good versus evil, loyalty, and sacrifice, making it appealing to readers beyond children.

- **Cultural Impact**: The films, merchandise, and theme parks created a global brand, extending the reach of Harry Potter beyond just the book world.

Conclusion: A Literary Legend

From facing rejections to becoming a global sensation, J. K. Rowling and the Harry Potter series have left an indelible mark on literature and popular culture. Harry Potter's success story is a testament to imagination, perseverance, and storytelling, with Rowling proving that even the most unlikely of dreams can turn into a worldwide phenomenon. Today, the magical world of Harry Potter continues to inspire and entertain readers, ensuring its legacy for generations to come.

—————

James Patterson's Success Story: From Adman to Literary Powerhouse

"Crafting a bestselling manuscript is like building a house. Every chapter a brick, every plot twist a beam, and every character a window into the soul of the story." — JAMES PATTERSON, PROLIFIC AUTHOR

"Formatting is to a book what tailoring is to a suit: it doesn't just fit the content comfortably on the page; it enhances the overall presentation, compelling readers to engage from the first glance." — JAMES PATTERSON, BESTSELLING AUTHOR

"Having a good agent and lawyer is like having a GPS and a good set of brakes: one helps you to find where you're going, and the other makes sure you can stop before anything crashes." — JAMES PATTERSON, AUTHOR

James Patterson has become one of the most influential and successful authors of all time, known for captivating readers with fast-paced, thrilling narratives. From humble beginnings in New York to a thriving career that spans multiple genres, Patterson's story is one of persistence, innovation, and strategic collaboration. His unique ability to produce gripping novels across diverse themes—from crime thrillers like the *Alex Cross* series to young adult hits like *Maximum Ride*—has solidified his status as a literary powerhouse. With more than 400 million books sold worldwide and an unwavering commitment to promoting literacy,

Patterson's legacy transcends publishing, inspiring generations of readers and writers alike.

Early Life and Career Beginnings

Born on March 22, 1947, in Newburgh, New York, James Patterson grew up in a working-class family. After earning a degree in English, he initially pursued a career in advertising, working his way up to become the creative director at J. Walter Thompson. During this time, Patterson nurtured his passion for storytelling, writing his first novel during early mornings before heading to work.

Breaking into the Literary World

Patterson's debut novel, *The Thomas Berryman Number*, was published in 1976 after being rejected by more than 30 publishers. The book went on to win the Edgar Award for Best First Novel, setting the stage for his literary career. However, Patterson struggled to gain mainstream popularity early on, experimenting with different genres to find his niche.

The Rise to Fame: Alex Cross Series and a New Model for Thrillers

Patterson's big break came with the release of *Along Came a Spider* (1993), the first novel in the Alex Cross series. The book became a bestseller, establishing Patterson as a master of suspense. Known for his short chapters, fast pacing, and unputdownable plots, Patterson pioneered a new style of thrillers designed to hook readers from the first page.

Collaboration and Innovation

One of Patterson's most successful strategies has been his use of collaboration. Working with co-authors, Patterson developed a prolific output, releasing numerous titles across various genres, including romance, non-fiction, and young adult novels. This collaborative model allowed him to reach broader audiences while maintaining high storytelling standards.

Global Success and a Publishing Legacy

Today, Patterson is one of the world's best-selling authors, with over 400 million books sold. His series, from Alex Cross to *Maximum Ride* and *The Women's Murder Club*, have captivated readers across generations. Patterson's success goes beyond sales; he has become a major advocate for literacy and education, donating millions of dollars to support reading programs and libraries worldwide.

A Legacy of Storytelling

James Patterson's journey from an ad executive to a literary giant showcases the power of persistence, innovation, and collaboration. His impact on the publishing industry is unparalleled, inspiring both readers and aspiring writers with his storytelling prowess and relentless work ethic.

David Ogilvy's Success Story: The Father of Modern Advertising

"In public relations, creativity is not just an asset, it's a necessity. The best campaigns are those that dare to innovate, turning the ordinary into the extraordinary and the mundane into the must-see."
— DAVID OGILVY, ADVERTISING TYCOON

"Each marketing idea is a tool, and how you use them will define the craft and impact of your campaign. Be bold, be inventive, and watch as your book leaves a mark on the world." — DAVID OGILVY, FATHER OF ADVERTISING

"Understanding advertising is like unlocking a puzzle; each question you ask reveals a piece, guiding you to see the full picture of how to captivate and convert your audience." — DAVID OGILVY, FATHER OF ADVERTISING

"On the average, five times as many people read the headline as read the body copy. When you have written your headline, you have spent eighty cents out of your dollar." — DAVID OGILVY, ADVERTISING TYCOON AND FOUNDER OF OGILVY & MATHER

"When you advertise fire-extinguishers, open with the fire."
— DAVID OGILVY, FATHER OF ADVERTISING

"An executive summary should capture the essence of your business with clarity and flair—think of it as your chance to make a powerful first impression."
— DAVID OGILVY, ADVERTISING PIONEER

David Ogilvy, widely regarded as the "Father of Modern Advertising," revolutionized the way businesses communicate with consumers. From humble beginnings to building one of the most influential advertising agencies in the world, Ogilvy's journey was marked by curiosity, discipline, and an unrelenting focus on understanding human behavior. His ability to blend creativity with research redefined advertising, setting new standards for brand-building and campaign strategy. Through iconic campaigns and his enduring book *Confessions of an Advertising Man*, Ogilvy left a legacy that continues to inspire and shape the world of marketing today.

Early Life and Foundational Experiences
David Ogilvy was born in 1911 in Surrey, England, into a family that valued education and discipline. However, Ogilvy's path was far from conventional. After attending Oxford, he left without a degree and embarked on a series of diverse jobs, including working as a chef in Paris, selling cooking stoves door-to-door in Scotland, and conducting consumer research at the Gallup organization in the United States. These early experiences gave Ogilvy a unique perspective on human behavior, which later became instrumental in his advertising career.

Founding Ogilvy & Mather
In 1948, Ogilvy co-founded the agency Hewitt, Ogilvy, Benson & Mather in New York. From the start, Ogilvy sought to elevate advertising by combining creative storytelling with meticulous research. He believed that understanding consumer behavior was the key to crafting effective campaigns and stood by the principle that "the consumer isn't a moron; she's your wife." His vision was to create ads that were both informative and engaging, focusing on the long-term value of building brands.

Breakthrough Campaigns and Impact
Ogilvy's agency gained recognition with a series of high-profile campaigns. One of his most famous was the ad for Rolls-Royce, with the headline: *"At 60 miles an hour, the loudest noise in this new Rolls-Royce comes from the electric clock."* This campaign set a new standard for luxury advertising. Another breakthrough came with the Hathaway Shirt campaign, which featured a distinguished man with an eye patch—a detail that captivated audiences and made the brand memorable.

The Legacy of Confessions of an Advertising Man

In 1963, Ogilvy published *Confessions of an Advertising Man*, a book that distilled his advertising philosophy and practical advice. The book became a bestseller and remains a cornerstone in the advertising industry, valued for its insights into branding, copywriting, and campaign strategy. Ogilvy emphasized honesty in advertising, understanding the consumer, and building brands with long-term value—principles that remain relevant today.

Building a Global Advertising Empire

Under Ogilvy's leadership, the agency grew into one of the most influential advertising firms in the world. His focus on data-driven insights, elegant copy, and cohesive branding set a new industry standard. Ogilvy & Mather expanded globally, working with prestigious clients such as Dove, Shell, and American Express, cementing its reputation as a leader in the advertising world.

Legacy and Influence

David Ogilvy's impact on the advertising industry is immeasurable. His pioneering work changed how companies approached branding, combining creative ideas with research-based strategies. Even decades after his passing in 1999, Ogilvy's philosophy continues to shape modern advertising, influencing how agencies craft campaigns and connect with audiences.

Ogilvy's legacy serves as a reminder that effective advertising is not just about creativity but also about understanding the people you aim to reach. His work remains a guiding light for marketers, proving that great advertising is both an art and a science.

Zig Ziglar's Success Story: From Salesman to Motivational Icon

"Success in sales is about innovation and engagement; use every strategy as a stepping stone to transform interest into investment and readers into lifetime fans." — ZIG ZIGLAR, RENOWNED SALES EXPERT

"Mastering sales is less about pushing a product and more about pulling the customer into a narrative where the climax is their decision to buy." — ZIG ZIGLAR, RENOWNED SALES EXPERT

Zig Ziglar, one of the most influential motivational speakers and personal development coaches of the 20th century, built his success on a foundation of optimism, resilience, and unwavering faith. Known for his captivating storytelling and Southern charm, Ziglar's life journey—from humble beginnings in rural Alabama to becoming an internationally renowned speaker and bestselling author—illustrates the transformative power of a positive mindset. With more than 30 books and countless speeches that impacted millions, Ziglar's message remains timeless: success is attainable not just through ambition, but by serving others and fostering integrity, faith, and perseverance.

Early Life and Humble Beginnings
Born on November 6, 1926, in Coffee County, Alabama, Hilary Hinton "Zig" Ziglar was one of twelve children in a modest farming family. After the untimely death of his father when Zig was five years old, his family struggled to make ends meet, which instilled in him a strong work ethic from a young age. This early experience with hardship shaped Zig's belief in the power of perseverance, faith, and optimism.

Finding His Passion in Sales
After serving in the U.S. Navy during World War II, Zig enrolled at the University of South Carolina. While he did not graduate, it was during this period that Zig discovered his natural talent for sales, working as a door-to-door cookware salesman. His charm, enthusiasm, and ability to connect with customers set him apart, and over time, Zig climbed the ranks to become a top-performing sales executive at multiple companies.

However, Ziglar's career was not without setbacks. Early on, he experienced rejection and self-doubt, but these challenges only fueled his passion for self-improvement. He began reading personal development books, attending seminars, and immersing himself in positive thinking practices.

Transition to Motivational Speaking and Writing

As Zig grew in his sales career, he discovered a deeper calling: helping others achieve success by sharing the principles that had transformed his own life. In the 1970s, he transitioned into motivational speaking and published his first book, *See You at the Top* (1975), which became an enduring bestseller. The book introduced readers to Zig's philosophy that success comes from cultivating a positive attitude, building strong character, and helping others succeed.

Ziglar's speaking style—marked by humor, Southern charm, and compelling storytelling—quickly made him one of the most sought-after motivational speakers in the country. His speeches resonated not only with salespeople but also with individuals from all walks of life, emphasizing personal responsibility, faith, and the importance of setting goals.

Building an Empire of Inspiration

As his reputation grew, Zig founded the Ziglar Corporation, which offered seminars, training programs, and personal development materials. He traveled the world, delivering thousands of speeches to corporations, churches, and educational institutions. Zig's message was simple yet profound: "You can have everything in life you want if you will just help enough other people get what they want."

Over the course of his career, Zig authored more than 30 books, many of which became bestsellers, including *Born to Win* and *Raising Positive Kids in a Negative World.* His motivational content also expanded into audio programs, which were widely popular among professionals seeking continuous self-improvement.

A Legacy of Positivity and Faith

Zig Ziglar's life was not only about achieving material success; he was deeply committed to his Christian faith and often integrated spiritual principles into his teachings. He believed in leading a life of integrity and was a devoted family man, often speaking about the importance of strong relationships and personal values.

Zig continued to inspire audiences well into his later years, often sharing the stage with his children, who carried on his legacy. Even after his passing in 2012, his teachings remain influential through the Ziglar Corporation, which continues to promote his philosophy of personal growth, leadership, and motivation.

Lessons from Ziglar's Success

- **Positive Attitude is Key:** Ziglar emphasized the power of optimism and how mindset directly affects outcomes.

- **Help Others to Achieve Success:** His philosophy centered on serving others to create mutual success.

- **Persistence through Adversity:** Zig's life showed that setbacks can become stepping stones with the right attitude.

- **Faith and Family First:** Zig exemplified the importance of maintaining strong personal values alongside professional achievements.

Conclusion

Zig Ziglar's journey from a struggling salesman to a globally recognized motivational speaker is a testament to the power of faith, hard work, and helping others. His ability to inspire people across generations with his timeless principles of positivity and service has left an indelible mark on the world of personal development. His legacy lives on, continuing to uplift and encourage individuals to become their best selves, one goal and one act of kindness at a time.

Walter Wriston's Success Story: Revolutionizing Modern Banking

"Good corporate governance is about 'intellectual honesty' and not just sticking to rules and regulations, capital flows where it is welcome and stays where it is well treated." — WALTER WRISTON, FORMER CEO OF CITIBANK

Walter B. Wriston was a transformative figure in the financial industry, known for shaping Citibank (later Citicorp) into one of the world's largest financial institutions. Born on August 3, 1919, in Middletown, Connecticut, Wriston developed a passion for economics and international affairs early in life. He earned a Bachelor of Arts in History from Wesleyan University and later pursued a Master's degree in International Law and Diplomacy at the Fletcher School of

Law and Diplomacy at Tufts University. His early education laid the foundation for his future influence in global finance.

Early Career and Military Service

After completing his studies, Wriston served as a lieutenant in the U.S. Army Signal Corps during World War II, spending time stationed in the Philippines. Upon his return, Wriston began his career in banking, joining Citibank's Comptroller's Division in 1946.

Over the years, he steadily rose through the ranks, proving to be both innovative and forward-thinking. By 1967, Wriston became President and CEO of Citibank, and just two years later, in 1969, he assumed the role of Chairman of Citicorp, the parent company. His tenure marked a turning point for the bank and the industry as a whole.

Innovating at Citibank: Transforming Global Finance

During Wriston's leadership, Citibank underwent profound changes, expanding globally and embracing new technologies. Wriston believed that information was as valuable as currency, which fueled his focus on modernizing banking practices. Under his guidance, the bank introduced several groundbreaking innovations, such as the first ATMs in the United States and credit cards, which reshaped how people accessed and managed their money.

Wriston also championed the negotiable certificate of deposit (CD), which gave depositors more flexibility and marked a significant development in banking products. His vision of international banking led to Citibank expanding its operations across the globe, making it one of the first truly global financial institutions by the late 1970s.

Contributions to Public Policy and Thought Leadership

In addition to his influence within Citibank, Wriston played a key role in public policy. He served on presidential commissions and economic advisory boards under U.S. presidents such as John F. Kennedy, Richard Nixon, Gerald Ford, and Ronald Reagan. His ideas about the importance of global capital flow and deregulation profoundly shaped economic policy during this period.

Wriston was not just a banker but also a thought leader. He authored influential works on economics, including "Risk and Other Four-Letter Words" and "The

Twilight of Sovereignty," where he discussed the impact of technology on governance and markets. His forward-looking ideas about the digital economy continue to resonate in today's interconnected financial world.

Retirement and Legacy

Wriston retired from Citicorp in 1984, leaving behind a legacy of innovation and global expansion. His leadership helped Citibank grow into the second-largest U.S. bank by assets, cementing its status as a powerhouse in global finance. In recognition of his contributions, President George W. Bush awarded him the Presidential Medal of Freedom in 2004, one of the highest civilian honors in the United States.

Walter Wriston passed away on January 19, 2005, in New York City at the age of 85. His legacy endures through the institutions he built and the financial innovations he pioneered, which continue to shape the banking industry today. His visionary approach to finance, focusing on the role of technology and information, remains a guiding principle for modern banking leaders.

Sloan Wilson's Success Story: An American Author's Journey to Success

"Success in almost any field depends more on energy and drive than it does on intelligence. This explains why we have so many stupid leaders."
— SLOAN WILSON, AMERICAN AUTHOR

Sloan Wilson, a celebrated American author, is best known for his insightful novels that delve into the complexities of post-war American life. His works, including the iconic "The Man in the Gray Flannel Suit" and "A Summer Place," captured the societal tensions of the mid-20th century, focusing on themes like ambition, conformity, and personal identity. Wilson's success as a writer reflects not only his literary talent but also his keen observations about human nature, ambition, and the challenges of balancing personal and professional lives.

Early Life: A Love for Writing and Exploration

Sloan Wilson was born on May 8, 1920, in Norwalk, Connecticut. He showed an early interest in writing and storytelling, a passion he would pursue throughout his life. Wilson attended Harvard University, where he honed his skills as a writer and developed a deep appreciation for literature.

After graduating from Harvard, Wilson's career took an adventurous turn. He served as a World War II officer in the U.S. Coast Guard, an experience that profoundly shaped his worldview. His time in the Coast Guard provided not only material for his writing but also the discipline and perspective needed to pursue a career in literature after the war.

The Big Break: "The Man in the Gray Flannel Suit"

Wilson's breakthrough came in 1955 with the publication of "The Man in the Gray Flannel Suit." The novel, drawing on Wilson's own experiences balancing a corporate career and personal aspirations, resonated with a generation of Americans grappling with the pressure to conform to societal expectations. The protagonist, Tom Rath, embodied the struggles of many post-war men—torn between ambition and authenticity.

The novel became an instant success, selling millions of copies and being adapted into a film starring Gregory Peck. Its impact on American culture was profound, with the "gray flannel suit" becoming a symbol of conformity in corporate America.

A Versatile Career: Exploring New Themes

Following the success of "The Man in the Gray Flannel Suit," Wilson published "A Summer Place" in 1958, a novel exploring themes of love, relationships, and societal norms. The book also became a bestseller and was adapted into a popular film. Through these works, Wilson established himself as a keen observer of the emotional and social challenges faced by Americans during the 1950s and 1960s.

Wilson's ability to blend personal insight with broader social commentary made his works resonate with readers across generations. His novels reflected the anxieties of the time while also exploring timeless themes of ambition, love, and self-identity.

Later Career and Personal Struggles
Despite his early success, Wilson faced challenges in his later career. The pressures of fame and personal struggles, including battles with alcoholism, affected his productivity and personal life. However, Wilson continued to write throughout his life, publishing both fiction and non-fiction, including his memoir "What Shall We Wear to This Party?," where he candidly discussed his struggles with success, personal demons, and the literary world.

Wilson's ability to reflect on his own flaws and the imperfections of society gave his works a lasting relevance. His personal journey mirrored the themes of his novels—navigating the complexities of ambition, personal fulfillment, and the cost of societal expectations.

Legacy: A Voice for a Generation
Sloan Wilson's literary contributions remain a significant part of American literature. His works not only captured the spirit of their time but also explored universal themes that continue to resonate with readers. Wilson's most famous quote—"Success in almost any field depends more on energy and drive than it does on intelligence. This explains why we have so many stupid leaders."— reflects his sharp wit and critical perspective on the dynamics of power and ambition.

Through novels like "The Man in the Gray Flannel Suit" and "A Summer Place," Wilson left behind a legacy that continues to inspire discussions about the balance between personal happiness and societal expectations. His insights into the nature of ambition and success remain as relevant today as they were during the mid-20th century.

Conclusion: A Legacy of Honesty and Insight
Sloan Wilson's journey to success as a writer was not without challenges, but his energy, drive, and honesty shaped a career that has stood the test of time. His works serve as a window into the emotional and social landscape of post-war America, offering timeless lessons on ambition, conformity, and authenticity. Wilson's story is a reminder that true success lies not just in professional achievements but also in understanding oneself and the society we live in.

Conclusion

Your Turn to Lead, Innovate, and Persevere

This volume, *70 Case Studies in Leadership, Innovation, and Resilience*, provides a comprehensive exploration of how individuals, organizations, and industries thrive in the face of complex challenges. The stories within illustrate that leadership, innovation, and resilience are not merely abstract concepts but essential pillars of success. Each case study offers practical lessons and strategies that can be applied across various sectors, demonstrating how these three principles are interconnected and vital for sustainable growth.

Leadership as the Cornerstone of Success

Great leadership is at the heart of every successful organization. The leaders featured in these case studies reveal that true leadership extends beyond titles or authority—it's about vision, responsibility, and empathy. They inspire others, make difficult decisions, and cultivate environments where teams feel empowered to perform at their best. These leaders understand the importance of building trust, fostering collaboration, and leading by example, especially during times of uncertainty.

Through real-world examples, this volume highlights that effective leadership requires flexibility. In a fast-changing landscape, leaders must navigate shifting priorities while remaining true to their mission. They must balance short-term needs with long-term goals, ensuring that they adapt without losing sight of their core values.

These case studies underscore that the most impactful leaders recognize the need to empower their teams—to delegate, mentor, and nurture future leaders within the organization. Leadership, as illustrated throughout this volume, is not about wielding power but about creating opportunities for others to grow and succeed.

Innovation as the Engine of Growth

Innovation is a defining characteristic of the individuals and organizations profiled in this collection. It's not limited to groundbreaking inventions or revolutionary ideas; instead, it encompasses creative thinking, continuous improvement, and bold experimentation. These case studies show that companies at the forefront of their industries are those willing to embrace change, take calculated risks, and challenge conventional wisdom.

Innovation demands the courage to fail and the agility to learn from failure. The stories featured here highlight that many of the most significant breakthroughs emerged from setbacks. Rather than fear mistakes, the innovators in these studies view them as opportunities for learning and growth. This mindset of iterative improvement allows organizations to stay ahead of market trends and respond effectively to new challenges.

Furthermore, the volume emphasizes that innovation thrives in environments where diversity of thought is encouraged. Leaders who foster a culture of openness—where employees are free to share ideas without fear of judgment—create the conditions necessary for continuous innovation. The case studies demonstrate that successful organizations invest in research, explore new technologies, and empower their teams to think creatively. Innovation is not a destination but an ongoing process, requiring organizations to continuously evolve to meet customer needs and market demands.

Resilience: The Ability to Thrive Amid Adversity

Resilience—the ability to bounce back from setbacks and persevere through hardship—emerges as a critical theme across these case studies. The stories illustrate that challenges, disruptions, and crises are inevitable. What sets resilient leaders and organizations apart is their capacity to adapt, recover, and come out stronger. Resilience is not just about surviving difficulties but about transforming challenges into opportunities.

The case studies highlight several strategies that foster resilience, including:

- Building strong support systems within teams and organizations.

- Cultivating emotional intelligence to remain calm and focused under pressure.

- Developing contingency plans to manage risks and unexpected disruptions.

- Embracing a growth mindset, where every challenge is seen as an opportunity to learn and improve.

In today's business environment, resilience also involves the ability to pivot—to change direction when needed and find new paths forward. The individuals and companies profiled in this volume exemplify the value of staying agile and adaptable. They show that resilience is not just about waiting out the storm but about actively creating solutions in the face of uncertainty.

The Intersection of Leadership, Innovation, and Resilience

Throughout these 70 case studies, it becomes clear that leadership, innovation, and resilience are deeply interconnected. Great leaders foster environments where innovation can flourish, and resilient organizations embrace change as a natural part of growth. These three elements work together to create organizations that not only survive but thrive in complex and competitive landscapes.

Leaders who understand the power of innovation inspire their teams to think boldly and act courageously. They know that resilience is not just an individual trait but an organizational strength, built through supportive cultures and shared experiences. Innovation fuels resilience by providing new solutions to challenges, and resilience strengthens leadership by demonstrating the ability to persevere in tough times.

The stories in this volume demonstrate that success in today's world requires a balanced approach—one that integrates visionary leadership, creative innovation, and unwavering resilience. Companies and individuals who excel at all three are better equipped to navigate uncertainty, seize new opportunities, and achieve long-term success.

Applying the Lessons from These Case Studies

The insights from these 70 case studies offer valuable guidance for leaders, entrepreneurs, and professionals across industries. Whether you are managing a small team, building a startup, or leading a multinational corporation, the lessons in this volume are applicable to your journey.

- Lead with purpose by setting a clear vision and empowering others to reach their potential.

- Innovate continuously by encouraging creative thinking and embracing experimentation.

- Build resilience by staying adaptable, learning from setbacks, and developing strong support networks.

By applying these principles, individuals and organizations can create a sustainable path to growth and success. Leadership, innovation, and resilience are not fixed traits—they are skills that can be developed and strengthened over time.

A Final Thought: Thriving in a Changing World

In a world marked by rapid technological advances, shifting markets, and unforeseen challenges, the ability to lead with vision, innovate with courage, and remain resilient is more important than ever. The case studies in this volume serve as a reminder that success is not about avoiding difficulties but about embracing them as opportunities for growth.

Whether you are at the beginning of your leadership journey or an experienced professional seeking new strategies, the lessons in this volume offer inspiration and actionable insights. The path to success is rarely a straight line, but with the right blend of leadership, innovation, and resilience, you can navigate the twists and turns with confidence.

As you reflect on the experiences shared in these case studies, consider how these principles can shape your own journey. The future belongs to those who dare to lead, innovate, and persevere. With these insights in hand, you are well-equipped to face challenges, seize opportunities, and build a meaningful legacy in your field.

This volume is not just a collection of stories—it is a toolkit for those ready to step into the future with courage, creativity, and determination.

Resources

The Empires Builders and Blueprint Series

Welcome to the Resource section of the Empire Builders Series: Masterclasses in Business and Law. Here, we provide a carefully curated collection of practical tools and materials designed to complement the strategies and insights discussed throughout the series. This section is your gateway to deeper understanding and application, offering everything from sample agreements and checklists to detailed case studies and guidelines. Whether you're forging a new business, protecting intellectual property, or planning for expansion, these resources are intended to empower you with the necessary tools to effectively implement and navigate the complex landscape of business and law. Embrace these resources as your companion in building and sustaining a robust empire.

Empire Builders Series:
Masterclasses in Business and Law

In the dynamic world of business, where innovation intersects with opportunity, success often hinges not only on creativity but also on a deep understanding of the legal and operational landscapes. The Empire Builders Series is meticulously designed to arm aspiring entrepreneurs, seasoned business owners, creative professionals, and legal experts with the comprehensive knowledge and strategies needed to navigate these complexities and build lasting empires.

Each book in the series serves as a foundational pillar, offering expert guidance and actionable insights in specific areas of business and law; tailored to foster growth, innovation, and success in today's competitive marketplace:

1. **Brick by Brick**: This guide acts as your blueprint for building a business from the ground up. It offers essential strategies, legal insights, and operational tactics crucial for establishing a solid foundation for any business venture.

2. **Mark Your Territory**: Dive deep into the world of trademarks with this essential guide, designed to help you protect and effectively leverage your brand in today's competitive market.

3. **From Idea to Empire**: Transform your entrepreneurial dreams into reality with this exhaustive guide to business planning. Learn how to craft a compelling business plan that not only attracts investors but also sets the stage for a successful enterprise.

4. **Beyond the Pen**: Safeguard your creative works and master the intricacies of copyright law with this expert guide, tailored specifically for writers, artists, musicians, and digital content creators.

5. **Legal Ink**: Demystify the complex legal landscape of publishing with practical advice on negotiating contracts and protecting intellectual property, essential for authors and publishers.

The Empire Builders Series stands as a testament to the power of knowledge and the importance of mastering the strategic and legal aspects of business management. Each book is designed not merely to inform but to inspire action and lead to success. Embark on this journey to build your empire, one masterclass at a time.

Brick by Brick:
The Entrepreneur's Guide to Constructing a Company

The first book in the Empire Builders Series: Masterclass in Business and Law is "Brick by Brick: The Entrepreneur's Guide to Constructing a Company."

Summary: "Brick by Brick" is an indispensable resource for entrepreneurs who are poised to transform their innovative business ideas into successful enterprises. This comprehensive guide meticulously outlines the complexities of business formation, providing detailed, step-by-step instructions and vital insights into the legal, operational, and strategic aspects of starting and running a thriving company.

Part 1: Laying the Foundation – Focuses on selecting the appropriate business entity, delving into the legal implications of each option and the economic considerations vital for establishing a solid foundation for your business.

Part 2: Operational Mechanics – Discusses the operational aspects of setting up partnerships and LLCs, navigating corporate governance, maintaining corporate records, and managing capital and shareholder relationships effectively.

Part 3: Advanced Strategic Planning – Offers insights into managing structural changes, handling stock and ownership issues, expanding operations across state lines, and deploying tax strategies to ensure compliance and optimize financial performance.

Part 4: Implementation Tools and Resources – Provides practical tools such as sample agreements, startup task checklists, and comprehensive guidelines for drafting business plans and the incorporation process, enabling entrepreneurs to effectively implement their business strategies.

"Brick by Brick" not only serves as a guide but acts as a complete blueprint for building a robust business capable of thriving in today's competitive market. It arms aspiring entrepreneurs with the necessary knowledge and tools to navigate the complexities of business formation. From drafting your first business plan to preparing for incorporation, this book delivers invaluable insights and practical advice to establish a strong foundation and sustain growth.

Mark Your Territory:
Navigating Trademarks in the Modern Marketplace

The second book in the Empire Builders Series: Masterclass in Business and Law is "Mark Your Territory: Navigating Trademarks in the Modern Marketplace."

Summary: "Mark Your Territory" provides an indispensable resource for anyone involved in the branding and legal aspects of their business, offering a comprehensive guide to understanding, acquiring, and effectively managing trademarks. This book is crucial for ensuring that trademarks, which are vital assets to any business, are properly protected and leveraged.

Part 1: Fundamentals of Trademarks – Introduces the basics of trademarks, including their legal framework, the process of trademark selection and registration, and their importance in identifying business sources and ensuring product quality.

Part 2: Strategic Trademark Management – Focuses on the ongoing management of trademarks, detailing strategies for maintaining rights, monitoring for infringements, addressing challenges in digital marketing, and managing global trademark portfolios.

Part 3: Advanced Topics in Trademarks – Delves into more complex issues such as preventing trademark dilution, managing renewals, understanding the specific needs of service marks in advertising, and navigating the intricacies of trademark licensing and emerging legal trends.

Part 4: Practical Tools and Resources – Provides practical aids like sample trademark filings, management checklists, and insightful case studies, equipping readers with tangible tools and real-world examples to apply the concepts discussed effectively.

Designed for entrepreneurs, business owners, and legal professionals, "Mark Your Territory" equips readers with actionable strategies and essential tools for effective trademark management. It ensures that readers can maintain their brand's uniqueness and legal protections, thus securing a competitive edge in the marketplace.

From Idea to Empire:
Mastering the Art of Business Planning

The third book in the Empire Builders Series: Masterclass in Business and Law is "From Idea to Empire: Mastering the Art of Business Planning."

Summary: "From Idea to Empire" offers an indispensable roadmap for entrepreneurs eager to transform their innovative ideas into successful businesses. This comprehensive guide equips readers with a strategic blueprint for drafting robust business plans that attract investors and serve as a roadmap for navigating the transition from startup to thriving enterprise.

Part 1: Conceptualizing Your Business – This section lays the groundwork by assisting readers in defining their business vision, understanding market needs, analyzing competitors, and setting clear business objectives. It also guides readers in selecting an effective business model that aligns with their long-term goals.

Part 2: Strategic Planning – Delve into creating detailed marketing strategies, operational plans, and financial projections. This part covers risk management and technological integration, ensuring the business plan is both innovative and executable.

Part 3: Articulating Your Plan – Focuses on the actual drafting of the business plan, including how to write an engaging executive summary, develop compelling proposals, and master communication and negotiation tactics with potential investors and partners.

Part 4: Execution and Review – Outlines the necessary steps to launch the business successfully, monitor its performance, and make adjustments based on real-world feedback and market dynamics. This section also explores strategies for sustainable growth and long-term viability.

"From Idea to Empire" is more than a mere planning manual; it's a strategic guide that provides budding entrepreneurs with the necessary knowledge, tools, and confidence to build a business capable of facing today's market complexities. With practical advice, real-world examples, and essential resources, this book is a vital tool for anyone ready to evolve their business concept from idea to a profitable empire.

From Idea to Empire: Abridged Edition

The third book in the Empire Builders Series: Masterclass in Business and Law is "From Idea to Empire: Abridged Edition."

Summary: "From Idea to Empire: Abridged Edition" delivers the essential roadmap for turning business ideas into successful enterprises—streamlined for readers seeking concise and actionable insights. While the original edition provides an expansive resource with success stories and detailed case studies, this abridged version focuses solely on the strategic elements of business planning, offering the tools needed to conceptualize, design, and execute a winning business strategy.

By eliminating supplementary stories and focusing on the practical frameworks, this edition is perfect for readers eager to dive straight into the mechanics of business planning without distraction. It provides the knowledge required to develop robust business models, articulate compelling proposals, and successfully launch and grow a business in today's dynamic marketplace.

Part 1: Conceptualizing Your Business – Laying the Foundation – In this section, readers learn how to define their business idea, identify market needs, analyze competitors, and set clear objectives. It introduces essential business models and helps entrepreneurs align their vision with long-term goals.

Part 2: Strategic Planning – Mapping the Path to Success – Here, readers will discover how to design effective marketing strategies, operational plans, and financial projections. Topics like risk management and technological integration are covered to ensure every business plan is both realistic and innovative.

Part 3: Articulating Your Plan – Communicating with Precision and Impact – This section emphasizes the importance of clarity in communication. Readers will learn how to craft compelling executive summaries, develop strong proposals, and master negotiation strategies for working with investors and partners.

Part 4: Execution and Review – Launching and Scaling with Purpose – The final section covers essential steps for launching a business successfully, monitoring performance, and making real-time adjustments. It also addresses strategies for sustainable growth, long-term resilience, and market adaptation.

About This Edition:
The Abridged Edition is crafted for readers who prefer a focused, no-frills approach to business planning. By presenting the core methodologies from the original book in a concise format, this version allows entrepreneurs to absorb key concepts quickly and efficiently. Whether you're a first-time entrepreneur or a seasoned business owner, this streamlined guide provides the essential tools needed to transform an idea into a thriving business.

Why This Edition Matters:
"From Idea to Empire: Abridged Edition" underscores that great business planning doesn't require lengthy explanations—it requires clear strategies and actionable frameworks. This edition emphasizes the importance of focus, discipline, and adaptability in building a successful business.

Designed to complement busy entrepreneurs, it delivers the same powerful strategies as the original book but in a more accessible format. Readers can quickly refer to specific sections, apply the knowledge, and move forward with confidence in their business endeavors.

"From Idea to Empire: Abridged Edition" is the perfect companion for entrepreneurs who need to move swiftly from concept to execution. With straightforward advice and practical insights, this edition equips readers to create robust business plans and take decisive action toward building their own empire.

Beyond the Pen:
Copyright Strategies for Modern Creators
The fourth book in the Empire Builders Series: Masterclass in Business and Law is "Beyond the Pen: Copyright Strategies for Modern Creators."

Summary: "Beyond the Pen" serves as a crucial guide for artists, writers, musicians, and digital creators who seek to effectively navigate the complexities of copyright law and protect their creative assets. This comprehensive resource provides a deep dive into the mechanisms, legal frameworks, and strategic practices necessary to safeguard intellectual property in today's rapidly evolving digital landscape.

Part 1: Understanding Copyright Law – This section lays the groundwork by covering the essentials of copyright, including how to register works, the extent of legal protection available, and the nuances of international copyright laws. It equips creators with the crucial knowledge needed to assert and defend their rights.

Part 2: Navigating Use and Fair Use – Focuses on the vital concept of fair use, offering real-world scenarios and detailed guidance on how to handle copyright infringements and resolve disputes effectively without compromising creative freedom.

Part 3: Licensing and Monetization – Explores strategic approaches to structuring and managing licensing agreements, understanding diverse revenue models, and handling collaborations, ensuring creators can monetize their works effectively while maintaining control over their usage.

Part 4: Copyright in the Digital Age – Addresses the challenges and opportunities presented by new technologies, digital rights management, and online content sharing platforms. This part also examines the impact of social media on copyright and anticipates future trends that could influence creators' rights.

"Beyond the Pen" is more than just a legal manual; it is a strategic resource that empowers creators to protect, manage, and prosper with their intellectual property in today's interconnected market. Packed with practical examples, expert advice, and actionable strategies, this book is an indispensable tool for anyone looking to navigate the legal challenges and seize the opportunities in the modern creative landscape.

Legal Ink:
Navigating the Legalese of Publishing

The fifth book in the Empire Builders Series: Masterclass in Business and Law is "Legal Ink: Navigating the Legalese of Publishing."

Summary: "Legal Ink" offers an indispensable guide for authors seeking to navigate the complex world of publishing contracts. This comprehensive book demystifies legal jargon and provides a clear roadmap to understanding and managing the intricacies of publishing agreements effectively.

Part 1: The Grant of Rights – This section explains the various types of publishing rights, offering guidance on how to negotiate and manage these rights effectively to safeguard the author's interests.

Part 2: Your Obligations – Details the commitments authors must uphold under publishing contracts. It emphasizes the implications of these obligations for an author's literary career and advises on managing multiple contractual commitments.

Part 3: Getting Your Book to Market – Covers the practical aspects of the publishing process from the final manuscript preparation to marketing and distribution. This part ensures authors understand the steps involved and their roles in bringing their book to market.

Part 4: Follow the Money – Breaks down the financial components of publishing contracts, including advances, royalties, and accounting clauses. It offers crucial advice on how to negotiate for fair compensation.

Part 5: Parting Ways – Discusses strategies for effectively managing the conclusion of a publishing agreement, including rights reversion and contract termination, providing tactics for authors to regain control of their work.

"Legal Ink" acts as more than just a guide—it's a strategic tool for any author looking to deeply understand and master the legal framework of publishing contracts. With this book, writers are equipped to make informed decisions, negotiate better terms, and ensure their rights are protected throughout their publishing journey. It is an essential resource for anyone looking to confidently handle the legalities of publishing and secure the success of their work in the competitive marketplace.

The Empire Blueprint Series:
Case Studies for Business Success

Welcome to the Case Studies section of The Empire Blueprint Series: Case Studies for Business Success. This collection serves as an essential companion to the theoretical knowledge presented in the earlier volumes. Here, we delve into real-world applications and successful business practices through detailed case studies, showcasing how various entrepreneurs and businesses have navigated challenges, seized opportunities, and achieved success in their respective fields.

In this series, you will encounter a variety of scenarios that illustrate the practical implementation of business strategies and legal frameworks. Each case study not only highlights successes but also discusses the obstacles faced and lessons learned along the way. Whether you're a budding entrepreneur, a seasoned executive, or a legal professional, these insights will provide you with invaluable perspectives and tools to enhance your own business endeavors.

Each book in the series includes:

1. **70 Case Studies in Vision, Strategy, and Personal Branding**: This volume explores the journeys of entrepreneurs who have effectively crafted their visions and built strong personal brands. It highlights strategies for aligning personal values with business goals and creating a lasting impact in the marketplace.

2. **70 Case Studies in Leadership, Innovation, and Resilience**: This volume examines leaders who have driven innovation and fostered resilience within their organizations. The case studies showcase their approaches to overcoming challenges and inspire others to cultivate a culture of adaptability and forward-thinking.

3. **74 Case Studies in Growth, Digital Presence, and Legacy Building**: This volume delves into the strategies employed by businesses that have successfully navigated digital transformation and growth. It emphasizes the

importance of establishing a strong online presence and building a legacy that resonates with future generations.

Each case study in The Empire Blueprint Series: Case Studies for Business Success is crafted to offer actionable insights and inspiration for readers. By examining these real-world examples, you will gain a deeper understanding of the strategies that drive business success and how to apply these lessons to your own ventures.

70 Case Studies in Vision, Strategy, and Personal Branding: The Foundations of Success, Volume 1

The first book in The Empire Blueprint Series: Case Studies for Business Success is "70 Case Studies in Vision, Strategy, and Personal Branding: The Foundations of Success," Volume 1

Dive deeper into the essential elements of business success with Volume 1: 70 Case Studies in Vision, Strategy, and Personal Branding. This volume not only presents a wealth of real-world examples but also serves as a practical toolkit for aspiring entrepreneurs and seasoned professionals alike. Here, you will find a curated collection of resources designed to complement the case studies and enhance your understanding of effective business practices.

From strategic planning templates and personal branding frameworks to time management guides and storytelling techniques, these resources empower you to implement the insights gleaned from the case studies. Explore practical tools for optimizing your online presence, launching impactful marketing campaigns, and engaging audiences across various platforms.

With a focus on innovation and adaptability, this resource section is your go-to companion for navigating the complexities of today's business landscape. Whether you're looking to craft an inspiring vision, develop effective strategies, or build a standout personal brand, the materials provided will equip you with the actionable insights needed to achieve meaningful success. Embrace the tools and inspiration within these pages, and take your entrepreneurial journey to new heights.

70 Case Studies in Leadership, Innovation, and Resilience: Building a Thriving Enterprise, Volume 2

The second book in The Empire Blueprint Series: Case Studies for Business Success is "70 Case Studies in Leadership, Innovation, and Resilience: Building a Thriving Enterprise," Volume 2

Enhance your understanding of effective leadership with Volume 2: 70 Case Studies in Leadership, Innovation, and Resilience: Building a Thriving Enterprise. This resource section is designed to complement the rich insights presented throughout the volume, providing you with practical tools and frameworks to elevate your leadership journey.

Within this section, you'll find a variety of resources that address the core themes of this book—leadership, innovation, and resilience. From templates for developing effective communication strategies to guides on fostering a collaborative corporate culture, these materials are crafted to support your growth as a leader. Explore negotiation techniques, emotional intelligence assessments, and frameworks for ethical leadership that will help you build trust and loyalty within your teams.

The resources also include practical tips for embracing digital transformation and integrating innovative technologies into your business practices. Learn how to leverage these tools to drive growth, enhance customer engagement, and maintain a competitive edge in today's dynamic market.

With a focus on creating lasting value and building a legacy, this section equips you with actionable insights and strategies to navigate challenges with confidence. Whether you are an entrepreneur launching a new venture or an executive steering an established enterprise, these resources will empower you to lead with purpose and resilience.

Dive into these valuable tools and insights, and discover how to turn challenges into opportunities, fostering an environment where innovation and sustainable growth thrive.

74 Case Studies in Growth, Digital Presence, and Legacy Building: Strategies for Long-Term Success, Volume 3

The third book in The Empire Blueprint Series: Case Studies for Business Success is "74 Case Studies in Growth, Digital Presence, and Legacy Building: Strategies for Long-Term Success," Volume 3

Unlock the secrets to sustainable success with Volume 3: 74 Case Studies in Growth, Digital Presence, and Legacy Building: Strategies for Long-Term Success. This resource section is designed to enhance your understanding and application of the powerful insights shared throughout the volume, providing you with practical tools and strategies for thriving in today's competitive landscape.

In this section, you'll find a wealth of resources that align with the key themes of this book—growth, digital engagement, and legacy building. From templates for strategic goal-setting and growth frameworks to guides on optimizing digital marketing efforts, these materials will help you implement the actionable insights gained from the case studies.

Explore best practices for storytelling and community engagement in the digital realm, along with practical tips for leveraging social media to amplify your brand's presence. Discover frameworks for navigating the complexities of innovation and operational efficiency, ensuring your business not only grows but flourishes sustainably.

The resource section also emphasizes the importance of legacy building, offering tools for effective succession planning and community involvement. Learn how to align your everyday decisions with your long-term vision, ensuring that your enterprise leaves a lasting impact for future generations.

Whether you are an entrepreneur embarking on a new venture, an executive scaling operations, or a professional seeking to elevate your digital presence, these resources will empower you to lead with purpose and confidence. Dive into the practical tools and insights provided here, and equip yourself to navigate challenges, innovate boldly, and create a meaningful legacy.

In conclusion, the Resource section of the Empire Builders Series and Empire Blueprint Series serves as valuable extensions of the learning journey you've embarked upon. By utilizing these carefully chosen tools and materials, you are better equipped to apply the principles and strategies discussed in the series to real-world scenarios. Each resource has been tailored to enhance your understanding and effectiveness in the realms of business and law, ensuring you have the practical support necessary to navigate challenges and seize opportunities. We hope these resources prove instrumental in helping you build and sustain your business empire, transforming knowledge into actionable success.

L. A. Moeszinger also known as simply "L" is the face behind the AuthorsDoor Leadership Program: AuthorsDoor Series: *Publisher & Her World*, AuthorsDoor Advanced Series: *Publisher & Her World*, and AuthorsDoor Masterclass Series: *Publisher & Her World*. The program comprises, books, courses, and workbooks. The courses expand upon the books. The workbooks go into further detail, outlining step-by-step instructions. Courses are *free*; books and workbooks are available for purchase on Amazon and other retailer sites. She has been launching the careers of self-publishers since 2009, and she also writes the AuthorsRedDoor.com blog on writing, publishing, and marketing. L is also the co-founder of The Ridge Publishing Group and its imprints.

She is an American author, publisher, and creator who resides in Coeur d'Alene, Idaho, with her husband and two dogs. She writes under the pseudonyms: Ann Patterson and Ann Carrington for her business law pieces; L. A. Moeszinger for her writing, publishing, and marketing pieces; Lori Ann Moeszinger for her biblical books and personal pieces; and a handful of others for her Manhattan Diaries series. She believes strongly in faith, blessings, and working her butt off. . . and she thinks one of the best things about being an author-publisher—unlike the lawyer she used to be—is that she can let her passion out.

Original Package Design
© 2024 AuthorsDoor Leadership Program
Cover Design: Eric Moeszinger
Author Photo © 2023 Edwin Wolfe

Parent Website: https://www.RidgePublishingGroup.com and

blog site https://www.PublisherAndHerWorld.com

Publisher Website: https://www.GuardiansofBiblicalTruth.com and

blog site https://www.Jesus-Says.com

Author website: https://www.LAMoeszinger.com and New Youniversity sites:

https://www.NewYouniversity.com, https://www.ManhattanChronicles.com

Bridge Website: https://www.AuthorsDoor.com and

blog site https://www.AuthorsRedDoor.com

Entertainment website: https://www.EthanFoxBooks.com and

blog site https://www.KidsStagram.com

Want More?

The ideas in this book are expanded upon throughout the AuthorsDoor Leadership Program of books, courses, and workbooks. Follow our Facebook page. Join our Facebook private group. Watch our YouTube channels (AuthorsDoor Group, Authors Red Door #Shorts, and Publisher and Her World at Ridge Publishing Group). Listen to our Podcast channel (Publisher's Circle); or email me: *Hello@AuthorsDoor.com*

AuthorsDoor Hubs

Get insights from the articles we write on our *website* (AuthorsDoor.com). You'll find more publications to help authors sell better, pitch better, recruit better, build better, create better, and connect better. You are also invited to visit our *blog* and find out what we're talking about now. Sign up for our *AuthorsDoor Leadership Program Newsletter* and join the conversations going on there with our private community (Publisher's Circle); visit: *www.AuthorsRedDoor.com*

Publisher & Her World Blogs

Enter a world where the sometimes shocking and often hilarious climb to the top as an author-publisher is exposed by a true insider. Faced with on-going trials and tribulations of the world of self-publishing, L. A. Moeszinger is witty and sometimes brutally candid in her postings. If you enjoy getting the inside scoop on the makings and thoughts behind self-publishing, this is the blog for you! *www.PublisherAndHerWorld.com*

This
book was art
directed by John Jared.
The art for both the cover and the
interior was created using pastels on toned
print making paper. The text was set in 10 point Times
New Roman, a typeface based on the sixteenth-century type designs
of Claude Garamond, redrawn by Robert Slimback in 1989.
The book was printed at Amazon and IngramSpark.
The Managing Editor was Jack Clark. The
Production was supervised by
Jason Reed and Ed
Warren.

www.ingramcontent.com/pod-product-compliance
Lightning Source LLC
Chambersburg PA
CBHW022113210326
41597CB00047B/256